Theology
for the Church

Writings by
Marlin E. Miller

Richard A. Kauffman and Gayle Gerber Koontz, editors

Institute of Mennonite Studies
Elkhart, Indiana

Text-Reader Series

Series Titles:

1. *Essays on Biblical Interpretation: Anabaptist-Mennonite Perspectives.* Edited by Willard M. Swartley, 1984.

2. *One Lord, One Church, One Hope, and One God: Mennonite Confessions of Faith in North America.* Howard John Loewen, 1985.

3. *Monotheism, Power and Justice: Collected Old Testament Essays.* Millard C. Lind, 1990.

4. *So Wide a Sea: Essays on Biblical and Systematic Theology.* Edited by Ben C. Ollenburger, 1991.

5. *Essays in Anabaptist Theology.* Edited by H. Wayne Pipkin, 1995.

6. *Understanding Ministerial Leadership: Essays contributing to a developing theology of ministry.* Edited by John A. Esau, 1995.

The Text-Reader series is published by the Institute of Mennonite Studies with the encouragement of the Council of Mennonite Seminaries. The series seeks to make available significant resource materials for seminary classroom use. By using photographic reproduction and/or desktop publishing technology, and marketing primarily through individual channels, the series seeks to make available helpful materials at relatively low cost.

Priority in accepting manuscripts will be given to material that has promise for ongoing use in the seminary classroom, with orientation toward or interest in the Anabaptist-Mennonite theological tradition.

The Institute of Mennonite Studies is the research agency of the Associated Mennonite Biblical Seminary, 3003 Benham Ave., Elkhart, Indiana, 46517-1999.

Copyright © 1997 by the Institute of Mennonite Studies
ISBN 0-936273-24-0
Printed in the United States of America

to speak or present papers at church-related conferences and consultations, to write articles for church papers and for volume five of the *Mennonite Encyclopedia,* and to prepare material for ecumenical information and conversation. Some of the writing draws on research and formulation developed in special projects for the church. For example chapter 9, "The Recasting of Authority," draws upon work done for the Mennonite Church study on "Leadership and Authority in the Church" completed in 1979. Miller served as the primary draft writer for this substantial document.

Although it is not reflected in this collection, a further theological contribution which Miller made to the Mennonite church which should be noted along with these writings is his involvement in the intensive ten-year work on the first confession of faith adopted by two of the largest Mennonite conferences in North America. The 1995 publication, *Confession of Faith in a Mennonite Perspective,* owes much in the formulation and implementation of the extensive church-wide process on which it was based, as well as in its theological content, to Miller who served as a co-chair of the confession of faith committee until his death a few months before the final document was presented to the church for adoption.

Miller's theological acumen was early demonstrated in his graduate work at Goshen Biblical Seminary in Indiana, at the University of Basel in Switzerland, and at the University of Heidelberg in Germany where he completed his Dr. Theol. *summa cum laude* in 1968. Miller wrote his doctoral dissertation in German on the reign of God in Friedrich Schleiermacher's theology.

Following this Marlin and his wife, Ruthann Gardner Miller, accepted a Mennonite Board of Missions assignment in Paris, France, helping to initiate a ministry among African students. During this time Marlin also served as a mission board consultant for program in West Africa and engaged in part-time post-graduate studies at the Ecole des Hautes Etudes in Paris.

In these European settings from 1963-74, Miller expressed and developed his ongoing interests in peace theology and in ecumenical dialogue. He served as the Mennonite Central Committee European Peace Section representative, participated in the "Puidoux Theological Conferences on Church and State," and was involved in various East-West conversations and travel in the German Democratic Republic and

Czechoslovakia. From 1970-74 he was president of Eirene International Service for Peace.

As relationships with European Mennonites deepened and options for part-time teaching in Paris began to open, the Mennonite church in North America issued a strong call to Miller to serve as president of the Goshen Biblical Seminary (one of two seminaries forming the Associated Mennonite Biblical Seminaries) and to teach theology there. In 1975 at age 37 Miller accepted this call and with Ruthann and their three children—Rachel, Eric, and Lynelle—relocated in Goshen, Indiana.

Although his primary energies were now focused on the North American Mennonite world, Miller continued close contact with European Mennonites. He helped European students who wished to study theology in this country find their way in the American academic setting. As a teacher he encouraged European students to see their theological task in the service of the church and the ecumenical community. He exhibited an ongoing interest in German theology, especially theology of baptism, and was a co-moderator of Reformed and Mennonite dialogue in Strasbourg, France, in 1984. For a dozen years he served as the Mennonite Central Committee liaison with "Christians Associated for Relations to Eastern Europe" and "Christian Peace Conference."

The ecumenical and peace theology interests Miller developed through his exposure to European Christians spilled into North American assignments as well. He was co-moderator of a Lutheran and Evangelical dialogue from 1979-81, an Anabaptist-Mennonite observer during a three-year process of the Commission for a New Lutheran Church in the mid-eighties, and a member of the Mennonite Central Committee Ecumenical Peace Theology Group from 1987 until his death. He was also a key participant in the National Council of Churches Faith and Order discussion on peace and the apostolic faith which issued in a book Miller co-edited, published shortly after his death.

In addition to the strong Anabaptist-Mennonite theological orientation apparent in this collection, Miller's twenty years of formal and informal writing and teaching show evidence of personal and critical appreciation for the Swiss Reformed theologian Karl Barth. Miller valued Barth's focus on Jesus Christ; his reaffirmation of the primary authority of the Scriptures for the church, theology, and ethics; the

vi

support in Barth's mature writing for baptism upon confession of faith; and his criticism of the Christian's participation in war.

Miller indicated that Barth's influence on him was first significant when Miller spent his junior year in college in Japan. He remembered this year as a "threshold year," a year of personal and intellectual struggle as he encountered Christian mission in a dramatically different culture. Disillusioned by much of what he saw, he considered dumping Christianity. One of the persons who gave him reason to continue as a Christian at that pivotal point was Karl Barth mediated through a Swiss missionary. Several years later (1961-62) Miller spent a year at the University of Basel studying with Barth who was completing the last year of his teaching career. Decades later, as a professor of theology and seminary president, Miller continued to affirm that "of the two or three people most influential in my thinking, Karl Barth is either first or second on the list."

While other theologians and theological streams were significant conversation partners along the way—Paul Minear and the biblical theology movement, Schleiermacher and Ritschl, John H. Yoder, among others—one influence on Miller's theological reflection that might be overlooked was congregational life itself. Although his work with the mission board and seminary required him to travel and relate to a variety of congregations, Marlin and Ruthann made intentional decisions over the years to remain substantially involved in the local Mennonite congregations where they were currently members. This commitment grew out of an Anabaptist-Mennonite ecclesiology which emphasized the priority of the local congregation in discipleship and discipline. Active in a Mennonite congregation near Paris, Miller was ordained to pastoral ministry in 1971. His theological interest in pastoral leadership and education was further fed by his involvement in two congregations during his years in Indiana as well as by talking with pastors from many other churches. His theological work on pastoral leadership not only shaped his thinking about congregational life, but his writing and teaching were shaped by the practical pastoral issues he observed and engaged as a congregational member and leader.

Among the work Miller left unfinished were notes based on years of special interest in the theology of the Gospel of John and notes from a series of lectures on atonement presented in Japan in the summer of 1994. Miller had hoped to work particularly on the theme of atonement in subsequent projects and had found the thought of Rene Girard regarding the dynamics of violence and the tendency to project communal sin onto scapegoats intriguing and potentially fruitful for this issue.

Although Miller may be remembered first as a gifted Mennonite leader—a bridge builder—the quality of his work in such a role was due in part to his incisive theological vision. That vision developed in the crucible of the believers church tradition carried by Anabaptist denominations who "share their accent on living as Christ taught and modeled." The following writings *for* the Anabaptist understandings of baptism, and on the role of the Bible in theology—are also *from* the church. They represent not only Miller's theological gifts to the church, but also the church's gifts to him. They distill not only segments of his theological thinking but also mirror the way he chose to follow Christ in life—joining hands with others in discipleship and service.

Richard A. Kauffman   Gayle Gerber Koontz
Carol Stream, Illinois   Elkhart, Indiana

Acknowledgments

We would like to thank the following people for their assistance in making this volume possible: Ross T. Bender, director of the Institute of Mennonite Studies, who oversaw the publishing process; Willard M. Swartley, dean at Associated Mennonite Biblical Seminary, who encouraged those of us involved in the project and gave us counsel; Ruth Liechty, also of IMS, who provided clerical support; and Jeni Hiett Umble, a student assistant at AMBS, who ran down many of the essays. We also wish to personally thank Ruthann Miller, Marlin's spouse, and her family for allowing IMS to publish these essays of Marlin's.

I

The Church and Its Witness

Chapter 1

The Gospel of Peace

Reprinted by permission from *Mission Focus*, Mennonite Board of Missions, vol. VI, no. 1 (September 1977) 1-5.

Many contemporary evangelical Christians refer to "the gospel" as if the word had a narrowly circumscribed content. "Preaching the gospel" presumably means proclaiming the message of forgiveness from past sin and guilt through the atoning work of Christ on the cross, inviting sinners to repent and accept God's plan of salvation, and extending the promise of eternal life to those who accept Christ as personal savior. Within the broader Protestant context of evangelical Christianity, "the gospel" also carries the connotation of pure grace, devoid of any ethical demands which might be construed as prerequisites for salvation or as conditions for remaining in a state of peace. Discipleship as the shape of Christian obedience is seen at best as secondary, as a fruit of faith's response to the gospel. It is however not understood as integral to the gospel message as such. Major dogmatic definitions have thus attached to the biblical term "gospel" a particular content which provides a capsule statement of the message to be preached. This content supposedly also serves as a critical safeguard against liberal deviations such as tendencies to seek salvation by education, material welfare, or social change rather than by preaching "the gospel."

The New Testament however employs a variety of terms to describe the comprehensiveness of the Good News. Jesus himself proclaimed the gospel of the Kingdom. The Apostle Paul speaks about the gospel of God, the gospel of Jesus Christ, the gospel of the glory of Christ, the gospel of salvation, and simply the gospel. Both Peter (Acts 10) and Paul (Ephesians 2, 6) refer to the "gospel of peace." This variety of New Testament terms certainly may not be construed to mean that there are several "gospels" which differ markedly in form and substance. The gospel of God is none other than the gospel of Jesus Christ. The gospel of salvation is the same as the gospel of peace. Even on the most superficial level, this multiplicity of descriptions should caution against too readily limiting our understanding of the gospel to one facet of the

New Testament message or against reducing all other dimensions of the Good News to one particular aspect. Such reductionist interpretations almost inevitably end up with a truncated gospel, an amputated Christ, and a crippled church. We should rather seek to understand the particular point of reference of each description and its roots and place within the global vision of the Good News.

Within the limits of this essay, we will focus on the description of the Good News as "the gospel of peace." This focus is prompted not by an attempt to reduce the Good News to a gospel of peace, but by specific shortcomings in broad streams of Protestant and evangelical thought and practice. Sometimes the gospel of peace has simply been omitted from the message as preached. Perhaps more often, "peace" has been reduced to the inner calm of an assuaged conscience, interpreted as "peace with God." Perhaps even more often "peace" has been separated from the gospel and assigned to Christian social ethics. As such it may arise when the topic is discipleship or Christian action in the society at large, but peace is not seen as the immediate focus of the gospel. This theological axiom has also been reinforced in the minds of many Mennonite missionaries as well as congregational members by the institutionalized division of labor between denominational mission boards and the Peace Section of the Mennonite Central Committee. In all of these ways, sometimes more explicitly, other times more implicitly, reconciliation of former enemies and the establishment of peace where prejudice, conflict, and injustice characterize human relations and social structures are not understood as integral to Christ's saving work on the cross.

In comparison to these omissions and interpretative schemes, we may summarize our thesis as follows: Peace as a present social and structural reality as well as an inner tranquillity and future promise inherently and explicitly belongs to a biblically adequate understanding of salvation through Jesus the Messiah. It therefore also inherently and explicitly belongs to a mission theology and practice which accepts the New Testament description and proclamation of the Good News as normative for Christian mission in our time.

In its major forms, the word "peace" appears over 100 times in the New Testament. The contexts of its usage also demonstrate its significance for the biblical message. God is repeatedly called the God of peace; Jesus is named the Lord of peace; the Holy Spirit is recognized to be the Spirit of peace. After Jerusalem's rejection of the messianic peace offered by Jesus, he gave it instead to his disciples. "Peace" was the characteristic greeting of the early Christians. In using this greeting, they most likely meant to follow Jesus' own practice and to witness to the fulfillment of the messianic peace. When he addressed Cornelius, a Gentile with whom faithful Jews were to have no close association, the Apostle Peter summarized God's message to his people as "the good news of peace through Jesus Christ" (Acts 10:36). The Apostle Paul encouraged the Christians in Ephesus to "stand firm" with their "feet fitted with the gospel of peace as a firm footing" (Eph. 6:15). In the same epistle, he summarized the purpose of Jesus' coming and of his death on the cross as the making of peace between Jew and Gentile.

We do well to remember that Jesus and his disciples stood in the tradition of the Old Testament law and prophets (Matt. 5:12). When they spoke about peace and identified the good news of salvation with the gospel of *peace,* they used the term in the Hebraic sense of *shalom.* John Driver has aptly summarized this understanding of peace in *Community and Commitment,* from which we quote extensively: "Shalom is a broad concept, essential to the Hebrew understanding of relationship between people and God. It covers human welfare, health, and well-being in both spiritual and material aspects. It describes a condition of well-being resulting from sound relationships among people and between people and God. According to the prophets, true peace reigned in Israel when justice (or righteousness) prevailed, when the common welfare was assured, when people were treated with equality and respect, when salvation flourished according to the social order determined by God in the covenant which he had established with his people. In fact, the prophet understood that God's covenant with Israel was a 'covenant of life and peace' (Mal. 2:5).

"On the other hand, when there was greed for unjust gain, when judges could be bought for a price, when there was not equal opportunity for all, when suffering was caused by social and economic oppression, then there was no peace, even though false prophets insisted to the contrary (Jeremiah 6:13-14).

"For the Hebrews, peace was not merely the absence of armed conflict. Rather shalom was assured by the prevalence of conditions which contribute to human well-being in all its dimensions. Not mere tranquillity of spirit or serenity of mind, peace had to do with harmonious relationships between God and his people. It had to do with social relationships characterized by his people. It had to do with social relationships characterized by justice. Peace resulted when people lived together according to God's intention. Peace, justice, and salvation are synonymous terms for general well-being created by right social relationships."[1]

To be sure, the concept of peace in the New Testament differs in significant ways from this composite image of shalom in the Old Testament. In this respect, the New Testament fulfills and transforms the expectations of the Old. But this fulfillment and transformation does not amount to replacing the Hebraic vision of peace with Greek or Roman views of peace, even though these may be more familiar to those of us shaped by western culture and accustomed to thinking with its categories. In contrast to a predominantly Greek view, the New Testament does not focus on peace as inner calm and tranquillity at the expense of peace as reconciliation in social relations and structures. Nor does the New Testament consider peace to be the balance of self-interest between power groups regulated by an extensive legal system and maintained by military might. Such a view is part of the Roman legacy to western culture. All too often Christianity has adopted this notion of peace when it has identified itself with a particular group or nation. The differences between the Old and New Testaments have to do rather with the way in which Jesus fulfilled the messianic expectations of the Old and the way in which shalom took shape in the church as the messianic community. These differences transform, but do not eliminate the structural and social dimensions, of peace understood in the Hebraic sense of shalom.

The messianic peace inaugurated by Jesus and characterizing the Christian community springs from Christ's sacrifice on the cross. As a mature missionary-theologian, the Apostle Paul summarizes in Ephesians 2 and 3 the "mystery" about the present age made known to him by revelation. According to the revelation of this mystery—something which had previously remained hidden from the sight and knowledge of humanity—God's intent at the present time is that his "manifold wisdom" be made known "to the rulers and authorities in heavenly realms" through the church. As made clear in the Apostle's summary, he does not mean simply that the church should transmit a particular message which in some curious way will be communicated to angelic powers. God would hardly have needed such a devious route of communication with angelic hosts. The crucial issue is rather that the church now exists as the messianic community made up of both Jew and Gentile. Those who had previously been divided by an insurmountable hostility of religious, social, cultural, and political dimensions now were reconciled and participated on an equal basis in the messianic shalom. The community made up of former enemies is itself the message—visible as well as verbal—of God's intent in creation, as in the cross of Christ. In the Ephesians summary, reconciliation and peace between former enemies even provides the context in which both may live in "peace with God." The peace between Jew and Gentile is the realm in which the reality of peace with God may be experienced—rather than a possible secondary and derivative consequence of a purely transcendent peace with God. The messianic peace encompasses both the reconciliation of enemies on the social level as well as the common access to the presence of God.

Contrary to several strands in the Old Testament expectations as well as among the Jewish people of the first century, Jesus as the Messiah made peace by suffering and death, rather than by righteous vengeance and the domination of the enemies of God's people: "But now in Christ Jesus you who were once far away have been brought near by the blood of Christ. For he himself is our peace, who has made the two one and has destroyed the barrier.... His purpose was to create in himself one new man out of the two, thus making peace, and in this one body to reconcile both of them to God through the cross, by which he put to death their hostility" (Eph. 2:13ff., NIV). The peace established by Jesus as the Messiah thus retains and even goes beyond the Hebraic understanding of shalom as including the social relations among God's people and between the people and God. It includes the realization of reconciliation and community unattainable by human efforts and therefore relegated to a utopian future age. What was considered utopian had now through the cross become present reality.

Traditional doctrines of the atonement have usually focused on the language of sacrifice and have understood the work of Christ for the salvation of humankind above all in relation to his death on the cross. Whether of Anselmic or Abelardian leanings, whether explaining Christ's death on the cross as a ransom paid to the devil or as a demonstration of his power over the evil one, the classic understandings of the atonement—whatever else their strengths or weaknesses—have overlooked or neglected any direct relation between the crucifixion and the social reality of the messianic peace. They have focused rather on the enmity between the sinful or guilty soul and God, thus abstracting from both the social reality of sin as well as of reconciliation.

The language of Paul's summary, however, emphasizes that the work of Christ inherently means the making of peace between human enemies as well as providing their common access to God. Peacemaking between enemies thus belongs fundamentally to the death and resurrection of Jesus Christ—not only to Christian social ethics once the enmity with God has been overcome. This making of peace includes both a destructive and a constructive action.

By his death on the cross, Jesus "has destroyed the barrier, the dividing wall of hostility, by abolishing in his flesh the law with its commandments and regulations" (Eph. 2:14f., NIV). Peacemaking in the sense of the biblical shalom means first of all negation of whatever causes division and hostility. It begins at the point of offense in the situation of conflict and confronts that offense rather than simply calling for greater toleration or balancing off one offense against another. The offense between Jew and Gentile was founded on "the law with its commandments and regulations." What had originally been given to the Jewish people as a part of God's covenant with his people had become a means of perpetuating and justifying division from and enmity with the Gentiles. The uniqueness of Jewish existence and of its relation to God was defined in such a way that it meant division from and enmity with the Gentiles. This division and hostility continued to shape the mood and actions of many early Christians—even though contrary to the leading of the Holy Spirit as recounted in Acts. But as Paul rightly insists, the fulfillment of the messianic peace in the Christian community means the destruction of the occasion for enmity and prejudice. The crucifixion of Jesus as the representative of God's chosen people means that he has taken the initiative to destroy the barrier between his people and their enemies rather than compelling the outsiders to submit to the spiritual and social domination of his people or simply leaving them outside the scope of his peace. In solidarity with Jesus, Jewish Christians were thus freed to die to the presumed necessity of finding their identity in a religious, social, and cultural reality which ratified enmity with all those outside their own ethnic group.

Nothing less than the cross of the Messiah could overcome a hostility as profound and pervasive as that between Jew and Gentile. In situations of radical enmity, the conflict may be overcome only by the elimination or defeat of the enemy. The elimination of the enemy, whether in personal or social conflict as experienced on the human level, however, rules out any reconciliation between the opposing parties. The defeat of the enemy in such conflict situations only reinforces the resentment on the part of the defeated and relegates him to the status of subjugated or second-class citizen in relation to the victor. And the defeat of the enemy only reinforces, on the part of the victor, his own personal or social identity, now further strengthened by the experience of having conquered the one who threatened that identity. These examples may serve as partial analogies to the way in which only the death of Jesus on the cross could overcome the hostility between Jew and Gentile. "Through the cross" the occasion for this conflict was destroyed without relegating the Gentiles to second-class citizenship in the messianic community. "Through the cross" the hostility was defeated without reinforcing the kind of Jewish existence which necessarily implied enmity with the Gentiles or spiritual or political subjugation to the Jews.

The making of peace and the reconciliation of former enemies has a constructive side. In destroying the barrier of hostility, Jesus' purpose "was to create in himself one new man out of the two, thus making peace." This constructive side confirms the Hebraic understanding of shalom which goes beyond mere absence of conflict to a reordering and restructuring of social relations between former enemies and between them and God. In this aspect of making peace the Messiah is the representative of a new humanity. He is the new "image of God" who incarnates a human identity in which reconciliation and peace rather than strife and division become a visible and social reality. Paul's language here is rooted in the creation account, but now oriented around the new creation in the person and corporate existence of the Messiah. Both Jew and Gentile are given a new basis for existence. Rather than perpetuating their uniqueness as experienced and defined over against each other, they are granted a new common existence in Christ. The new humanity created by the Messiah is his own corporate existence, the messianic community in which hostilities are overcome and former enemies live in peace. The messianic peace thus includes a change of attitude, but also an equally fundamental restructuring of social realities in the messianic community. National, racial, class, and cultural division and enmity are replaced by a peace which overcomes such divisions and reflects the unity of humankind in Jesus Christ.

The creation of a new corporate existence in which hostility and conflict give way to a new social and religious identity does not however amount to a kind of cosmopolitan universalism, in which the "Gentiles" gain the upper hand. The new community in which the messianic peace takes on social reality is not the realization of a humanistic universalism, but the participation of former enemies in the particular corporate existence of the Messiah. The Apostle Paul can therefore speak of Gentiles, Jews, and "the church of God" (1 Cor. 10). Nor does the fulfillment of the messianic shalom provide a rationale for the elaboration and imposition of a "Christian culture" upon all. The peace of the messianic community is a dynamic rather than a static reality which begins ever anew at the points of offense and hostility between conflicting peoples with the message of reconciliation between themselves and God. As such, the messianic community by its corporate and social existence points toward the final peace and reconciliation of all creatures, which God will establish in his name (Col. 1).

In addition to the continuity with the Hebraic vision of peace and the Pauline summary of Christ's work on the cross as reconciliation between former enemies, the broader testimony of the New Testament speaks for the structural and social dimensions of the messianic peace. In the messianic community, peace and reconciliation include the creation of new relations between men and women, relations which had been marked by alienation and structures of domination since the fall as described in Genesis. Shalom means a new social and structural relation of mutual service between men and women rather than hostility or domination based on sexual difference. The work of Christ similarly transformed the structure of relations between slaves and masters in the messianic community. Even though the legal and economic structures which perpetuated the "institution" of slavery continued in the broader society, the social reality of these relations began to take on the shape of shalom in the messianic community (Philemon, 1 Corinthians, Ephesians).

The social dimensions of the messianic peace also extend to the economic area, where wealth becomes another form of power which engenders hostility, oppression, and conflict. The Apostle Paul, who proclaimed the gospel of peace between Jew and Gentile, also helped organize the redistribution of material resources between Jewish and Gentile Christians. Not only was this redistribution to respond to the particular material needs under which Jewish Christians suffered, but it was to be carried out according to the "rule of equality" (2 Cor. 8). Far from being limited to a subjective attitude about the charitable sharing of excess wealth, the collection organized by Paul was a means of making the final equality between former enemies part of the messianic peace. Even though the economic inequalities and divisions of the broader society continued to engender hostility and conflict, the church began to live out this dimension of reconciliation and peace. In making material sharing according to the "rule of equality" part of the gospel of peace, the Apostle Paul continued the tradition of the early Jerusalem Christians who had "all things in common."

The gospel of peace thus integrally belongs to the Good News about Jesus Christ. The message of peace means that through no merit of our own, we are in Christ reconciled to our enemies and called to participate in the social realities of a new community where old structures of personal, social, and economic hostility are replaced by those of reconciliation. In this sense the gospel of peace is a social gospel. It differs from other social gospels, however, which would attempt to establish peace and overcome conflict by domination and power rather than by inviting men and women to participation in the messianic community. The gospel of peace is also the proclamation of a present reality which has begun to take shape in a world characterized by strife, injustice, and power struggles—not simply a utopian vision of a desirable future. Finally the gospel of peace is both a message and a corporate existence. The credibility of the message will therefore depend in large measure upon the community which proclaims it.

Understood as part of the gospel of peace, several New Testament passages usually cited as support for an almost exclusively individual and subjective understanding of reconciliation and peace with God, in fact express a more comprehensive perspective. For example, most translations of 2 Corinthians 5 encourage an understanding of God's reconciling work in Christ limited to an inner and personal transformation. Instead of the familiar "if anyone is in Christ, he is a new creature" (or an equivalent rendering), a more accurate translation of verse 17 would read "'therefore, if anyone is in Christ, [there is a] new creation—the old has gone, behold the new has come." Through reconciliation in Christ there is thus a whole new perspective, a whole new way of looking at the world. Rather than others being judged from the worldly perspective of status, nationality, culture, class, gender, or race, they are now seen as befits their common participation "in Christ." Reconciliation thus means both peace with God as well as with those previously considered enemies. Another example is the familiar opening verse of Romans 5: "Therefore, since we have been justified through faith, we have peace with God through our Lord Jesus Christ...." Even though the immediate context of Romans 5:1 does not explicitly refer to the social dimensions of shalom, it does not exclude them either, particularly in view of the Hebraic understanding of shalom which includes both spiritual and social reconciliation. Moreover the broader setting of Romans 5 has to do with the theological foundations of the gospel addressed to both Jew and Gentile. Just as the shalom of the messianic community may not be reduced to a purely social reality, so this social dimension may not be excluded from the peace with God incarnate in Jesus Christ.

A renewed vision of the gospel of peace as an integral part of the Good News of Jesus Christ would have far-reaching consequences for missionary thought and practice. It would mean a theological reorientation with respect to central, traditional, doctrinal formulations which have not been foundationally shaped by the social dimensions of the Good News. It would mean an understanding of the Apostle Paul as a peacemaker, continuing the teaching of Jesus on peace as well as his reconciling way of the cross in the cities of the Roman Empire. It would mean an extension of the missionary proclamation in our time to include the messianic peace addressed to situations of enmity and injustice. It would mean giving priority to theological and missionary efforts which focus on points of conflict and reconciliation rather than reinforcing or totally undergirding given social and economic conflicts and enmity. It would mean the renewal of the church as a messianic community whose basis for existence derives not from national, ethnic, or cultural givens, but from an ever new corporate identity in Christ. To all of this and more we are called and freed by the "good news of peace through Jesus Christ."

---

[1] John Driver, *Community and Commitment* (Herald Press, 1976) 71.

Chapter 2

Preaching the gospel of peace
Ephesians 2:14, 17

Reprinted by permission from *Gospel Herald,* vol. 76, no. 35 (August 30, 1983) 593-96.

Early last March the National Association of Evangelicals gathered at Orlando, Florida. Among the many speakers and preachers were two Ronalds: Ronald Reagan and Ronald Sider. Ronald Reagan, as we doubtless all know, currently serves as president of the United States. Ronald Sider, as some of us may know, presently serves as president of Evangelicals for Social Action. Both Ronalds came to the NAE meeting with a message about peace.

As reported by the *New York Times* Ronald Reagan admonished Evangelical Christians to speak out against recent demonstrations of anti-Semitism and ethnic and racial hatred in this country. "Use the mighty voice of your pulpits and the powerful standing of your churches to denounce and isolate hate groups...preaching ethnic and racial hatred in this country.... The commandment given us is clear and simple: 'Thou shalt love thy neighbor as thyself.'"

The first Ronald went on to warn the Christians gathered at Orlando against other Christians who are promoting a bilateral freeze on strategic nuclear arms between the United States and the Soviet Union. He contended: "The truth is that a freeze now would be a very dangerous trend, for that is merely the illusion of peace. The reality is that we must find peace through strength." Accordingly we ought to "pray for the salvation of all those who live in totalitarian darkness." But until "they discover the joy of knowing God they are the focus of evil in the modern world." Until then peace through strength rather than through a bilateral freeze demands the support of American Christians.

Two days later the other Ronald addressed the Florida assembly. He challenged evangelical Christians to speak out in *favor* of a bilateral nuclear freeze. But he launched this challenge after sounding several notes which had not been heard in the first Ronald's sermon. He reminded his listeners that Jesus had focused the love of neighbor in the love for the enemy: "Jesus taught us to love our enemies.... Loving our enemies at least means refusing to put them in the category of enemies to be hated or eliminated, refusing to put them in the category of subhuman beings whose lives are less important than ours. Loving our enemies means insisting that even the wicked are still persons for whom Christ died, neighbors to be loved and understood."

The second Ronald also pointed out that millions who live in the Soviet Union confess the name of Jesus Christ. There are 70 million professing Christians in that country. A higher percentage of them go to church each Sunday than in Great Britain, France, and West Germany. The church of Jesus Christ lives not only in the West, but also in the East. The first Ronald didn't even mention this; the second Ronald made it a launching pad for Christian peacemaking: "American Evangelicals could take the lead in developing a worldwide movement for peace in the church. Since the one we worship is the Prince of Peace who commanded his followers to be peacemakers, surely the place to start working for peace is the worldwide body of Christ."

Just as the first Ronald, the other Ronald also called upon his listeners to pray. But he focused the appeal to prayer quite differently: "Let's pray for a mighty revival that brings millions of sinners into a living personal relationship with Jesus Christ.... Let's pray for a peace revival in which people see that Jesus is the only way to peace and that peace is the way to Jesus."

Two Ronalds and two sermons. Two preachers of peace. Both cited Scriptures. Both exhorted their listeners to pray. Both challenged them to action. Both proclaimed the way to peace. For the one, peace with military strength is the message, and an expanded nuclear arsenal the way. For the other a peace revival which includes loving the enemy is the message and Jesus is the way. Which peace shall we preach? Which peace will you preach as you take up or continue your ministry in the Christian church?

Two kinds of peace

President Reagan proclaims the kind of peace that has a long and venerable tradition in human history. In Western civilization we call it the Roman idea of peace, the *pax romana*. For the *pax romana*, peace depends on the empire's military strength, a strength superior to all real and potential enemies. This wall of defense is needed to defend the law and order within the empire from the chaos and disorder without. This wall of defense protects the civilization inside from the barbarism which is rampant outside. The pax romana assumes that the good is on the side of the empire and the empire on the side of good. The security of the empire, indeed of the entire civilized world, depends on the strength of the *pax romana*. Peace with strength is the message; a superior military arsenal the way.

In fact, there are two major contenders for the *pax romana* in the world today: the United States and the Soviet Union. The *pax romana* has split into a *pax sovietica* and a *pax americana!* Each claims to incarnate the true movement of history. Each claims the ancient role of the Roman Empire as the modern guardian of civilization.

President Sider proclaims the kind of peace that also has a long and venerable tradition, but in a different history. Its source is the covenant history that comes to fulfillment in Jesus Christ. This kind of peace goes back to Abraham and Sarah who were called out of their nation in order that God could make them a blessing for all nations. This kind of peace depends on God's miraculous intervention to gather a motley crowd of slaves into a people and to preserve them as a holy people called to be different in the midst of other peoples. This kind of peace is the *shalom* which includes both a new quality of relationship to God and to human beings. It encompasses forgiveness from sin, a new birth in relation to God, and justice and love in human relations. This *shalom* comes to its fulfillment in the Messiah Jesus "who is our peace," who has "broken down the dividing wall of hostility...who came and preached peace to those far off and to those near at hand." Because this kind of peace comes to its fulfillment in Christ, we can call it the *pax Christi.*

Today I would like to invite you to join the second Ronald in preaching this kind of peace. Just as the apostle Peter proclaimed the "gospel of peace" to the Roman centurion Cornelius (Acts 10:36), let us renew the proclamation of peace to all in our time. Let us be preachers of the *pax Christi* rather than propagandists of the *pax romana.*

Preaching the "gospel of peace" in our time will do at least three things. It will recast our call to conversion. It will renew the priority of Christian community. And it will witness to the cosmic consequences of the *pax Christi.*

Comprehensive conversion

Preaching the gospel of peace calls first for a *comprehensive vision of conversion.*

In the Protestant tradition the peace of the gospel has come to mean peace with God. From Martin Luther's anguished conscience in search of a gracious God was born a Reformation emphasizing justification by faith and an inner peace with God. From John Wesley's desire to experience renewal was born a revival which emphasized a change of heart and a vital sense of peace with God. The call to conversion in the Protestant and revivalist heritage has focused on an inner transformation of the heart and on the individual believers relationship to God.

Unfortunately, the emphasis on an inner transformation of the heart and a personal relationship to God has usually cut the biblical scope of conversion and renewal in half. According to Ephesians 2, Christ is our peace not only with God, but simultaneously with those who have formerly been our human enemies. Gentiles and Jews who previously hated each other have "been brought near in the blood of Christ...who has broken down the dividing wall of hostility." Through Christ the heart is indeed transformed. Through Christ there is indeed access to a gracious God. But the same blood of Christ breaks down the walls of hostility between human beings and creates *one* new humanity where there have been enemies. The gospel of peace through Christ envisions a conversion and a rebirth which transforms both our relationship to God and our relationship to our enemies or to those for whom we are enemies. Anything less is a half conversion, half a new birth.

The second Ronald who preached peace at Orlando, Florida, proclaimed this vision of *comprehensive conversion.* He entreated his listeners to pray for a revival which would bring sinners into a living relationship with Jesus Christ. He also challenged them to pray for a revival which would convert their acceptance of enmity with others to breaking down the nuclear wall of hostility.

Christian community

Preaching the gospel of peace will secondly renew the *priority of Christian community.*

In the *pax romana,* the national community takes priority over all other communities and groups. On the North American continent the United States became a nation by overcoming particular and regional interests and molding them into a "new world." On the Asian continent, the Soviet Union became a nation by overthrowing a decrepit czarist regime and welding a multitude of peoples and provinces into a world power. In both cases, the nation claims priority over detractors from within and those who threaten from without. The first Ronald who preached peace at Orlando last spring clearly exhorted his listeners to assert this nation's priority against detractors from within and enemies from without.

Unfortunately, this emphasis on the nation's priority in the *pax romana* tradition has usually blinded Christians to the priority of the Christian community in the *pax Christi* heritage. According to our text, Jesus Christ has made Jewish and Gentile believers "both one, and has broken down the dividing wall of hostility...that he might create in himself one new man in place of the two, so making peace...." In the first epistle to the Corinthian Christians the apostle Paul even speaks about three types of human beings: Jews, Greeks, and the church of God (1 Cor. 10:32). Because our peace is in Christ, we are a new people, a new "nation" if you will, whose boundaries are measured by faith rather than by geography. The millions of Christians in the United States and the millions of Christians in the Soviet Union belong first of all to this transnational Christian community and only secondarily to our particular nations. That Jewish and Gentile believers should become a new people in Christ seemed incredible to the first generation of Christians. That American and Soviet believers belong to a community which takes precedence over ethnic and national loyalties seems equally incredible to many Christians today. Nevertheless this priority of Christian community belongs at the heart of Christ's peace.

In the late 1940s a young student from Eastern Europe came to the United States to study theology. During his years here, he married an American woman. When the communist party came to power, he and his wife struggled with whether they should remain here or return to his home country. After prayer, counsel from friends and teachers, they decided to return.

The young minister served briefly as a pastor in a large city. They then moved to a small Protestant congregation in a large industrial town. In the early 1950s, he was arrested. His arrest came during the Stalin years of repression against the church. He was suspected of being a spy: why else would he return to an Eastern bloc country after marrying an American woman? During the years he worked in a forced labor camp, his wife held the congregation together in spite of her broken language and the care of two small children.

When he was released, they began to seek ways to incarnate Christian community beyond political and ideological walls. They invited Christians from Eastern countries and Christians from Western countries to their congregation and to the churches in their country.

Participants in these encounters discovered a common faith. They discovered sisters and brothers where they had previously written off everyone as either enemies or victims of enemies. The biblical vision of a new people in Christ began to light up the eyes of believers again.

Cosmic consequences

Preaching Christ's peace witnesses to its *cosmic consequences.*

The apostle Paul shares the vision of Christ's peace in Ephesians 2. He goes on in 3:10 to say: "Through the church the manifold wisdom of God might now be made known to the principalities and powers in the heavenly places." These heavenly principalities and powers represent the structures of created order. They guide the social and political institutions. They reflect the balance of national and ideological loyalties which shape human life in this world. Common sense would have seen these principalities and powers preserving the divisions between Jews and Gentiles, between Romans and barbarians. The *pax romana* didn't challenge these divisions or this structured balance between hostile groups. It sought to channel them and to preserve them.

But the *pax Chrtsti* incarnated a new reality that must have startled the principalities and the powers. The peace of Christ changed from within the way reality "really is." The peace of Christ challenged the way things "had always been" by the very existence of this new humanity in Jesus Christ. The peace of Christ demonstrated this new humanity not only by preaching the gospel of peace, but also by the very existence of the new Christian community.

It is fitting that the second Ronald who preached peace at Orlando challenged his listeners to start working for peace in the worldwide body of Christ. The Eastern European-American pastoral couple began to work in precisely this way. They touched the lives of many people both in their country and in other countries.

About two years ago they planned to travel together back to the United States to visit family, friends, and churches. In the more than thirty years since they had left, they had not returned to the States together. Two months before their scheduled trip, the wife took ill and died within a week.

Her funeral became the occasion for a unique gathering of people. People who did not speak to each other in public, and very rarely in private, because of political and church tensions, came to the funeral. Survivors from the forced labor camp came. Christians from the local congregation and other congregations came. Both government representatives and political dissenters came. Christians and those professing no faith came. All had somehow seen in the ministry of this couple and the church there something which transcended their usual categories. They had seen something of God's wisdom being revealed through the life and ministry of that church. They had glimpsed something of the cosmic consequences which flow from the peace of Christ.

Chapter 3

The Word of the Cross

Reprinted by permission from *The Way of the Cross and Resurrection*, John M. Drescher, ed. (Herald Press, 1978) 99-108.

For the word of the cross is folly to those who are perishing, but to us who are being saved it is the power of God. 1 Corinthians 1:18.

The Apostle Paul sometimes summarized the gospel as the "word of the cross." Far from narrowing the New Testament message down to a handy cliché, this short phrase binds together the life of Jesus and the early church, the work of Christ and Christian conduct. The "word of the cross" is rooted in a particular historic event, signifies the forgiveness of sins through Jesus Christ, points to the faithfulness and sacrifice of Jesus Christ on our behalf, and symbolizes the Christian lifestyle in the world.

Many religions zealously tally the number of miracles wrought by their founders and followers; only the New Testament proclaims the cross of Christ as the decisive act of God. Many religions recount stories of divine beings taking on human form; only the Christian faith focuses on God Incarnate suffering the ignominious death on the cross.

Several religions hope for life after death; only the Christian hope lives from the resurrection of the Crucified One. Little wonder that the apostle reminds his readers that the word of the cross appears as foolishness and weakness in the eyes of the world.

Human power and wisdom

In the early chapters of 1 Corinthians, Paul emphasized one facet of this unique word of the cross. The Corinthian Christians had apparently relegated the cross to the margin of faith and life. In their perhaps even well-intentioned enthusiasm for the gospel they had translated the word of the cross into categories compatible with the wisdom and power coveted by the society around them. They may even have replaced the message of the cross with Corinthian versions of human power and wisdom.

The consequences were devastating. Instead of welding Christians of diverse ethnic and religious origins into a new community in Christ, conformity to Corinthian wisdom and power began to fragment the young congregation. Instead of shaping a Christian lifestyle which could be a light in a religiously and morally decadent society, the conformity to Corinthian wisdom and power added a halo to their immorality and justified it in the name of Christian liberty.

In this context the apostle vigorously called the Corinthian Christians back to the centrality of the cross. Conformity to the cross and nonconformity to the surrounding society would lead to church unity and faithful Christian conduct; nonconformity to the cross and conformity to the surrounding society would deepen the congregational divisions and undermine Christian obedience.

Let us look more closely at why and how the Christians at Corinth departed from the "word of the cross" because of conformity to the surrounding culture and society.

Why did early Christians change their thinking?

The Corinthian Christians were doubtless impressed by the many philosophical schools and groups in their city. Each had its wise teacher who vied with others in thinking the deepest thoughts and attracting the most brilliant students. These philosophers taught the latest fads as well as the most venerated traditions. They sought to give a wise and profound account of human experience, about the world of nature and society.

Many of the Corinthian Christians apparently transferred the customs of Christian "schools" and groups to the church. They saw Paul, Peter, and Apollos as their wise men, each bringing new insights and teaching. The Corinthian church, which had little educational or social standing, could now boast about "their philosopher." They could also be somebody. Like other groups in Corinth they began to argue the merits of their teachers and the demerits of the others. One group boasted of Paul but *not* Peter as their wise man. Another claimed Peter but *not* Paul as theirs. One group even claimed Christ rather than Paul, Peter, or Apollos as theirs.

The congregation thus became a reflection of the Corinthian pagan society—divided into groups which disputed conflicting claims of wisdom and loyalty to their "wise man." Conformity to the wisdom of the world around them threatened to divide the congregation permanently.

This conformity to the society and the nonconformity to the cross expressed itself not only in the congregational relations, but almost certainly in the content of the message as well. As an illustration of how Christians of Greek origins would have valued wisdom and how sophisticated non-Christians would have therefore criticized the "word of the cross," we may refer to Celsus' attack on Christianity.

Celsus, even though writing a generation after the Apostle Paul, spoke out of the same mentality which would have been present in first-century Corinth. He vigorously tried to demonstrate the utter senselessness of the cross. Celsus recognized that the Christians proclaimed "the Son of God to be the Word." But for the Greek philosopher, *Word* represented beauty, goodness, and the profound rationality of reality.

The Word preached by the Christians by contrast grated Celsus' sensibilities and challenged reasonable standards of truth. He disdained those "who do not bring forth a true and holy Word, but a man who was arrested most disgracefully and crucified." Had Jesus been genuinely divine—Celsus argued—he should have displayed his divine power and greatness by "suddenly disappearing from the cross" rather than submitting to its shame and accepting the insults against him and his Father. Celsus' conclusion: the message of the cross is indeed foolishness.

Faced with such values in the surrounding culture, the Corinthian Christians apparently began to emphasize the wisdom of God in such a way that it would be more palatable to the Greek way of thinking. Because the cross fit least well into a vision of wisdom focused on beauty, goodness, and rational order, they may well have begun to concentrate rather on eloquent wisdom, spiritual gifts, wise speech, and knowledge at the expense of the word of the cross. Conformity to the wisdom of the world around them threatened to empty the cross of its meaning for the Corinthian Christians.

Finally, many of the Christians at Corinth were apparently also fascinated with both spiritual and material power. The city of Corinth boasted not only many philosopher schools but many religious groups and currents. Each offered its own version of power: power to accomplish the extraordinary, power to open deep religious mysteries, power to ascent to the heights of religious experience. Those who demonstrated special powers also expected and claimed special privileges—easily enough obtainable from the crowds fascinated by the mysterious. Spiritual ratings were prevalent: the spiritual ones distinguished themselves proudly from the less spiritual. And those who exhibited extraordinary spiritual powers simultaneously claimed privileges of higher honor, respect, financial, and social status.

This fascination with spiritual and material power also led to deviations and divisions in the Corinthian congregation. Some considered themselves spiritually superior to others because they could perform extraordinary miracles or speak in unknown tongues. Some criticized the Apostle Paul because his rhetoric was not eloquent and powerful, or because he maintained a humble social and economic status. Some rationalized that their spiritual power and freedom raised them above the petty considerations of faithfulness in marriage. Some discounted the resurrection because they had already attained the "new life." Some had moved up in society and were using the levers of the courts to obtain greater economic status.

This conformity to the power of the world around them threatened to shatter the Corinthian Christians' fellowship and empty the cross of its power. Paul reminded his readers by their own experience and by the heart of the gospel story that God, however, chose what was weak in the world to shame the strong and begged them to return wholeheartedly to "Christ crucified," indeed the power of God. Conformity to the word of the cross would correct the Corinthian Christians' fascination with signs and power as manageable proof of divine intervention and justification of their own spiritual and material status.

What is the "word of the cross"?

What is this "word of the cross" which the apostle repeatedly placed before the early Christians? How does "Jesus Christ and him crucified" represent the power and wisdom of God—the kind of wisdom and power which differs radically from the kind prized and promoted by an unbelieving society and culture?

The Apostle Paul reminded his readers that none of the rulers of this age understood the wisdom and power of God in Christ. Had they understood and accepted it rather than desperately trying to preserve their own power and wisdom, "they would not have crucified the Lord of glory" (1 Cor. 2: 8).

Those who crucified Jesus were precisely the ones who stood for the kind of wisdom and power which exercised a tantalizing influence on the Corinthian Christians. The Jewish leaders, preoccupied with signs and manifestations of divine power, clamored for the crucifixion of him who offered them only the sign of Jonah and entered Jerusalem on a humble donkey instead of a magnificent war horse. The Roman leaders, representing traditional wisdom, political might, and legal power, cross-examined Jesus by pressing for his definition of truth as well as a confession of his complicity in a movement seeking political power. To preserve their synthesis of wisdom and power, they sent Jesus off to be crucified.

In another epistle, Paul used three verbs to express more adequately what happened to these kinds of wisdom and power at the cross. At the cross God "disarmed" worldly power and wisdom and made a public example of them, "thus triumphing over them" (Col. 2:15). In what way did God make a public example of unbelieving wisdom and power at the cross, triumph over them, and disarm them?

It is first of all precisely in the crucifixion that the true nature of unbelieving wisdom and power has come to light. Prior to the cross, they were accepted as basic and ultimate realities of this world, as standards by which to measure human experience and religious endeavor.

Previously people had not perceived that this belief was based upon an illusion. Philosophers had believed that such power enabled the preservation and guaranteed the security of society and individual persons, that such wisdom provided the necessary insight to understand the meaning of life and to solve the riddle of human existence.

But when the one true God appeared on earth in Christ, it became apparent that the highest human wisdom and the greatest human power of the time were his adversaries rather than his instruments. Now the belief in them and the dedication to them is unmasked as deceptive and illusory: they are made a public spectacle.

By unmasking the claims of worldly wisdom and power to be the final arbiters of human experience and piety, God also "triumphs" over them. The unmasking is already their defeat. During the present time, however, only the men and women who know that God himself has appeared on earth in Jesus Christ can see what has happened. Only those "who are being saved" (1 Cor. 1:18) hear the word of the cross as a word of genuine power rather than of weakness. To "those who are being lost," the cross appears as weakness on the part of Christ and power on the part of those who ordered his crucifixion. But what Christ already accomplished at the cross became manifest in his resurrection, namely, that in Christ God challenged the best of human wisdom and power, penetrated their territory, and demonstrated that he remains stronger and wiser than they.

The evidence of this triumph is that at the cross Christ also disarmed human power and wisdom in their claims to attain the highest truth and deploy the greatest strength. As Hendrik Berkhof has pointed out, the weapon of this kind of wisdom and power "was the power of illusion, their ability to convince men that they were...regents of the world, ultimate certainty and ultimate direction, ultimate happiness and ultimate duty for small, dependent humanity. Since Christ we know that this is an illusion. We are called to a higher destiny: we have higher orders to follow and we stand under a greater protector.... Unmasked, revealed in their true nature, they have lost their mighty grip on men. The cross has disarmed them: wherever it is preached, their unmasking and disarming take place."

The word of the cross, therefore, frees "those who are being saved" from the kind of wisdom and power which crucified Christ and opens to them a vision and reality of the alternate power and wisdom manifest in him. What is the shape of this alternate power and wisdom? And how does conformity to the word of the cross lead to church unity and faithful Christian conduct?

The cross and servanthood

The power of Christ crucified is the power of servanthood. In Philippians 2:7 the Apostle Paul recounted how Christ Jesus "emptied himself, taking the form of a servant." In his first letter to the Corinthians, the apostle stated that he and Apollos were nothing more than servants. They could make no claims to final authority over the Christians at Corinth. The power which had been given them was the power to execute faithfully the task of building up the body of Christ, not the power to dominate others and acquire an elevated status in the church or in the surrounding society. As servants of Christ they both belonged to all the Christians in Corinth, who in turn all belonged to Christ, the Servant par excellence.

Paul thus admonished the Corinthian Christians to conform to the word of the cross as it takes the shape of servanthood rather than to a society bent on the acquisition of power as domination. Serving, rather than dominating, becomes the principle of Christian unity and fellowship; sacrificing, rather than the manipulation of personal and material status, the path to congregational solidarity. Common subordination to the servanthood of Jesus Christ, rather than the proud promotion of extraordinary spiritual powers, charts the course to Christian excellence. Seeking to demonstrate the mind of Christ—rather than glorifying individual uniqueness—leads the way to church unity and Christian obedience.

The same may be said of the alternate wisdom rooted in the word of the cross. The wisdom of God in Christ reveals a new creation which transcends and judges the fallen world that unbelieving wisdom seeks to justify. As someone has observed, human rationality at its best still "seeks its foundation and its justification in the forces which hold the world in its eternal order, and which also surround with superior forces the mighty human spirit itself."

The wisdom revealed by the word of the cross, however, does not seek to understand and justify fallen creation apart from Christ and then to fit Christ into the scheme of things so understood. It rather recognizes that the inner structure of the world is transitory. The alternate wisdom of the cross, therefore, begins with the new creation in Christ and understands the world in that light. The alternate wisdom of the cross recognizes that even though the world in its effort to probe the depths of truth and reality rejected Christ, God has revealed in him the beginning of a new humanity and will make all things one with himself in Christ (Col. 1). Conformity to this vision of reality will become visible in a Christian obedience discernible by its resemblance to the cross of Christ rather than by whether it fits well within the acceptable moral standards of an unbelieving society.

Chapter 4

The Missionary Method of Jesus

Reprinted by permission from *Gospel Herald*, vol. 69, no. 8 (February 24, 1976) 150-53.

Some of my earliest memories are of childhood fantasies that I would someday be a missionary. I managed to combine the idea that mission was the great task of the church with the belief that it was exciting because you could go to places like Australia, where they knew how to make boomerangs. In the course of personal and spiritual growth the boomerangs fell away, but a certain kind of mission idealism remained a part of my thinking and motivation. Partly for that reason, and partly because of the encouragement of friends and others, I left the United States to spend a year in Japan as a college student.

One of the reasons for doing this was to see what missionaries looked like when they were out there, and to see what missions looked like in that kind of a setting. It was in part a traumatic experience, beginning already on a ship where I met some missionaries. The trauma continued throughout several of the first months that I was in Japan as a young student. I began to see that much of what I had understood in the light of my missionary idealism did not at all measure up to the gospel, and that what was happening very often was the exporting of American power and self-righteousness and denominationalism more than it was the sending of the gospel.

The experience was so difficult that for several months I was involved in a personal debate about whether it was still possible to remain a Christian. Through the help of God and some missionaries I began to see that there is also another kind of mission and that this other kind has much more to do with what Jesus was asking his disciples to do.

Some time after returning from the Japanese experience, still with deep convictions about the mission of the church, but with the romanticism and the idealism shattered, my wife and I left to work in Europe. We also spent time itinerating in West Africa. During that time of examining and testing mission methods and messages I came to a deepened and renewed appreciation of what we observe in Matthew 10. I have concluded that if we would see this Scripture in all its relevance before we turn to the Great Commission, the shape of mission would be radically changed.

Jesus first sent out his disciples at a time when Jewish people were probably more missionary than before or since. Great effort was expended to demonstrate the uniqueness of the Jewish faith in terms other people could understand. It was a time when some of the restrictions of what it meant to be a Jew were relaxed so that other people could become Jews without having to change all the customs. It was like changing Mennonite disciplines so that people in Africa don't have to live as we do in Eureka or Elkhart.

This whole missionary outreach met with a certain measure of success as we know because early Christians scattering throughout the Roman Empire found numerous Jewish proselytes. Many of the first Christians came from those groups of Jewish proselytes.

Riding the waves

There are, of course, differences between that situation of the first century in the Roman Empire and ours of the twentieth century in North America and in Europe. Yet we too are riding the waves of a powerful missionary stream that has changed the course of world history. It began in the eighteenth and nineteenth centuries. Today there are between 35 and 40 thousand American and Western European missionaries in countries other than their origin, working, preaching the gospel, and doing various other kinds of things that are involved in a holistic mission outreach of the church. Since the World War Two, the vast majority of those foreign missionaries are North Americans, and more specifically from the United States.

It's beginning also to work the other way. There are approximately 2,500 missionaries who have been sent out from different countries of the Third World, some of them coming to the United States and Canada, and some to France. There is also a measure of success in this whole missionary wave going in all directions.

There are thousands of Christian congregations and millions of Christians around the world because of this missionary wave of the past two centuries. In many respects there have been noble motivations and great results. But it is a mixture of good and bad. However, those of us who want to be sons and daughters of the kingdom need not only to recognize the mixture, but distinguish the good from the bad. We should begin by going back to Jesus to see what he said and did about mission.

It is striking that Jesus did not have a lot to say about this great missionary wave of the first century, except one rather cryptic statement. In Matthew 23 he addressed himself to the missionary activists of his time: "Woe to you, teachers of the law and Pharisees, you hypocrites! You travel over land and sea to win a single convert, and when he becomes one, you make him twice as much a son of hell as you are" (23:15, NIV).

That is not a very polite thing to say about foreign missionaries. It is not very affirming, nor does it tend to encourage dialogue. We should remember that the Pharisees were a renewal movement among the Jewish people and they had, for the most part, good intentions. Jesus was not criticizing their intentions. He was criticizing what was happening in comparison to the coming of the kingdom of God. The question that has often troubled me is whether Jesus would say something like this in relation to much of the missionary awakening of the past centuries.

We ought to examine this kind of question very carefully. And it would be a question of distinguishing between different cases. At the least we need to recognize that Jesus did not simply ride the current missionary movement. There are very good reasons for that. If we learn those reasons we can also be the kinds of missionaries that Jesus was calling his disciples to be.

Let's return to our text (Matt. 10:1-23) and lift out several things. The first thing he said was: "Do not go among the Gentiles or enter any town of the Samaritans. Go rather to the lost sheep of Israel." Begin, in other words, in Galilee. Do not start by moving out there where all the missionary activity is happening. Begin right here where you come from, right in your backyard. The other side of this missionary method also seemed to strike in the face of what was understood as successful missionary strategy. Do not take along any gold or silver or copper in your belts. Take no bag for the journey or extra tunic or sandals or a staff.

But how are you going to carry on anything if you don't have some kind of base from which to operate? We would usually establish this first of all. Jesus, however, was saying: Learn to be a missionary by making yourself vulnerable to those to whom you go. Do not go to them out of a position of power where you look down on them and they have to look up to you. Why did he do it that way? Because that is the kingdom way to do it. That is the kind of King he is and the kind of missionary Jesus wants.

It is difficult to understand why Jesus, the Son of Man, the King of this new kingdom, the Prince of this new kingdom, the Messiah, said, "I have no place to lay my head." The King of all and no place to lay his head! He had no position from which he could get a lever on everyone else. He made himself weak and vulnerable and dependent on others in going out to them and in reaching to them.

One could give examples of North Americans and others who have understood and lived out this kind of missionary stance. But one could give more examples of those who have not understood and lived out their lack of understanding. I could give examples where there were deep struggles in the church because the missionary would say, "You cannot tell me what to do because you do not pay me." On the other hand, I could mention missionaries who would say, "Yes, we could get around faster and reach more people if we had cars, but since everyone in town has a bicycle, we will ride bicycles." You can trace the development in the preaching of the gospel and the building of Christian community by whether missionaries have adopted the one stance or the other.

Particular American temptations

As Americans we have particular kinds of temptations. We are in general a practical and pragmatic people. We measure success in terms of doing it faster and better and bigger, and we don't understand that this often means wielding power and crushing people, rather than being vulnerable and sensitive to them. When we want to measure the success we can say how fast something was done, but we don't measure how long afterward it took to repair the damage. Jesus taught another way and he put his disciples through the paces of this other way before he ever talked to them about going beyond Galilee and making disciples of all nations.

Now why is that? On the more superficial level what Christians have learned to do at home they tend to do when they go somewhere else. Jesus was not simply talking about what the disciples were going to do when they got out there, but how they were living and witnessing in Galilee. He was talking about how they were going to their neighbors. He was talking about their style of life at home.

If we keep on translating we could say he was talking about the congregational structures at home. He was talking about how people worship at home. He was talking about the models of church leadership at home. He was talking about whether or not we have learned to be conformed to his Spirit instead of the spirit of the world. If we have not learned all those things, or even if we have, we tend to repeat what we have done there. So each local congregation in Galilee or Eureka or Paoli or Harrisonburg is the primary training ground for missions "out there." Jesus was really liberating his disciples and those who would be citizens of the kingdom from the temptation to use mission and service as a stepping-stone to power, to personal gain, to the fulfillment of romantic idealism, and to the satisfaction of personal ambition.

This is important because the method is part of the message. As Mennonites we still need to learn that the medium is the message because we have sometimes confused personal or denominational ambition with our understanding of the proclamation of the kingdom of God. And I say this not in order to criticize those who have led us into mission, but that we might learn to distinguish serving Christ from serving ourselves.

In *A New Rhythm for Mennonites,* a study of American Mennonite mission outreach until the latter part of the nineteenth century, Theron Schlabach points out that Mennonites in the first part of the nineteenth century and earlier had very little concern for evangelism. Then toward the end of the nineteenth century one began to hear them say that their fathers had sinned in not being involved in evangelism. There was a strong motivation to become involved in evangelism and mission. That was honorable, and we can be grateful for the way God has led.

However, there was at the same time an ambition to become a part of the larger missionary movement, something which had not been a part of the mood in the earlier time, says Schlabach. It shows that even with honorable motives we can become involved in the cultural mood that surrounds us. We can easily see missionary outreach and service as a part of becoming more respectable as individuals and as a denomination as well as becoming more Christian.

Schlabach gives several examples. One was an invitation from John F. Funk to John S. Coffman to help with the publishing efforts in Elkhart, Indiana. Coffman hoped his response was not motivated by "vain aspiration," and wished "to serve my Master in the best way and place that I can." He observed that not only farmers were needed in the church and he wanted to have his sons consider church publishing.

Further, he did not sense a need for his services as a minister in Virginia, where people had little interest in his preaching. Working on Funk's staff would give him "abundant opportunity to improve myself" and also make the whole Mennonite Church his forum. Finally Coffman wanted "to better my worldly circumstances though I crave only a comfortable living" (pp. 27, 28).

We are no less ambitious

This is not to throw stones. For if there was a note of ambition among those who have helped to renew our brotherhood and our sisterhood in the last part of the nineteenth century, we have not grown less ambitious since that time. So we need to ask ourselves to what degree our mission and service springs from this kind of ambition, and to what degree it is ready to return to the kind of vulnerability and servanthood which Jesus talked about and lived.

What does this mean? Does it mean that for the next two years we tell our mission boards not to send out foreign missionaries? I don't think so. However, I believe that it should mean at least several things for each of us and our congregations. For example, we have been talking much about peoplehood and about what it means to be a part of a charismatic community. We have heard what it means to be a part of the black people and the Latino people.

We have also heard ambivalent feelings expressed. Some ask why should we be Anabaptists—let's simply be Christian. I think that if we are to go back to the kind of stance that Jesus emphasized we will need to return to a different kind of peoplehood which does not depend upon its own tradition and which does not depend upon itself for its power to move forward.

Jesus was creating a new people. He called together the twelve disciples and sent them out as a beginning of this new community. He sent them out so that they would remain vulnerable, and sensitive, so they would remain dependent upon the people to whom they went. But he did not send them out to preach a message which would make their Jewish peoplehood the focus of concern. He sent them out, if I can translate, not to preach the kind of message which would make charismatic community the focus of concern. He sent them out, if I may translate, not to make Latin-American community the focus of concern.

He sent them not to make North American Mennonite community styles the focus of concern. He sent them out to emphasize God's kingdom. Because this is God's kingdom it could not be equated with one of the other definitions of peoplehood, which the Jewish people would have liked to have had, or which perhaps we would also like to have.

It has been exciting for me at the Mennonite Church General Assembly to see black and Latino brothers becoming associate secretaries. It reminded me of what happened in Acts 6 where the church had to be reorganized because the Jewish Christians were running away with things and the Greek Christians didn't have much of a say. But there were other steps after that. The other steps had to do with making sure that this was God's kind of peoplehood, God's kind of kingdom, and not simply a mixture of various types with no one very sure about what was going on. God's kind of people and God's kind of community was something that was created anew out of these various kinds.

There was something Jewish about this new community. There was something Greek about the new community. But because it was God's community, it was not either one or the other. When we understand that God takes those elements of the Anabaptist tradition which are right without letting them become a means of power and self-rationalization and justification, then they can become a part of his kingdom. When we understand that he uses those elements of charismatic community which are right for renewing the church, then they can become a part of his kingdom. When we understand that he uses those elements of the black Mennonite community, or of Latino or of white, to become a part of his kingdom, then we can understand how it is God's people and God's community rather than one of our own.

When we understand that, we will quit playing off Anabaptists or charismatics or blacks over against others. That is a difficult process. It requires repentance, growth, renewal. It is something that can happen only in mission and it is something that can happen only if we begin our mission in our backyard and only if that mission is carried on in a spirit of humility and vulnerability and servanthood.

I would like to commend this vision of the missionary method to each one of us. Let us begin in the way we structure our congregations, in our personal relations, in the message that wives and husbands and fathers and mothers and businessmen and church leaders and doctors and nurses exercise in their daily walk.

If we learn to live, to incorporate, and to proclaim the message in this way, God will then call us to extend this message and this mission beyond the borders of Galilee. It will have a power to build up rather than crush, and a strength to continue to the ends of the earth rather than being the exportation of our own provincialisms and ambitions.

Chapter 5

The Church in the World:
A Mennonite Perspective

Reprinted by permission from *The Covenant Quarterly,* vol. XLI, no. 3 (August 1983) 45-50.

This essay attempts to summarize, according to a Mennonite perspective, the nature and the shape of the Christian reality in the world. An attempt to carry out this assignment adequately in the context of ecumenical dialogue would require giving serious attention not only to articulating a Mennonite "position" but also to the varied ways of perceiving and posing the question. To grasp what a Mennonite understanding of discipleship and the church intends in relation to the Lutheran understanding of the Christian life would mean giving an account of the frames-of-reference within which these understandings have been formulated, debated, reformulated, and taught. It would also mean giving an account of how these respective understandings have been perceived by their interlocutors and how these perceptions have shaped one's own understandings. Time does not allow me to pursue such methodological concerns in any detail. I shall therefore only summarize three major points which merit attention in this kind of discussion.

Sola Gratia—but in what sense?

Recent scholarship has proposed that an Anabaptist/Mennonite understanding of discipleship and of the church as the community of committed believers presupposes a concept of grace which differs significantly from the classic Lutheran view. To be sure, the shape of the Christian reality in both its individual (discipleship) and corporate (church) expressions is based on grace alone rather than upon a combination of divine grace and human accomplishment or upon grace and the practice of specified works of righteousness. The distinctive emphasis of a Mennonite perspective is therefore not grounded in something besides grace; it does however perceive the reality of "grace alone" differently than traditional Lutheran theology.

In an article on "Grace in Dutch Mennonite Theology," J.A.
Oosterbaan compares the concept of grace in Thomas, the Lutheran
Reformation, and in the theology of Menno Simons. He concludes:

> ...grace is not, as for Rome, a thing that is poured out by God
> and gives as a mere accident to the soul of man a certain
> quality. Grace is also not, as in Lutheran-Calvinistic theology, a
> specific soteriological term which points to the favor and
> readiness of God to forgive. No, for Menno, and I believe on
> this point he is representative of a great part of his Anabaptist
> contemporaries, grace signifies nothing less than the creating
> love itself, which is the essence of God. Therefore Menno can
> say that God has created the human race out of grace and that
> He also has the power to recreate man out of the same grace....
> Grace, therefore, is not only given for nothing, but also calls
> into existence out of nothing. Grace is not a strength that is
> poured into nature, as for Rome, but is God's creating love
> through which nature itself is created and, when it has
> degenerated, is recreated.... No disposition or worthiness is
> needed; no conditions or means are needed to mediate grace or
> its gifts. In the beginning it created entirely out of nothing; just
> as easily it recreates the new man out of the nothingness of his
> lost manhood.[1]

This understanding of grace has not been systematically unfolded
and developed in terms which would easily compare to a Lutheran
theology of grace. If it were, we might call it a "creative" rather than a
"forensic" view of justification and divine grace.

Alvin Beachy comes to a similar conclusion in his Harvard
dissertation on *The Concept of Grace in the Radical Reformation*. He
also suggests that these differing understandings of grace were not
clearly perceived by either the Protestant reformers or the Mennonites in
the sixteenth century.[2]

If Oosterbaan and Beachy are correct, a Mennonite theology of
discipleship and of the reality of the church in the world presupposes a
shift in the basic paradigm rather than simply another point along the
continuum of what is affirmed and rejected by a distinctively Lutheran
view of grace and justification.

Christian life as a life of discipleship

In a Mennonite perspective the life of faith is a life of discipleship. Accordingly, the life of faith is not understood primarily in terms of giving assent to the correct doctrinal beliefs, even though right teaching remains important. Nor is the life of faith understood primarily in terms of an inner attitude abstracted from any visible expression, although faith includes a real attitude of trust. Nor is faith to be understood primarily as coming to life in a particular type of experience, although the reality of faith will also express itself experientially. The life of faith is rather understood primarily in terms of a commitment to "following Jesus Christ in life." As a recent statement formulates it: "The believer in Jesus Christ manifests a new quality of life which many of us have preferred to call discipleship."[3]

This understanding of the life of faith has implications for the theology and practice of baptism. The life of discipleship begins with a voluntary response to God's call. Baptism marks the occasion when this commitment to following Christ in life becomes publicly manifest. Balthasar Hubmaier, a sixteenth-century Anabaptist who wrote most extensively on baptism, outlined the coming to faith in a way characteristic of Anabaptist and Mennonite understandings. To cite Beachy's summary of Hubmaier:

> First, one must be led through the Word of God to a knowledge of his sins, and he must confess that he is a sinner. Second, one must be taught again by the Word of God that he should cry to God the Father, for the forgiveness of his sins for Christ's sake. Third, where one now does this in faith and does not doubt, God cleanses his heart in faith and trust and forgives him all his sins. After one experiences this grace and goodness, he gives himself to God and pledges himself inwardly in his life to lead a new life after the rule of Christ.[4]

The pattern for a life of discipleship is "the perfect humanity of Jesus Christ."[5] This means that the life, teachings, and cross of Jesus Christ constitute the normative pattern for shaping the Christian's life in the world. Christ works in the life of the disciple in such a manner that the disciple's life in the world visibly corresponds in some measure to the perfect humanity of Jesus Christ.

The enabling of a life of discipleship may also be formulated in pneumatological terms. For example, the 1968 "Believers' Church" statement maintains: "Discipleship is brought about by the regenerating and sanctifying work of the Holy Spirit, who enables and sustains a life otherwise impossible."

Anabaptists/Mennonites, whether in the sixteenth or the twentieth century, have not understood this view as perfectionism. They have not assumed that human beings can attain sinlessness. One sixteenth-century Anabaptist who did make such a claim was repeatedly warned to desist from this assertion. When he did not, he was excommunicated.[6] The "Rule of Christ," that is, the exercise of church discipline according to Matthew 18 among Anabaptist/Mennonite groups, also implies the rejection of any claims to perfectionism in a practical as well as theoretical way.

Discipleship includes both the personal and social dimensions of the Christian life. Anabaptists/Mennonites would agree with Luther that in God's sight the work of a priest or a monk is no better than that of a "rustic toiling in the field or a woman going about her household tasks."[7] Their rejection of the separation of secular and sacred vocations, however, derives not from the differentiation between *coram deo and corarn mundo*. It arises from the disciple's commitment to follow Jesus Christ in all of life: in the church and in society, in the family and in relation to the states, in personal and in occupational pursuits. They could therefore also not accept the Lutheran distinction between "public" and "private" person when this distinction justified concomitantly different ethical standards in the "public" and the "private" conduct of Christians. Jesus' teaching in the Sermon on the Mount as well as the Pauline ethical admonitions are therefore meant to shape Christian conduct. The way of servanthood rather than of hierarchical rule in church or society, the love of enemy rather than coercion and warfare, the sharing of material resources rather than the accumulation of wealth, and the trustworthiness of one's word rather than the regulation of truthfulness or political loyalties by the swearing of oaths are to characterize the life of the Christian disciple.

Because discipleship so conceived extends into the social as well as the personal arenas of human life, it may sooner or later come into conflict with the social and political order. In such cases, Jesus' acceptance of suffering and the cross as the alternative to violence and as the way of overcoming evil remains paradigmatic for his disciples.

In the sixteenth century the refusal of the Mennonites to use the sword and participate in warfare also meant that they could not (or would not) become magistrates or soldiers. But the question is less a matter of whether under any circumstances and in all situations discipleship necessarily implies the refusal "to engage in civil functions" (CA 16). Menno Simons, for example, did not categorically deny that a Christian could be a magistrate. He rather maintained that if a magistrate is a Christian, he is called to live as a disciple, according to the "teachings, life, and spirit of Christ." Whether such a magistrate would be allowed to or would remain in office may then be an open question.

The church as the community of grace

In an Anabaptist/Mennonite perspective, the new life in Christ takes shape not only in the individual Christian, but fundamentally in the corporate reality of the Christian community in the midst of an unbelieving world. According to the 1968 Louisville statement, "the most visible manifestation of the grace of God is His calling together a believing people."[8] Beachy reflects a broad consensus in recent scholarship when he points out that different concepts of the church prevailed among the sixteenth-century Protestant reformers and the Anabaptists. For the latter:

> The Evangelical Anabaptists sought to maintain the Church as the holy community.... The Church so understood was a community of individuals who had availed themselves of the new opportunities that were now open to mankind because of the grace of God in Christ. The Church was indeed the community of the new covenant of grace, formed by God's regenerating act of grace.[9]

This means that the renewal of the church in an Anabaptist/Mennonite perspective includes a critique of and dissent from any form of "Constantinian" or "establishment" Christendom for which voluntary commitment does not have constructive character in defining the visible community. The renewal of the church therefore has sociological and ethical implications as well as doctrinal and ecclesiastical significance. The church can no longer be construed as the means by which grace may be transmitted to the entire society, but is itself the community of the new covenant of grace. The church is therefore the community created by the grace of God and so constituted that it manifests this grace in its corporate existence and in its service and mission in the world.

We have already noted the significance of baptism for this understanding of the church. Grace also manifests itself through the believers' fellowship, loving concern, mutual support, and material sharing by the believers. This fellowship and mutual sharing is reinforced by participation in the Lord's Supper. The partaking of the bread and wine is a remembrance of the death of Christ on behalf of the world, a reminder that our salvation depends entirely upon Christ, and simultaneously a sign of the community of the new covenant:

> Now in taking the bread and giving it to his disciples, Christ desireth to show and explain the community of his body to his disciples, that they had become one body. one plant, one living organism and one nature with him...cleaving to him in one Spirit.... Thus, the meal, or the partaking of the bread and the wine of the Lord, is a sign of the community of his body, in that each and every member thereby declareth himself to be of one mind, heart and spirit with Christ.[10]

Further, the church as the community of the new covenant of grace constitutes the primary locus of moral discernment and accountability for the Christian. Anabaptists/Mennonites have usually considered the "Rule of Christ," namely the fraternal binding and loosing process of Matthew 18, central to their understanding of the Christian community. From the earliest "church orders" of the sixteenth century to baptismal covenants in many contemporary Mennonite congregations, church discipline in this sense constitutes a visible mark of the church. In the Louisville statement discipleship "is sustained by the mutual discipline of the congregation, which supplies discernment, admonition, moral solidarity, and forgiveness." [11]

Church discipline in this sense does not belong exclusively to a particular church office, but to the common life of the Christian community. Moreover the functions of Christian moral discernment and accountability belong to the church rather than to the non-believing society.

Finally, the church as the community of grace is to exist not for itself but for the world.

The congregation is called out of the wider society for a communal existence within and for, yet distinct from, the structures and values of the rest of the world. This distinctness from the world is the presupposition of a missionary and servant ministry to the world.[12]

As a distinctive community created and sustained by God's grace, the church is called "out of the world" in order to carry out a missionary and servant ministry "in the world."

---

[1] J. A. Oosterbaan, "Grace and Dutch Mennonite Theology," in C. J. Dyck, ed., *A Legacy of Faith* (Faith and Life Press, 1962) 82-83.

[2] Alvin J. Beachy, *The Concept of Grace and the Radical Reformation* (B. de Graaf, 1977).

[3] James Leo Garrett, Jr., *The Concept of the Believers' Church: Addresses from the 1968 Louisville Conference* (Herald Press, 1969) 316 B.

[4] Beachy, 105.

[5] *Ibid.*

[6] Walter Klaassen, "The Anabaptist View of the Christian Life," *Canadian Journal of Theology*, vol. 9 (1963) 107.

[7] Beachy, 122.

[8] Cited in Garrett, 315 I.

[9] Beachy, 88.

[10] Klaassen, 110.

[11] Cited in Garrett, 316 B.

[12] *Ibid.*, 318 C.

Chapter 6

Non-violent Witness for Justice and Peace
An Historic Peace Church View

Reprinted by permission from *Justice Through Violence?* Eckehart Lorenz, ed. (1984) 96-111.

The Lutheran World Federation study on "Violence and Non-Violent Methods in the Maintenance of Order and in the Struggle for Change" specifically requests conversation with the "historic peace churches." The prospectus for the study correctly notes that these churches have "often taken a very different stand to the majority of the churches of the Reformation...on matters of political ethics." It suggests that the peace churches may be "particularly noteworthy interlocutors in the attempt to understand the relation between justice, power and violence from a theological and ethical point of view" because of their "eminent and credible praxis" during the past four and a half centuries. The project description also rightly observes that "the theology of the peace churches represents a fundamental view...which is not only their own but is shared by many groups." Finally the interest of the LWF focuses on the eventual "answers which their theology provides on contemporary questions," namely the ecumenical debates on violence and non-violence which have been precipitated in the last two decades particularly by liberation and/or revolutionary movements.

Before summarizing the "answers" of the historic peace churches in the context of current debate, I shall make introductory comments on the "historic peace churches" and on the nature of conversation between that tradition and the mainstream Protestant churches, particularly the Lutheran tradition (A). For the purpose of orientation both to the dialogue and to the potential responses to current issues, I shall then summarize significant perspectives which have shaped and have been shaped by the historical experiences of the peace churches (B). Finally, I shall enumerate the major assumptions and points the historic peace churches have made in several recent statements on peace and justice, and on the church's mission and service tasks in situations of injustice and oppression (C).

A. On the simplest level, the term "peace church" should apply to any Christian community in which a pacifist commitment belongs to the shared faith. The label used in this way would exclude a significant number of Christian pacifist individuals, small groups, and voluntary associations without the support of institutional church bodies. Nevertheless, such persons have had a significant ecumenical impact in our time. Some have been notable as individual figures, such as Harry Emerson Fosdick, André Trocmé, Friedrich Sigmund-Schultze, Albert Luthuli, and Martin Luther King Jr. Many have contributed effectively through the common witness of agencies like the Women's International League for Peace and Freedom, the Fellowship of Reconciliation, and the Southern Christian Leadership Council (USA).

A second category of Christian pacifists shall also be excluded from this report on "an historic peace church view" of violence and non-violence. There has been a considerable number of Christian renewal movements whose initial pacifist position was not elaborated over a longer time and did not survive until the present. Sometimes the group itself did not continue. Sometimes the group neglected or disavowed the peace position with the passage of time. Even so, it is important to recognize how many such groups there have been. A "peace church witness" is in fact more widely present across the memory of church history than most churches recognize. Because they have not continued to the present or have moved away from a common and consistent peace position as a church or Christian movement, the following groups shall however be excluded from the present analysis:

1. The *Waldenses,* who held a pacifist position from the twelfth to the sixteenth century, but abandoned it in 1534 by allying themselves with the Reformed churches.

2. The *Czech Brethren,* who arose in the old-fifteenth century and were formally constituted in 1467 as the Unitas Fratrum. Their pacifist commitment diminished during the sixteenth century. Their communities were wiped out by the Thirty Years' War.

3. The *Disciples,* who began in nineteenth-century America. Among their contemporary heirs, a pacifist commitment has considerable strength. However, the Disciples' church policy and discipline have not effectively implemented this pacifist orientation.

It has therefore become a minority position. The Disciples' experience parallels the development of other American "restoration" groups in the nineteenth century, such as the *Church of God* (Anderson).

4. The *Doukhobors* and the *Molokhans,* Russian groups who were inspired by reasoning patterns endemic to Russian culture in a fashion similar to Leo Tolstoy. They were crushed in the Russian empire and the Soviet Union or scattered elsewhere (for example, Western Canada) as refugees in insignificant numbers.

5. *American Pentecostalism,* which until the 1920s was racially integrated and pacifist. It rapidly lost the peace commitment in a process of rapid growth and cultural accommodation.

6. The *Mu-Kyo-Kai* or "No-church Church" founded in the 1930s by Uchimura Kanzo. It still contributes part of the anti-militaristic thrust in present Japanese society. Because of the breadth and diffused quality of Japanese anti-militarism, it has not developed a strong confessional commitment to pacifism as a distinctively Christian stance. Moreover, the *Mu-Kyo-Kai's* minimal church structure does not make the peace commitment a matter of community discipline.

7. The *Kimbanguist* community of Congo basin, which first established contact with other Christian churches through the channel of the Fellowship of Reconciliation. Its anti-military testimony has lost some clarity because it overlapped with the anti-colonial witness before independence. It was therefore not well prepared to maintain a pacifist stance once Zaire became an independent nation with an indigenous military elite.

Even though these groups are not generally labeled "historic peace churches," it is ecumenically important to notice the breadth and length of this list. It points to the perennial naturalness of a peace witness which repeatedly surfaces in times and places of renewal. I shall return to this observation in the next section.

According to Don Durnbaugh the specific phrase "historic peace churches" was apparently coined in the mid-1930s by leaders of the

Mennonites, Quakers, and Church of the Brethren in North America. World War I had surprised them and put before them challenges for an effective peace witness and for the administration of common efforts in relation to military service. Although they did not create an institutional federation, the leaders of the service agencies of these three bodies met regularly for several years in an informal "continuation committee." This committee also convened larger study conferences as needed. During the 1930s, concerns focused on countering developments which seemed to be leading the United States to war, and on obtaining, should war indeed break out, a better way of dealing with conscientious objectors than had been available in World War I. In the 1940s and the 1950s, the same structure was used to coordinate relief and reconstruction services, particularly in Europe. The three denominations found themselves involved in these services to a degree out of proportion to their small membership. For dialogical purposes, I shall characterize very briefly and in an oversimplified way the origins and historical experiences of the Quakers and Mennonites. I shall seek to do so typologically with a view to the systematic and structural differences between a Lutheran and an historical peace church political and social stance.

The Quaker peace witness arose in the near-apocalyptic enthusiasm of mid-seventeenth-century England. It was rooted in the experience that Christ's Spirit has the power to reconcile and renew. The sinner who had been overcome by the power of the "light" in his own heart knew that the power could move others as well. This power would remove the causes of war as violence could never do. The Quaker peace witness ripened and was tempered through the collapse of the Puritan revolution, when it became progressively clear that Cromwell and the Puritan parliament could not fulfill the hopes of a religious commonwealth which had sustained their wars and regicide.

Beginning in 1689, Quakers (as well as the non-historically pacifist Baptists and Congregationalists) have demonstrated that a morally committed minority in a tolerant society can make a significant contribution to combat social injustices and to develop a wholesome economy and political culture. William Penn was able to demonstrate in Delaware, New Jersey, and Pennsylvania that, in the light of his perspective of faith and hope, a society could be constructed which would resolve in distinctive ways the problems of relating to the original Americans, expressing religious liberty, immigrating freely, and treating the poor and offenders. Quakers to this day continue actively in conflict resolution ministries between groups, classes, and nations. They also contribute significantly to creating alternative patterns at major junctures in our social pathology: criminal corrections, labor conflicts, and race relations.

The American Friends Service Committee has for two generations been largely supported by funds from other Christians, Jews, and even non-religious people who have been convinced that their peace-making style is fundamentally valid. They have facilitated readiness to dialogue between political and social opponents, when brought together in the light of the Quaker vision.

The effectiveness of the Quakers in such efforts amounts to a practical refutation of some assumptions made by classical Reformation thought about the need for law and gospel, or about the need for distinguishing between secular common sense and the witness of Jesus Christ. To the Friends, the fact that non-Quakers and even non-Christians understand their ethos seems to confirm George Fox's conviction that the opponent in a conflict is also a bearer of dignity and is able to perceive God's speaking. This has been confirmed experientially by a long history of effective reconciliatory efforts, even across cultural and social lines. This Quaker insight has been rejected most deeply by defenders of the Christian tradition rather than by those who, according to Reformation doctrine, ostensibly know nothing of grace in Christ.

To be sure, Friends have not engaged in their special ministries of communication and reconciliation to prove anything in the debate with mainstream Protestant thought about law and gospel. They have intended simply to live out the universal relevance of Christ's renewing work in the midst of a hostile world. Nevertheless, their conclusions at least partially seek to confirm their hopes.

Furthermore, Quaker testimony does not operationally confirm a Lutheran division between law and gospel which establishes different patterns of ethical insights and moral value. Their historical experience has not validated the split between generosity and toughness which many have taken to be the meaning of Lutheran dictum that "you cannot run the world with the gospel." More traditionally soteriological concerns, which may still support a distinction between law and gospel, are not thereby necessarily set aside. But whatever this difference may otherwise mean, the Quaker stance would claim that it cannot support a division between two kinds of ethics, one kind based on love and practicable only in an ideal world, and the other kind more effective in the real world because it justifies violence and killing under certain conditions.

The Quaker corrective to the disjunction between the two ethical frameworks does not necessarily claim that love and gentleness are effective. It seeks rather to clarify, as George Fox had already done, that the gospel judges and renews as it forgives and promises. Contemporary Quaker political witness "speaks truth to power" with respectable technical expertise and factual documentation (see bibliography at end of paper). It calls opponents in a conflict to take manageable steps toward one another. Such steps depend upon a measure of trust in the truth. But they do not make utterly impossible demands or impose the cross upon those not ready to practice sacrificial love as an expression of Christian faith.

The Mennonite experience has differed significantly from the Friends' history. Quakerism came into the British reformation just a generation before the advent of religious toleration. Continental Anabaptism, whose survivors are represented by the Mennonites and the Hutterian Brethren, had to survive two or three centuries before benefiting from access to citizenship, freedom of movement, and public approval of their independent existence as a worshipping community. Before that time, persecution was not always harsh. Occasional friendly arrangements with local authorities provided them with more freedom than the dominant theologies theoretically tolerate. Occasionally, as sometimes also happened with Jews, a prince or local ruler specifically favored a minority group in consideration of their reliabilities as tax payers or renters or artisans. This, however, only reinforced their ghettoization.

More frequently, their migrant status was prolonged by the official ecclesiastical ostracism. Anabaptists continued to move: from the Netherlands eastward to the shores of the Baltic and toward the Steppes of Central Asia, and from the Swiss heartland eastward along the Alps to Austria (then Moravia), Hungary, and then Transylvania. The early migratory history and the longer leap of the eighteenth and nineteenth centuries to North America as well as to South America in the twentieth, kept the relevance of a "stranger and pilgrim" language vitally alive. Mennonites have exercised little social responsibility, usually because they were not permitted to share in it rather than because they chose to reject it.

In a manner others may best understand by comparing them to diaspora Jews, even though on a much smaller and less tragic scale, Mennonites and Hutterites have demonstrated the possibility of participating in a healthy social order and being good citizens without having access to governmental authority. Sometimes their civil responsibility expressed itself in a degree of faithfulness to Christ's ethic which resulted in their being expelled as unwanted conscientious objectors. At other times the conscientious participation in social progress led to leadership involvement disproportionate to their limited numbers, especially in the Netherlands. In neither case has their historical experience confirmed the axiom of mainstream western Christendom, which claims that the only or even the primary way to be socially responsible is to govern, with all the prerequisites for gaining, maintaining, and defending the power to rule implied by that axiom.

In the twentieth century, Mennonites (along with other historic peace churches) have developed relief, reconstruction, "peace," and development services, conceived as alternatives to participation in military service and war. As we shall note in the last section of this essay, the historic peace churches' development of peace witness and service efforts, increasing participation in the broader society, and recent invitations to ecumenical conversation have challenged them to address issues of justice as well as of peace, and of power as well as the rejection of war. The ways in which they presently seek to address these questions in theory and in practice are informed by a theological-ethical-practical framework which has shaped their traditions and which has been influenced by their historical experiences. Let us turn now to a schematic summary of major elements which have historically contributed to that frame-of-reference.

B. One may begin with a broad generalization about Christian pacifism in relation to thorough-going church renewal, particularly with respect to patterns of renewal and reformation in situations where political control is not constitutive. The three "historic peace churches" do not exhaust the history to which the label points. There have been similar churches across the centuries. In almost every century, and at least once in every century since the fifteenth, movements of church renewal rejected participation in war as part of their confessional identity. Usually, these movements did not begin with the rejection of violence as their first purpose. They were usually preoccupied with such matters as biblical exegesis or revival preaching, or with restoring a New Testament pattern of church order, or with renewing the deep authenticity of personal religious experience in the spirit. Nevertheless, they regularly came to reject participation in war as belonging to their confessional identity. The phenomenon is striking in its widespread appearance. It is all the more noteworthy because their pacifism was often not the product of profound thought and sometimes became embarrassing to the second generation of these groups. From an historic peace church perspective, this recurring pattern seems to confirm that a paradigm of thorough-going and consistent church renewal and Christian faithfulness includes the rejection of violence, even if a particular movement begins at another point.

Secondly, the historic peace churches have reiterated the imperative that the church have a visible membership distinguishable from that of the entire society, in order that we know of whom we speak with reference to Christian ethics. Being a "peace" church means being a "free" church (*eine freie Kirche*).

Usually this separation begins to take visible shape by baptizing only those who confess their faith, rather than all in a given society. (It is interesting to note that pedobaptism is being challenged in some Lutheran and other Protestant churches.) Whether this will eventually be linked to a new ethical frame-of-reference remains to be seen.

There would also however be other ways to create a visible body of believers. The vision for a "third truly evangelical order" which Luther advocated in 1526 (but had already abandoned as impractical) proposed a distinctiveness made visible by meeting in a different place than the parish church building, by having members put their name on a list, and by making a personal pledge to an evangelical order of life. Pietism later followed this pattern in one sense in numerous new beginnings with Lutheran history. Another functional equivalent would be to take a pattern of historic catechism in early adulthood seriously, followed by celebrating a confirmation which is not obligatory for all baptized children of Christian households. Finally, on the other side of the scale, a visible community may be formed even without the use of baptism such as is the case in the Society of Friends or the Salvation Army.

Those groups which have been most clear about defining and retaining an integral peace position have also been most clear about the imperative that there be a visible viable form for the local Christian community. The separate histories of the Czech Brethren in the middle of the fifteenth century, the Swiss Brethren and other Anabaptists between 1525 and 1535, the Society of Friends between 1650 and 1670, the Church of the Brethren between 1720 and 1730, and the Christian Church between 1830 and 1860 all focused first on the proper pattern for the life of the Christian community. They derivatively came to reject the sword and to their various attitudes toward holding public office even while rejecting violence. On the grounds of biblical ecclesiology, they first became "free churches," and then "peace churches." In this sense, the term "free church" does not refer primarily to the relation between a church's administrative organization and the civil government. It means rather the believing community as a whole. A free church is a church distinct from the rest of society along the lines of belief and unbelief or of obedience and disobedience to the Christian faith.

Thirdly, the underlying free church ecclesiology has several implications for the social ethics of the historic peace churches. Lutheranism, for reasons derived both from Constantinian Christendom sociology and Augustinian theology, denied the theological importance of the visible structures of the Christian community. But the movements which issued in the historic peace churches, along different historical paths and with different language, insisted upon forming a visible community of committed believers. This commitment has obvious implications for Christian social ethics.

One implication for social ethics is that where this visible community is a numerical minority, as early Christianity was and the peace churches have been for most of their history, how a believer ought to behave socially is not based upon establishment assumptions about how to govern a society. These majoritarian reflexes may take several forms:

a) There is a simple pragmatism which asks: "If most people in a society were to behave this way, what would happen to the society?" The answer to this question is different and its pertinence is less relevant if we are asking the question for a small minority within a given society.

b) In the free/peace church perspective there is also less reason to focus on rulers and office holders as exemplary social agents and to test ethics by asking "what should a ruler do?" In the Protestant Reformation, social action was not thought of as being done by people in general or by "the people" as a whole. It was understood as being done by people in stations of social leadership where they acted on behalf of the entire community. A believing community not involved in social domination is less likely to phrase the *paradigmatic* question about a social issue as if the person in office were a member of the community.

c)   Underlying these numerical indications of majoritarian assumptions are more important logical ones. The axiom that a moral obligation can be conceived as binding only if one can wish that all people fulfill it eliminates any consideration of the fact that "all people" have not made the same value assumptions or commitments. Nor does it take into account that all people do not have the same spiritual and community resources for nurturing moral fidelity.

Another implication of a free/peace church orientation is that the question of whether people at large are likely to accept such a stance need not carry normative ethical significance. The New Testament ethic is sometimes described as apocalyptic or radical, as if it requires a special kind of courage (or foolhardiness) for people to take those risks and pay those prices. In one sense, it is important to affirm within the discipline of Christian ethics that New Testament ethics is meant for everyone rather than only for moral heroes and that it is meant for the Christian community in time rather than apocalyptically. Nevertheless, New Testament and peace church ethics presuppose that the moral agent whose conduct is being talked about has made a commitment to Christ's Lordship, to the identity of Jesus who is confessed as Lord, to his teachings and his example, in short, to his authority.

This recognition that Christian ethics is for Christians does not mean, as it is often interpreted, that there can be little to say from a Christian perspective for people who do not claim to be Christians. That conclusion would follow if Christian ethics were thought to have an esoteric source or an esoteric content which did not fit in the same world where others are. Christian ethics is for Christians because it is a non-coercive and nonviolent ethic which can be refused. Christian ethics is for Christians because it lets people free not to confess Christ in faith and therefore not to make assumptions on which Christian ethics depends. Non-believers need not be expected to act on the basis of Christian ethics. Ethics need therefore not be tailored to fit everyone, especially those who deny the faith. This does not mean that faith or the obedience of faith is not for everyone. It means that God grants, to those who claim it, the freedom not to believe and to therefore not be considered as disciples of a cross-bearing Lord.

Thus, the existence of a distinctive ecclesiastical reality is important in social ethics. The believing community cultivates—in worshipping, in recounting holy history, in making decisions, and in maintaining contacts with the rest of the world—the awareness of a value system which differs from the self-affirming values of family, clan, race, and nation. This does not deny those more selfish values their place. Nor does it condemn them as evil, seek to destroy them, or deny that they may be understood in some sense as orders of creation. But in themselves and when accepted as self-authenticating and self-evidently valuable, these provincial values are less normative than the kingdom and the Christian church which is worldwide. They need to be corrected and balanced by other social experiences giving visibility to wider community realities.

The visible distinctness of church and world is foundational in another direction as well: it is needed in order to affirm the freedom of unbelievers to remain that, the freedom of those who are not ready to take up the cross to avoid that suffering, and to incarnate the respect that the God of the gospel has for the rebelliousness of his creatures. When Luther maintained that "you cannot rule the world with the gospel," the free/peace churches think he was wrong in making the gospel uniquely "spiritual" or otherworldly, or considering it ineffective. But he was correct in assuming that moral choices derived from faith in Christ cannot be imposed on unbelievers.

Fourth and finally, the historic peace churches have learned over the centuries to mistrust certain ethical and theological dichotomies which frequently shape debates about non-violence and violence/coercion. This mistrust of biased dichotomies has also surfaced most pointedly in more recent history, when the initiative has moved from the historical peace churches to the non-violent activities of the twentieth century, such as Gandhi and King.

According to one such dichotomy, the moral dilemma of moral purity versus practicality required an ultimate choice between an ethic of means and an ethic of ends. We are told by this way of phrasing the question that an ethic of means must ultimately disregard the consequences and stand for what is intrinsically right, "even if the heavens fall." Such an ethic will presumably focus on one's faithfulness to "principle," and be ready to leave the practical outcomes of one's behavior to divine providence or to others. Such an ethic will presumably remain unconcerned with a detailed analysis of the consequences, if one acts in a certain way. An ethic of ends, on the other hand, will presumably take responsibility not only for right actions, but also for the outcomes; not only for personal intentions, but also for the effects, not only for individual moral rightness, but also for the most just results. Applied to the issue of non-violence, this framework postulates a profound abyss between a pragmatic non-violence and a non-violence of principle. The pragmatic type may be creative in the search for less destructive means, and more effective in advocacy and conflict. The principled type will supposally be ultimately unconcerned about results and effectiveness.

This mode of reasoning appears practically self-evident to the majority of western Christians (some would also link it theologically to the division between law and gospel). It however reflects a distinct social situation in which those formulating this dichotomy can conceive of themselves as being at the top of the social and political structure, so that

- they are in a position to make decisions in the function of their vision of the total social process;
- the decision they make can be implemented efficaciously.

People and groups, such as the historic peace churches, who are accustomed to thinking in genuinely minority or non-ruling terms do not make these assumptions. Thus it is fitting that the peace church tradition denies the split between ends and means as normative in both intellectual and practical ways.

The earlier free/peace church vision may well have stated its rejection of this dichotomy in terms which traditional Lutheranism was trained to consider *schwärmerisch*, because it saw potential for real change in the individual or for authentic progress in human history or for divine interventions to save. Gandhi however spoke of the unity between ends and means in terms of a pre-industrial world-view. And Martin Luther King Jr., spoke of the unity in a post-industrial sense of sociological realism. He recognized that only a common commitment to principle, namely truth-telling and promise-keeping, can effectively hold a community of resistance together. He realized that when individuals claim a sovereign right to sacrifice morally faithful means for the sake of an expected effectiveness of ends, community accountability is destroyed.

In an historic free/peace church perspective, moral insight is not served by contrasting effectiveness and faithfulness as if believers normally are compelled to choose between them. If a clash between faithfulness and effectiveness seems unavoidable in a particular situation with no time for further analysis, believers are called to choose what appears to be "faithful." Such a choice does not however imply an ultimate unconcern with results or a preoccupation with one's own righteousness. It means that acknowledging that the world is in God's hand will likely be more "effective" on the average and in the long run, even if we cannot readily see the connections between faithful means and effective outcomes. Moreover, it is not clear that we should always be able to perceive the continuities which make faithfulness "work." They have to do with the nature of the resurrection, in whose light alone the cross is meaningful. They have to do with God's providence, whose definition means that we cannot always spell out the consequences ahead of time as the basis for our decisions.

Further, according to an historic free/peace church perspective, those approaches to social ethical issues are most valid which do not simply allow the existing authority structure of a given society to be taken as defining justice. This orientation does not amount to an unrealistic or utopian optimism about attaining perfection in this world. It does mean that all structures, whether institutional or intellectual, which claim to resist the transforming power of the gospel, are to be relativized.

Thus, for example, the historic peace churches would be suspicious of the notion that we can be logically compelled to give a sweeping yes or no to some general value like "the civil order," in the sense that saying yes would amount to a basically uncritical stance toward the civil order from that point on and in the sense that saying no would necessarily mean "withdrawal" from participation in the civil order. The Augsburg Confession condemns the Anabaptists for withdrawal. But the Anabaptists "withdrew" from a government in which they in any case had no possibility of participating as citizens. In that historical and political context, the same government simultaneously denied them freedom of religion as individuals and their local congregations any voice in determining their own order. The "*Obrigkeit*" Anabaptists found before them in the sixteenth century represented a late feudal absolutism which denied political rights to its subjects and religious freedom to everyone. In that context, Anabaptists said that Christians cannot consistently participate in government. In situations where a greater degree of freedom to participate in the political process was granted to subjects (who, strictly speaking, then become "citizens" rather than merely "subjects"), sectarian-type Christians in a minority have generally participated conscientiously in the pluralistic political process. Indeed they have often done proportionately more than their share, as minority groups tend to do in open societies.

Thus the paradigm for peace church experience with respect to the matter of participation in the social and political process is not a kind of voluntarily chosen and systematic "withdrawal" which confirms the condemnation of Augustana XVI. It is exemplified rather in the qualities of pluralistic participation acted out by the Quakers in England, the exceptional experience of social leadership exercised in Penn's colonies in America, and by the Doopzsgezinde in the Netherlands.

Thus, in an historic church perspective, civil authority does not represent a bloc which can and should either be affirmed uncritically as a whole or rejected globally in either sociological or theological terms. "Civil authority," "society," "political process," etc., are concepts which represent many kinds of activity and value. In some of these activities and values the disciple of Jesus will not be welcome or will not be effective or will not be free. The selection of emphases and accents should however be determined on the basis of opportunity rather than sweeping moralism. For that reason, the biased dichotomy of participation-withdrawal is also one which the historic peace churches have also increasingly learned to mistrust as a framework for Christian ethical discernment, judgment, and action.

C. We turn now to an historic peace church perspective on the more recent discussions about violence and/or non-violence in relation to oppression, injustice, and liberation movements. The historic peace churches have traditionally rejected violence in the form of war as contrary to God's will. They have done so within a theological and ethical frame-of-reference which confessed Jesus as normative for Christian conduct, presupposed the visibility of a freely believing church as distinct from unbelieving society, understood Christian ethics to be for Christians and offered to others without being imposed upon them, and included the Christian community's witness to the gospel and sacrificial service in the world.

During the last thirty years, ecumenical dialogue challenged the historic peace churches to articulate more clearly their rejection of war and their stance with regard to peace. In the last twenty years, their own mission and service efforts, their increasing participation in a broader range of social, economic, and political institutions, as well as ecumenical debate and dialogue, have confronted the historic peace churches with contemporary forms of racism, oppression, social and economic injustice, and struggle for justice and liberation. Faced with these challenges, they have begun to rethink their understandings of peace and non-violence. Faced with many forms of violence, they are seeking to establish guidelines and priorities for action and witness. It would be premature and inaccurate to speak of a consistent and systematic historic peace church understanding of violence/nonviolence, justice and peace as "answers" to these current questions. Nevertheless, I shall attempt to summarize the direction which historic peace churches' responses are beginning to take. This summary is limited in scope, drawing upon several representative statements from historic peace church groups and agencies in North America.

The historic peace church rejection of violence has seldom, if ever, begun with a precise conceptual definition of violence, in order to then reject it as a justifiable option for Christian ethics and conduct. The recent statements are no exception. They do not offer a systematic concept of violence with a careful delineation of its causes, eventual criteria for distinguishing between legitimate and illegitimate violence (which might amount to another "biased dichotomy"), or the goals of violence. Nevertheless, violence is seen as present in several "forms," as distinguishable from power, and as describable in discrete and concrete ways.

In contemporary ecumenical discussions, the notion of "structural" or "systemic" violence has been employed to indicate the use of violence not only in wars or revolutions, but also its presence in unjust and oppressive economic, social, and political structures. One function of this concept in ecumenical debate has been to recognize that violence may be present (or in fact *is* present) not only in revolutionary movements, but also in the "status quo," where its legitimacy may be equally questionable and where it may justify the use of revolutionary violence as an *ultima ratio* by Christians. This broadening of the notion of violence has not produced an agreed upon concept of violence. But it has rendered more evident that the revolutionaries are not the only agents of violence.

In their response to the Cardiff Report, several historic peace church representatives note that there appears to be not one, but "multiple ways of discussing structural violence." Some of them question whether the term is "precise enough to guide a careful analysis'" of what they all oppose. When they have adopted the language of structural or systemic violence, recent historic peace discussions and statements have often tended to describe phenomena of oppression, injustice, and coercion in terms not unlike those in ecumenical discussion. One such statement, for example, speaks about "systemic or structural violence" as "the violence often hidden in the usual and customary institutions and practices." In this sense, structural violence "refers to violations of personhood such as malnutrition, oppression of apartheid, or denial of equal opportunity because of one's class, race, age, or sex." Other statements use different terms to refer to similar realities. Regardless of the availability or lack of a clear definition of structural violence, historic peace church representatives would tend to agree that the realities to which it points are often present and that many Christians are implicated in them. But they would not accept the presence of injustice and oppression as legitimating the participation in revolutionary violence for Christian ethics and conduct. Nor would they see in the rejection of revolutionary violence a rationale for engaging in violence to maintain order. The grounds for rejecting both "structural" and revolutionary violence are derived from the biblical testimony to the way in which Christians are called to work for justice and liberation. "The world confronts us with the temptation to use violence in war, to acquiesce and participate in structural violence, and to support violent revolution against structural violence. Although we seek to identify with the oppressed, to these three types of violence we make a uniform response: the Scriptures call us to reject all forms of violence and to undertake nonviolent acts to exercise our commitment to human liberation and justice."

Before summarizing the major reasons why Christians are called to reject violence in their commitment to liberation and justice, we should note that an historic peace church orientation distinguishes violence from power. "Power is essentially the ability to get things done and may be exercised through non-violent techniques available to the so-called 'powerless' as well as through military and economic force." There are at least two reasons for differentiating power from violence in this context.

In the first place, the concept of power should not univocally be linked with force and violence because there are many other forms of power. Jesus demonstrated the power of forgiveness, the power of an alternative community in the calling of the disciples, the power of confronting religious and political authorities with a greater righteousness. Historic peace churches would maintain that love has the power to effect justice and to change human hearts as well as structures. The experiences of a Gandhi and a Martin Luther King Jr. demonstrate the power of truth-telling in situations where the perversion of truth is used to cover up injustice and oppression, the power of solidarity in suffering in situations where repressive structures and regimes defend an unjust status quo, the power of non-violent confrontation in the struggle for justice and peace. In their response to the Cardiff Report, the historic peace church representatives observed that greater differentiation and discrimination between different kinds of power would be necessary in order to more critically and carefully assess the complexities of violent and non-violent action in relation to social change: "The opportunity for illumination of the issues of liberation and systemic change from many contemporary psychological, social, and political analyses of power has been bypassed in the report. Some of the perplexities of the effect of violent or non-violent tactics might be resolved if discriminations between cooperative, persuasive, utilitarian compromises, manipulative and coercive forms of power were discussed. The discussion of moral and/or spiritual power and the demonic effects of assumed innocence on the part of the crusader for the cause of liberation, as on the part of the conscious or unconscious oppressor, is not treated."

Secondly, the concept of power ought not be equated with force and violence in a way which normally legitimizes the use of violence by those in positions of power and authority. Depending upon their respective emphases and historical experiences, the historical peace churches may harbor greater or lesser expectations about the readiness and ability of older or newer rulers to govern and maintain order without resorting to violence or without misusing power in oppressive, brutal, and lethal ways. They may assume, in terms of historical realism, that those who rule in positions of political, social, and economic power do so by resorting to violence and coercion. They may assure, in terms of historical realism, that those who seek to replace current rulers of oppressive and unjust regimes, in order to take their place, will do so by resorting to violence and force. Nevertheless, a realistic observation and expectation that violence is and will be used does not render the moral legitimacy of violence and force less ambivalent, nor does it commend violence as an acceptable pattern for Christian ethics and conduct. In an historic peace church perspective, violence is used because of human sin and the fallenness of the structures, not because in some ultimate sense God wills it to be so or because it lies in the nature of human institutions and structures as such.

One recent statement claims that this perspective is biblically grounded and normative for Christian social ethics in which the concern for justice is fundamental: "The biblical concern for justice grows from the failure of humankind to live up to the divine image in which they were created. Instead of creating culture and structures for the glory of God and for mutual benefit, human sin has subverted potentially good structures for the service of human pride and selfishness.... The Bible speaks of this process when it refers to 'principalities' and 'powers' created by God..., but now fallen, ruling over the disobedient...and seeking to separate believers from the love of God. Even in their rebellion, however, the powers and structures operate under the providential sovereignty of God. In spite of their fallenness, God can use them to exercise an ordering function, as in Romans where the sword of the state serves to protect good and punish evil (13:1-4), or in Isaiah where God uses pagan Assyria as the rod of his anger against Israel" (10:5). Further dialogue will doubtless be necessary in order to ascertain the similarities and differences between this orientation and a traditional Lutheran perspective. From an historic peace church view, the Lutheran stance tends to equate the exercise of power with the legitimate use of violence and coercion and thus to justify morally the use of legal violence for the maintenance of order.

Recent experiences, debates, and renewed theological and biblical study have challenged the historic peace churches not only to review their understandings of violence and power, but also to rethink the relation of peace to justice. The challenge to consider more seriously the imperative of justice has reminded them that they have often "limited the way of peace and love...to nonparticipation in the hurts of the world." This has led to attempts to elaborate a concept of justice which is biblically grounded, consistent with the rejection of violence, and integrally related to peace. Peace without justice can be only a contradiction in terms. And a justice which ostensibly depends on the sanction or instrumentality of violence cannot be the kind of justice to which Christians are called and empowered.

Because of limited space, I shall forego the attempt to systematically report and analyze the concept(s) of justice which inform recent historic peace church discussions. The reader may consult particularly the Church of the Brethren and the Mennonite statements. In general terms, both seek to develop a *theological* concept of justice based upon the way in which God is a God who acts to liberate the oppressed and to establish both justice and peace. Accordingly, definitions of justice which suggest that justice consist in "fairness to all concerned" or "equal rights under law" or "giving to each his or her due" or "equal access to resources" are considered inadequate. These definitions omit the concern for reconciliation between hostile and opposing persons and groups which is at the heart of justice (*mishpat*) in a biblical sense. They do not speak to the "concern for reconciling relationships which is implicit in biblical justice, a justice which seeks more to restore and maintain covenant than to assign blame or punishment." We may note in passing that this focus on reconciliation is also translated into programmatic and operational terms of peace church agencies which include both expressions and actions of solidarity with the oppressed and the poor as well as witness to and confrontation with the oppressors and the wealthy.

Although it can hardly be considered to represent an historic peace church consensus, the recent Mennonite Church paper on "Justice and the Christian Witness," which has been submitted to the churches for study and evaluation, is based upon a "working definition" of justice which in some measure reflects the more recent historic peace church orientation. According to this description:

> Justice in the Bible is characteristic of the rule of God which is rooted in the demand of the relationship established by God's election and covenant,
> • a covenant founded upon his act of spiritual, social, and economic liberation, which is then to be maintained among covenant equals,
> • and an election whose goal is to extend this rule to all the earth.

The statement then seeks to elaborate this understanding of justice by describing the character of justice in the Bible, by positing love and peace as the way to justice, and by suggesting guidelines for the Christian community's task in witnessing to and establishing justice.

This conceptualization of violence, power, and justice in contemporary peace church discussions draws upon several foundational elements in their traditional theological and ethical stance with respect to non-violence and their rejection of war. I shall enumerate these elements briefly and again refer the reader to appropriate sections in recent representative statements. These elements include the normativeness of Jesus for Christian social ethics, the mandate of the church to be a sign and witness of peace and justice, and the task of the Christian community to work for peace and justice in its mission and service in the world (see, for example, the 1953 statement "Peace is the will of God" in the Durnbaugh anthology where these axioms figure prominently in the case for Christian pacifism and the rejection of war).

First of all, Jesus' solidarity with the poor, his initiation of a new order of justice and peace, and his willingness to accept the way of the cross rather than the way of coercion and violence remain normative for Christians, both individually and corporately. An historic peace church view therefore challenges biblical interpretations and ethical constructs which contend that Jesus did not in fact face the issues of power, violence, and justice; or that if he did, his way retains little relevance or normative significance for Christians in today's world. They would rather understand the biblical account as demonstrating that Jesus did indeed speak and act in ways which directly address these issues and that the manner in which he did so carries normative theological and ethical significance for discipleship in our time.

Secondly, because the church as the visible community of discipleship is itself to be a sign and witness of peace and justice in the world, it is called first of all to incarnate in its own structures and life the justice to which it testifies. This incarnation of justice will include confession and repentance where the church has acquiesced in practices, structures, and rationalizations of injustice and violence. It will require renewed commitment to practice justice and change its own structures in a way which reflects the good news of liberation and justice. This repentance and renewed commitment to be a sign and witness which incarnates peace and justice should not be limited to the "internal" life and structures of the church in the narrow sense, but include the church's corporate presence in the world as well as its presence through individual Christians in society.

Finally, the church is called in a particular way to work for peace and justice in the world. On the one hand this will include solidarity with those suffering from injustice and oppression: "As Christians, we find ourselves compelled to stand solidly against injustice and oppression wherever that is identified and we must respond to the situation in the interest of justice. In this we stand solidly with all persons participating in movements of liberation and social justice. However, this does not mean we find ourselves in complete agreement with the affirmative goals of all or perhaps any of the current movements."

On the other hand, the universality of non-violent love and justice means that it includes the oppressor and the enemy as well: "Past movements which have been demonstrably effective in non-violent empowerment have consciously included the 'liberation' or 'humanization' of the oppressor as both end and means." The historic peace church representatives found this dimension missing in the Cardiff Report. More broadly, this aspect of justice seems to be lacking whenever Christian ethics seek to define justice apart from the concept of reconciliation and divorced from the biblical vision of the church as a "universal" community of peace and love.

Bibliography

Examples of "Speaking Truth to Power":

The United States and the Soviet Union: Some Quaker Proposals for Peace. Report prepared for the American Friends Service Committee. New Haven, Yale University Press, 1949, 39 pp.

Steps to Peace: A Quaker View of U.S. Foreign Policy. Report prepared for the American Friends Service Committee. Published by AFSC, 1951, 64 pp.

Speak Truth to Power: A Quaker Search for an Alternative to Violence. A study of international conflict prepared for the American Friends Service Committee. Published by AFSC, 1955, 70 pp.

A New China Policy: Some Quaker Proposals. Report prepared for the American Friends Service Committee. New Haven and London, Yale University Press, 1963, 68 pp.

Peace in Vietnam: A New Approach in Southeast Asia. Report prepared for the American Friends Service Committee. New York, Hill and Wang, 1966, 132 pp.

Search for Peace in the Middle East (revised edition): Report prepared for the American Friends Service Committee. Greenwich, Connecticut, Fawcett.

Chapter 7

The Church in the World as the Community of the Kingdom:
A Radical Reformation Perspective

Reprinted by permission from *Brethren Life and Thought,* vol. XXXV, no. 1 (Winter 1990) 52-70.

The general theme for this consultation, "Eschatology and Social Transformation", arose from last year's discussion on the potential significance of the First and Radical Reformations for church, social, ethical, and theological renewal. This focus on eschatology and social transformation gathers up several interests. It first inquires into one aspect of the First and Radical Reformations, namely a particular view of eschatology and its implications, which presumably distinguishes them in some fashion from other patterns of church life and thought. Secondly it brings this heritage to bear upon a preoccupation of many twentieth-century social and intellectual movements, namely a deep concern and struggle for social transformation in situations of injustice, violence, and oppression. Thirdly, it orients this theme in an implicitly apologetic direction, toward countering the criticism that Christianity has appealed to the hope of blessedness in heaven to rationalize its frequent acceptance or even blessing of social oppression and injustice on earth. Fourthly, it acknowledges that churches and faith communities claiming the First and Radical Reformation heritages may need to be challenged to renew in appropriate ways insights and commitments which have dimmed, diminished, or been discounted in the meantime.

Our theme presupposes a relatively modern way of phrasing the question. The formulation of the topic depends upon concepts which were neither current nor central during the fifteenth and sixteenth centuries. The term "eschatology" appears to have entered the theological vocabulary at the beginning of the nineteenth century as the doctrine of the "eschaton" or the "last/end time." This was also the period in western cultural and intellectual history when historical consciousness and a preoccupation with the purpose and meaning of historical movement gained considerable importance. In one way or another, theological concepts of eschatology since then refer not only to traditional Christian doctrines about a chronological end of time, the resurrection of the dead, and eternal life, but also to the purpose and meaning of history.

Similarly, concepts of social transformation, and the aspirations and realities to which they refer, have become a lively part of church and theological discussions in the twentieth century, prompted by political, economic, and social revolutions in the late eighteenth, nineteenth, and twentieth centuries. Minimally, this historical observation means that our spiritual ancestors may not have addressed precisely our questions, or that they struggled with similar issues in other terms, or that their stance may articulate and incarnate a challenge to us as Christians in our time.

Radical Reformation "eschatology"

Sixteenth-century Anabaptists shared with other Christians the hope of Christ's return, which they articulated in traditional terms. Although their extant writings do not include extensive treatments on the doctrine of Christ's return and the Last Judgment, Anabaptist leaders such as Hubmaier, Menno, and Riedemann occasionally refer to them in passing or summarize them in terms consistent with the Apostles' Creed.[1] However these passing references couched in traditional orthodox terms take on a distinctive orientation when understood in relation to their emphasis on discipleship (*Nachfolge*) and to their experiences of persecution and suffering. Repentance and following Christ in life were reinforced by references to the Last Judgment. Then the godly and the ungodly will be rewarded according to their faithfulness in following Christ in life, rather than according to their status or mere lip service to Christianity. And the assurance of deliverance to the faithful when Christ returns provided encouragement for the Anabaptists to persist in the face of their present suffering, persecution, and even martyrdom which was ordered and implemented by "Christian" authorities.

In addition to their adaptation of traditional views on the return of Christ and the end time, many Anabaptists also shared with other Christians an almost apocalyptic sense of living in the "last days." Observers in the sixteenth century regarded the ecclesial, social, and political upheavals of the period as signs that they were living in the last times and that the return of Christ was immanent. Some Protestant

Reformers as well as the Radical Reformers expected the world to end in the very near future. Luther thought the second advent of Christ was near at hand. He saw great similarity between the ecclesiastical and political situation of that time and the biblical description of the time immediately preceding the Last Day. He hoped that the astronomers' prediction of a great flood for 1534 signified the Last Day, but also reminded the people that none knew the hour or the day except God. Similarly, Menno Simons and other Anabaptist leaders referred to the scriptural passages on the last days and found similarities between contemporary events and biblical prophecies.

Some Radical Reformers even attempted to chart a kind of apocalyptic calendar. Hans Hut, a disciple of Thomas Müntzer, initially predicted that Christ would return at Pentecost in 1528. Melchoir Hoffman, who significantly influenced the entire Dutch and North German Anabaptist-Mennonite movement, expected the end to come in 1536 and Strasbourg to be the center of the kingdom. Hoffman's visionary thought also influenced the Münsterites, who adopted revolutionary violence as agents of the divine judgment in the end time, even though Hoffman himself did not support violent rebellion against the authorities. Most Radical Reformers thus lived and thought within the apocalyptic mood of the times. But they differed in their relative emphasis upon eschatology, in whether they attempted to coordinate contemporary events directly with biblical prophecies about the last day, and in the way in which they expected to participate in the events of the end time.

Twentieth-century Mennonites have generally sought to distance themselves from the type of eschatalogical expectations represented by Hut and Hoffman, to say nothing of the eschatology of the Münsterites.[2] Similar lines of disagreement were drawn already in the sixteenth century. Hut, for example, agreed at the Augsburg synod of Anabaptist leaders in 1527 to give up appeals to usher in the kingdom violently and to execute God's punishment upon evildoers.[3] Jacob Hutter and Peter Riedemann, early leaders of the Hutterite communities, rejected Hut's calculations of the end time and the appeal to violence. Menno Simons and Dirk Philips, who set the direction for Dutch Anabaptism after the events of Münster, similarly refused all attempts to calculate dates and places and sharply rejected the Münsterite holy war theology. Historians have therefore differentiated several groups within the Radical Reformation. The Canadian Mennonite historian Klaassen calls the eschatology of Anabaptists such as Menno Simons and Jacob Hutter "restrained." The American Methodist historian Franklin Littell used the term "quiet eschatology" for the views of such groups as those around Grebel, Menno, Marpeck, and Hutter to distinguish them from Thomas Müntzer and the Münsterites.

Both Littell and Klaassen have argued that all these groups of the Radical Reformation shared more common ground than recent apologetically oriented interpretations have frequently admitted. These similarities as well as the differences merit particular attention in the light of our focus on eschatology and social transformation. I shall therefore seek to summarize what appear to be significant similarities among the Radical Reformers of different tendencies. This may also help to focus the points at which important differences and disagreements arose and the significance of those disagreements for our discussion on the relation between eschatology and social change.

First, most Radical Reformers identified the Roman church of the time with the apocalyptic figures of the Anti-Christ or the Babylonian harlot.[4] In so doing they in one sense followed Luther who had used the same language. However, the Radical Reformers sometimes also characterized the Protestant Reformers with similar terms. In this respect Menno and the Münsterites shared similar perspectives. Sattler or Menno Simons occasionally sounded remarkably like Bernard Rothmann. According to Sattler, the Holy Spirit had awakened and raised up the Protestant Reformers to denounce the false doctrines and wrong practices of Roman Catholicism. They "were to arise and to attack with great zeal the Roman Church, the congregation of the work-saints, seize everything, and consume all the gold, silver, and other goods which she had brought together, condemn her as heretical...." Sattler then went on to say that unfortunately Protestant theologians "... would again take the side of the beast, that is the Roman school, and defend it, and again cast away the kingdom of God which previously come to them."[5]

This identification of the Roman Church and the Protestant groups with the beast or the Babylonian harlot or the Anti-Christ was based on what they were in fact doing and teaching, rather than primarily upon purely speculative or polemical considerations. In the Radical Reformation perspective, not only the Roman Catholics but also the Protestant Reformers persecuted those who were seeking to restore the church according to New Testament standards, namely the Anabaptists themselves. Both Protestants and Catholics thereby demonstrated their opposition to Christ by persecuting and opposing those who sought to follow Christ. Furthermore, the Protestants as well as the Roman Catholics perpetuated the unholy alliance of spiritual and temporal powers which had characterized the church since the age of Constantine. This intermingling of the temporal and spiritual powers stood in opposition to the teaching and example of Christ. It constituted unfaithfulness to the reign of Christ, and could therefore be fittingly described as "harlotry" or with the figure of the "Babylonian harlot."

Because of the church's unfaithfulness, the impending Judgment would fall first upon it: "Then shall the almighty God judge and punish the Babylonian harlot, because she is the mother of all abominations on earth (Revelation 17:5), and the blood of all the saints is found in her (Revelation 18:24). She has deceived the world with her beautiful appearance (being arrayed in purple and scarlet color, and decked with gold and precious stones and pearls, having a golden cup in her hand full of all abominations and gives all her lovers and paramours to drink thereof); and the kings of the earth have committed fornication with her and all nations have been made drunk with the wine of her fornication and sorcery. Therefore God shall punish her, and her plagues shall come unawares, and all who adhere to her and will not separate from her shall not go unpunished."[6] In the eschatological perspective of the Radical Reformers, the doctrine of the Judgment focused first of all upon the unfaithful Christians rather than, for example, upon the unbelieving Turks, who were seen by Roman Catholics and Protestants as the major threat to European Christendom at that time.

Second, most Radical Reformers characterized the present age as a time when faithful Christians can expect suffering, persecution, and martyrdom. But the imminent return of Christ and the impending judgment meant that this time of suffering and persecution will be limited by divine intervention or that it is circumscribed by God's will. Here again the gamut of Radical Reformation groups shared similar perspectives. Hans Hut reportedly claimed that "... God the Lord had given three and one-half years for repentance according to Revelation 13. Whoever repented would be persecuted and would have to suffer, as we read in 2 Timothy 3. All who would lead a godly life would have to suffer persecution."[7] Jacob Hutter, without attempting to develop an eschatological chronology like Hut, also said that there would be "struggle and strife" before the imminent deliverance of the Christians.

They should not be deterred by tribulation and suffering, but persist "with meekness, with great patience in righteousness and truth, in godly love and with strong faith and confidence."[8]

Similarly, Menno spoke much about the way of "*lydsaemkeit*" or willingness to suffer to which all believers are called by the cross of Christ.[9] True followers of Christ can expect to suffer persecution and even martyrdom, just as Christ himself suffered and was crucified. Menno did not hold out an easy hope that the end would come immediately and rescue the suffering believers from their tribulations. Nevertheless, he continued to comfort them with the assurance that the "way of the cross is the nearest way to eternal life."[10] Regardless of how long their suffering might last or how intense it might be, believers could take hope that they would be vindicated and that earthly tyrants would not defeat them. The faithful and suffering church would be transformed into the church triumphant only by Christ at his return. In the meantime, it should not resort to violent means either to establish the kingdom or to defend itself against the enemies of the kingdom, including the forces of Christendom, as the Münsterites did. Suffering and persecution could be expected by Christians who follow Christ and do not resort to the sword. Suffering and persecution are therefore not understood simply as a result of evil in the world or as the fatalistic result of an unfolding apocalyptic drama. They are the world's response to those who are committed to following the way of Christ.

Third, Radical Reformers of varying tendencies shared the conviction that they were called to restore true Christianity. In 1539, three years after his conversion and four years after the events of Münster, Menno Simons summarized this objective: "Therefore I and my brethren in the Lord desire nothing ... than that we may to the honor of God so labor with his fallen city and temple and captive people according to the talent received of him, that we may rebuild that which is demolished, repair that which is damaged, and free those who are captives with the Word of God by the power of the Holy Spirit. And we would bring it back to its earlier estate, that is, in the freedom of the Spirit to the doctrine, sacraments, ceremonies, love and life of Christ Jesus and his holy apostles."[11] In his 1526 interpretation of Daniel, Hoffman wrote: "God is now again present with his Spirit and angel and intercedes for his children and chosen ones. He is again cleansing his holy temple, which the angels of God are now rebuilding and erecting in a time of struggle. But however much the enemy of God's people with all his angels and false teachers seeks to prevent this rebuilding of God's temple, he will not succeed. It will be rebuilt."[12] This restitution of the church was not a backward-looking objective. It was the call to acknowledge the present shape of the inbreaking new reality.

In their common interest for renewing the visible church, the Radical Reformers of various tendencies differed from "spiritualists" such as Caspar Schwenkfeld. These differences were based in part on their different assessments of eschatology. For the spiritualists, the visible restoration of Christianity would be ushered in only at the end of history. They supported a futuristic eschatology which undermined attempts to incarnate realities of the new age. The new age expresses itself only in spiritual or inner realities during the present time, not in any "externals" such as sacraments, church structures, or a visible practice of Christian discipleship with social and economic implications.

However, significant differences as well as similarities existed among the Radical Reformers who rejected the spiritualist critique of "externals." Contemporary Mennonite interpreters have tended to emphasize the differences among the Radical Reformers. Social historians have perceived their common interest in restoring true Christianity as an alternative to Christendom. Littell, for example, contends that most Radical Reformers expected the imminent coming of Christ to bring judgment and the restoration of peace and justice in the world. Some of the Anabaptists quoted Isaiah 2:4 as a picture of this restoration. According to Littell: "The quiet eschatology which became exclusive after Münster did not change the world view nor the expectation of a Kingdom on earth.... The expectation of a coming Kingdom of God on earth...can be seen to link the revolutionaries and the nonresistants. The lack of historical concern in the secular sense, which is frequently noted in Anabaptist thinking, was not truly nonhistorical, but rather it stemmed from a contempt for the traditional things upon which God had already passed judgment and which were soon to pass away. Their unconcern with present matters was rooted in a great vision of things to come...."[13]

Littell and other social historians are doubtless correct in their contention that both types of Radical Reformers shared a vision of restoration which directly required or at least implied social and economic as well as ecclesiastical change. Nevertheless, there are significant differences on the primary "place" of restoration, and on the "time" when the conflict will be resolved.

The one tendency, represented by Hans Hut and others, insisted upon "the earth" as the place where the conflict would be resolved in the near future. According to the report on his November 1527 statement he contended that "...the new heaven and earth and a habitation for all the pious and elect [would appear] here on earth.... This he called the future world according to Ezekiel 37 and Psalm 37, when the godless would be rooted out and the just would live in the land in perpetual peace."[14] Similarly, Bernhard Rothmann contended: "The Scriptures say that everything must be finished on earth. The Lord our righteousness will do justice and righteousness on earth. The mouth of the godless must be stopped on earth. All evil, and everything that the heavenly Father has not planted must be rooted out and done away with. There must be one sheepfold and one flock and one king who rules over all. All creatures must be set free. In summary: God's people which survive and which must remain unspotted and clean in all obedience will inherit the earth and will be at the service of Christ the King over all the earth. All this will happen in this time and on earth where righteousness shall dwell. Those who understand the Scriptures to say that this will happen after the judgment day and that it must be fulfilled then do not understand."[15]

The other tendency among the Radical Reformers agreed that the restoration would take place "on earth" rather than simply "in heaven." The church is called to be the community of the kingdom in the present time. As long as there are people in the world who do not repent, conflicts between a restored Christian community and its opponents may be expected to characterize the present earthly life. Marpeck, for example, assumes that these differences will continue until the "separation": "For evil and good now exist together in this physical life undifferentiated and unseparated until the day when judgment takes place and good and evil are separated. This will take place when the last person to be saved is brought in. Then all worldly authority will be dissolved, one house will fall upon the other, there will be war and the cry of war without any means of peace or rescue, and all piety, faithfulness, love, truth, faith, and confidence will cease. For the pious and the godly, for whose sake the world with its wickedness is spared, will be saved. They will be separated from all wickedness and gain rest and eternal joy as Chist said...."[16]

Marpeck, Menno, and others of similar orientation thought less about establishing peace and justice "on earth" in global terms and focused more on the Christian community as their central locus "on earth." This emphasis may have been conditioned by their experiences of persecution. They may have also found confirmation of this emphasis in their understanding of eschatology. But it likely had more fundamentally to do with their understanding of the church as the community of the kingdom and with the way Christians are called to participate in the restoration of peace and justice in the world. We shall return later to their understanding of the church.

Fourth, the various groups in the Radical Reformation differed strongly on whether the Christians' vocation in the latter days included acting as agents of divine judgment. Some contended that God has chosen the godly to carry out the divine punishment of the "ungodly" (which referred primarily to the unfaithful Christians, rather than, for example, to the Turks or other non-Christians). Hut, for example, argued in 1527 that "... all who would lead a godly life would have to suffer persecution. Daniel 13 says that they will all be scattered. He also talked about the three and one-half years and predicted famine, pestilence, and war. Only after these had happened would the Lord gather his own in all countries, and in each country they would punish the governments and all sinners." Similarly Ambrosius Spitelmaier declared, also in 1527, "All the just who have remained will come together from the ends of the earth in a moment and kill all the godless."[17]

Other Anabaptists interpreted these eschatological events in ways which did not make the "godly" agents of divine wrath and punishment. Riedemann understood that the judgment given to Christ at the second advent somehow included this role, but not in a way which would make believers the agents of divine judgment: "We confess also that the Father has committed judgment unto the Son, who will come, and that right terribly, namely with flaming fire, to take vengeance upon all that is ungodly and all the wrong brought by men...."[18] It is precisely at this point that Menno Simons' rejection of violence on the part of Christians has its "Sitz im Leben." The only sword which Christians may wield is the "sword of Christ's mouth," i.e., the Word. In his polemic against the Münsterites, Menno cites Revelation 17:16 as evidence that God will punish "Babylon" by "heathen hands." Usually Menno speaks simply in terms of punishment or vengeance taking place through divine intervention after the second coming of Christ. Therefore all the arguments of the Münsterites that Christians are called to punish the "Babylonian harlot" or to kill the ungodly are false. Neither the interpretations of the apocalyptic or any other biblical passages may be so construed. "Let every one of you guard against all strange doctrine of swords and resistance and other like things which is nothing short of a fair flower under which lies hidden an evil serpent which has shot his venom into many...."[19]

Fifth, Radical Reformers of both tendencies interpreted contemporary events in the light of scriptural passages from prophetic and apocalyptic literature. They obviously differed in the relative emphasis on these passages, on whether they sought to establish a precise apocalyptic chronology, and on the practical implications they drew from their ways of understanding the times. Thus significant differences existed on the criteria for interpreting the "signs of the times." These differences were based on their understandings and experiences of the relation between "Spirit" and "Word." For Hoffman the Spirit of God mediated through a prophet took priority in granting insight into the signs of the times. The prophet or prophets were to speak God's word to the people and provide direction for them.[20] For Menno the Spirit is mediated supremely through the "word, spirit, and example of Jesus Christ" according to the Scriptures. The words of "prophets" need to be examined by their consistency with that criterion and tested by the church.

In summary the Radical Reformers shared with many other Christians in the first half of the sixteenth century a sense of living in the latter days. In various ways and with differing emphases, they described and interpreted contemporary events in eschatological and even apocalyptic terms. Their expectation of the imminent return of Christ and impending judgment offered them hope in the face of suffering and persecution. It also motivated their call to repentance and their admonitions to persist in Christian discipleship in spite of adversity. In no instance did they understand the imminent return of Christ and the impending Last Judgment as justifying the existing ecclesial and social order until the end actually arrived. Nor did they accept the "spiritualist" view that all "external" changes were insignificant and should be postponed until the end actually came or withdraw into a purely inner and individual piety to await the end. Rather than implicitly or explicitly justifying the existing order of things even for an interim time the Radical Reformers fundamentally denounced and critiqued the unfaithfulness and injustice of Christendom in apocalyptic terms.

The Radical Reformers differed among themselves in the relative emphasis they put upon "the end time," but even more on the criteria for discerning the signs of the times and on the implications of eschatology for Christian conduct for reforming the Christian community and for the kingdom of God "on earth." Some such as Menno, Marpeck, and Riedemann insisted that any claims of prophetic insight be consistent with the biblical account of Jesus Christ and of the first Christian communities. They also rejected all interpretations of the end time which made Christians agents of divine judgment upon evildoers or of establishing and defending the kingdom by violent means. And they understood the presence of God's kingdom or reign on earth in terms that focused in a particular way on the Christian community within the world rather than in relation to the world in an undifferentiated fashion. This focus is consistent with their view of the "end time." It also has to do with their understanding of the church and Christian ethics.

Within the limits of this paper I cannot discuss the ecclesiology of the Radical Reformers in detail. Nevertheless the relation between the kingdom and the radical restoration of the Christian community brings us again to the question of what we mean by "eschatology and social transformation" in a way which goes beyond eschatology in the limited sense of a doctrine of "last things" or an intense expectation of imminent end to history. I shall turn first to the question of "social transformation" and explore in what sense it is appropriate to speak about social transformation in relation to the Radical Reformation and what model of social transformation corresponds to such a view of Christian faith and life. I shall then return to concepts of eschatology in relation to that model of social transformation.

Implications of Anabaptist eschatology for social transformation

In this section I shall focus upon the Anabaptists which adopted what Klaassen has called a "restrained" eschatology, rather than continuing to summarize the similarities and differences among the broader range of Radical Reformers. That comparison has been instructive for historical reasons and for correcting tendencies to either associate or dissociate various Radical Reformation tendencies too sharply. Pursuing the comparison in detail might well be interesting and instructive. But the Anabaptists who both represented a "restrained" eschatology and rejected the sword make the question of social transformation particularly challenging. If Christians refuse to participate in lethal violence not only as a legitimate means of social maintenance, but also as a legitimate last resort for necessary social change, do they in fact become accomplices in social and economic injustice?

In his chapter on "Radical Politics: Anabaptism and Revolution," Walter Klaassen reports that the religious and civil authorities of the time viewed all sixteenth-century Radical Reformers "as social revolutionaries." Klaassen concludes that this identification was essentially correct. But this does not mean that all the Radicals set out to overthrow the established order or that they programmatically aimed to create a social revolution in the entire society. With the exception of the Münsterites, this was not their explicit concern. They were concerned rather to follow Jesus in all of life, in the social and political as well as in the religious spheres.[21] Out of this concern they insisted on religious freedom, developed a new economics, refused to take the oath, and did not participate in warfare. In the context of the sixteenth century, these beliefs, protests, and alternative practices in effect made Anabaptists "socially revolutionary" in some sense. Without examining all these examples more carefully, let us look briefly at economics as one illustration. We shall then seek to clarify the sense in which the Anabaptists who subscribed to a restrained eschatology and nonviolent social stance may be characterized as "social revolutionaries."

To begin with, the Radical Reformers sharply protested the disparities between the rich and the poor, the exploitation of the poor by usury, and profit-taking in commerce. In his "Reply to False Accusations," Menno Simons criticized the ineffectiveness of the Protestant Reformation in relation to economic change in the broader society as well as in the church. "Is it not sad and an intolerable hypocrisy that these poor people boast of having the Word of God, of being the true, Christian church, never remembering that they have entirely lost their sign of true Christianity? For although many of them have plenty of everything, go about in silk and velvet, ...have their coffers filled, and live in luxury and splendor, yet they suffer many of their own poor, ...(notwithstanding their fellow believers have received one baptism and partaken of the same bread with them) to ask alms; and poor, hungry, suffering, old, lame, blind, and sick people to beg their bread at their doors.... Shame on you for the easygoing gospel and barren bread-breaking, you who have in so many years been unable to effect enough with your gospel and sacraments so as to remove your needy and distressed members from the streets...."[22] According to Menno, the sharing of economic resources is apparently as much, or perhaps even more, a "sign of true Christianity" as the Lord's Supper. At the very least, breaking bread in the Lord's Supper is an empty ritual without a corresponding economic practice in the Christian community.

In addition to protesting economic practices which perpetuated great economic disparities, some Anabaptists sought to implement an economic attitude and practice which would eliminate material need. One group, the Hutterians, developed a community of goods beginning in 1533 in Moravia, including what may be called a community of production and consumption. According to Peter Riedemann, such a community of goods represents God's original intent for humankind. Indeed, departing from God's original design that human beings share both God's spiritual and material gifts has even caused them to forget God. The accumulation of private property has contributed to unbelief: "...One sees in all things created, which testify to us still today, that God from the beginning ordained nothing private for man, but all things to be common. But through wrong taking ... man drew such things to himself and made them his property, and so grew and became hardened therein. Through such wrong taking and collecting of created things he has been led so far from God that he has even forgotten the Creator."[23] Riedemann goes on to argue that the Christian community is called to hold material as well as spiritual things in common and so incarnate God's original intent for the entire human community. Indeed, the Holy Spirit restored this kind of community again in Jerusalem with the birth of the church.

Other Anabaptists also taught a community of goods, but allowed for personal property which was to be treated as common. They too sought to implement an economic practice and attitude which would eliminate need, but did not consider a community of production necessary.[24] Had these Radical Reformation groups been able to grow without persecution, such attitudes and practices may well have had major economic consequences.

Some tensions existed between the Hutterians and Anabaptists which allowed for personal property without claiming it as their own. But to the Protestant Reformers and most magistrates, both groups appeared to threaten the established economic order for at least two reasons. During the first two thirds of the sixteenth century, the poor suffered from a combination of sharply rising prices for goods and a constant level of wages. There were also other economic problems and conflicts. Even to say in that setting that Christians should not claim anything for their own seemed like throwing a torch in a tinderbox. Furthermore, the common ownership of property and its association with other practices in Münster doubtless cast a long shadow. Menno and others tried to distance themselves from the Münsterites by emphasizing the importance of voluntary commitment in the context of church discipline for their economic practices. But their attitudes and practices looked to the Roman Catholics and Protestants like they had been born in Münster and would produce similar offspring.

What we have summarized in terms of Anabaptist economic attitudes and practices could be repeated with reference to other examples. In all such cases, the Radical Reformers developed attitudes and practices which in effect challenged major issues in the social, economic, political, as well as in the religious setting. In this sense they did not voluntarily withdraw from society or from the problems of society. They protested against economic practices and theological rationalizations which they considered contrary to God's will for human society. They called the church to incarnate social and economic attitudes and practices which would represent an alternative to the dominant social and economic system. These protests and alternative practices were sometimes explicitly related to and otherwise implicitly consistent with their eschatological perspectives. Nevertheless, they did not explicitly articulate or initiate a specific program of social change for the entire society which could be established without reference to repentance and following Christ in life. The "society" which they sought to transform most directly was the Christian church. But can one meaningfully speak of social transformation in relation to the Radical Reformation in any other sense?

Jean Séguy, a longtime student of the Radical Reformation, has raised this question from a sociology of religions perspective. He builds upon Ralf Dahrendorf's understanding of class conflict in industrial society and Ernst Troeltsch's analysis of "sectarian" movements throughout Christian history. Séguy distinguishes between movements of "implicit" and "explicit protestation" in relation to religious and social change.[25] He notes that earliest Christianity did not directly intend to be a movement of social protest and change, but that it implicitly transmitted a social critique in its historical and social setting. Séguy applies the concept of "implicit protestation" to numerous other historical and contemporary religious movements, including the

Anabaptist groups represented by Menno, Marpeck, Hutter, and others of similar persuasion.

These Anabaptists manifest several characteristics of the "implicit protestation" type. Such movements usually express a latent social conflict in somewhat ambiguous and other than explicit social categories. These Radical Reformers similarly express certain latent social conflicts in terms of Christian faith and practice rather than in terms of global social protest and change. The adherents of this type frequently are not fully conscious of the broader social implications of such a movement. Less frequently its opponents are not aware of its potential social ramifications. Consistently with this type, the Anabaptists appeared to be social revolutionaries in the eyes of the religious and civil authorities, likely more than they themselves intended.

Further, the implicit protestation type frequently appears in societies which emphasize unity and unanimity as one of their structural characteristics. This also describes the social situation of European Christendom in the sixteenth century to a significant degree. Finally, this type frequently includes both a distinctive community practice and an eschatological conviction. The distinctive community practice constitutes a realization of the projected ideal in a limited space in the broader society. The projected ideal is considered the desirable and desired goal for the entire society even though it has not yet been accepted by the entire society. And the eschatological conviction provides a basis for the hope of an impending generalization of what has already been partially realized in the more limited community through the intervention of a transcendent reality into history or through some immanent dynamic. In sociological rather than theological and ethical terms, these characteristics also aptly describe the Radical Reformation groups which gathered around Grebel, Menno, Marpeck, and others.

These Radical Reformers set out to reform the church in faith and practice as well as in structure. They did not intentionally and explicitly seek to impose this transformation on the larger society. But they sought to renew the Christian community in a way which implied broader social change and potentially contributed to social transformation beyond their immediate congregations. The degree to which this model actually effects broad social transformation remains difficult if not impossible to measure with precision. Its social effectiveness will depend in part upon the given set of circumstances and upon its acceptance by the broader society. And its potential contribution to broader social change will most likely also depend upon the degree to which it combines a sustaining eschatological hope, a distinctive community practice, and a fitting challenge to what constitutes the contemporary forms of human sinfulness in the broader society as well as in the church.

It would be instructive to evaluate this model in terms of biblical and theological as well as sociological considerations. Irrespective of its potential significance for social transformation either in sixteenth century Europe or in contemporary settings, does it represent a (one among several or the most appropriate) normative orientation for biblical and theological reasons? Does it provide a normative framework for addressing contemporary issues of justice and peace? Instead of pursuing this inquiry along those lines, I shall turn to a remaining issue which merits clarification, namely the concept of eschatology.

The kingdom of God and the Christian community in the world

So far, I have been using the term "eschatology" primarily in two senses, in order to interpret Radical Reformation perspectives relevant to our discussion of eschatology and social transformation. In the first sense, eschatology referred to the traditional doctrine of the "last things" such as the return of Christ, the Last Judgment, and the Resurrection of the Dead as beliefs in their own right without attempting to locate them in relation to some grand scheme of history. In the second sense, eschatology referred primarily to an interpretation of contemporary events informed by the overwhelming conviction that the return of Christ was imminent and that history would soon end. In both senses, "eschatology" has implications for Christian life and thought.

In contemporary biblical and theological studies, it has become commonplace to refer to the centrality of the kingdom of God in Jesus' proclamation and to its "eschatological" reality. Biblical interpreters acknowledge that according to the Gospels, the kingdom is in some sense both present and future; it has already come and is yet to come. To be sure, interpretations differ with regard to the relative weight of emphasis on the present or on the future reality of kingdom. And understandings of the kingdom of God and of "eschatology" appear to be almost as numerous as there are scholars and theologies. Nevertheless, some common concerns appear in many contemporary understandings of "eschatology."

At the risk of great oversimplification, I am suggesting that most contemporary understandings of eschatology focus on the attempt to understand the goal and purpose of history theologically. "Eschatology" may still be used in the traditional sense to refer to the doctrine of "the last things." It may secondly be used to refer to an apocalyptic expectation of an imminent and cataclysmic end of the old world and the advent of a new world. But concepts of eschatology have been extended to describe the present and future reality of the kingdom of God as the new reality of God's reign which has already come in Jesus Christ and which is the final goal of human history. Concepts of eschatology in this third sense do not refer primarily to an understanding of the "end" of all things. Eschatology has frequently come to mean a theological understanding of the all embracing goal and purpose of history, of its present as well as its future shape, and of the way in which the goal of history gives meaning to human existence and to all of reality.

This is not a mere semantic shift without substantive implications for theology and ethics. Some of these implications may be helpful and consistent with Scripture. Some of them may be problematic or even misleading. Furthermore, eschatology in this third general sense overlaps with the concerns of eschatology in the first and second senses. In some ways it also recasts some of those concerns. And in some ways it raises new issues.

Within the limits and focus of this essay on eschatology and social transformation, I can at most indicate two points in contemporary discussions which are of particular interest from a Radical Reformation perspective. First, in what sense is the kingdom of God "eschatological," particularly in relation to Christian ethics? Second, what is the relation between the kingdom of God and the Christian community? In a Radical Reformation perspective, these two points are closely related. Let us turn first to the relation between the church and the reign of God.

I earlier suggested that the Anabaptists who assumed what may be described as an "implicit protestation" view on establishing peace and justice on earth linked their understanding not only with eschatology, but directly to their understanding of the church as the kingdom of God.[26] This correlation and differentiation between church and kingdom presupposed that they understood the kingdom of God in a way which did not simply postpone it to an indeterminate future. Nor did they identify the end-time kingdom with the shape claimed for it in Münster, even though they understood it as both a present and a future reality.

Menno Simons, as well as others of similar persuasion, referred to the church as the kingdom of God. For our purposes, we can take Menno as representative of this orientation. To begin with, he understood the kingdom of God in relation to Jesus' proclamation, ministry, and life. Jesus had called the people to repent because the kingdom of God had come near; Menno therefore emphasized the importance of repentance for entering the kingdom of God as a new order of life in the midst of the world. This emphasis was necessarily related to the Christian community as well as to the individual. The church is called to witness to the kingdom by word, deed, the lives of its members, and the quality of its community life. Where the church's life and witness contradict the kingdom of God, the church is called to repent. The faithful church is the place in the midst of the world where human beings respond in faith and obedience to the reign of God through Christ. In this sense, Menno Simons and others spoke of the church as the kingdom of God.[27]

This did not mean for them that the reign of God had already been fully realized in the Christian community. Nor did it mean that God's kingdom was limited to purely spiritual or religious or ecclesial matters apart from social and economic realities. The church as the community of the kingdom of God is also a social and economic reality and lives in the midst of and in dynamic interaction with other social and economic realities.

Menno mentions several characteristics of God's reign, which are to he visibly manifest in the community of the kingdom. Because Jesus Christ is the one King, no other king may reign in this kingdom. Further, the kingdom of God is a kingdom of peace rather than strife. "Neither this King nor his servants bear any sword but the sword of the Spirit, which pierces even to the dividing asunder of soul and spirit."[28] In this kingdom, the only form of marriage which is in effect is a monogamous relationship, which should not he dissolved by divorce except for fornication. Furthermore, this kingdom is to be a kingdom of humility, where people do not "parade in gold, silver, pearls, ...and costly finery," but adorn the spirit with zeal and diligence. Menno continues this description which includes truth-telling, a useful and sober style of life, following the "ordinances of Christ" on all matters related to ecclesial matters (baptism, communion, ministry, etc.), and witnessing to "Jesus Christ with the mouth, conduct, possessions, and blood, if divine honor requires it." Thus the kingdom of God has social and economic as well as spiritual dimensions which are to take on visible expression in the church.

If we were to examine these characteristics of the church as the kingdom of God in more detail, we would see that several of them are implicitly meant to counter Münsterite views and practices (appointment of a king, use of the sword, polygamy, etc.). Similarly they are meant to correct what the Anabaptists considered misuses in the churches of Christendom. Indeed, it appears that this understanding of God's kingdom has been influenced in large measure by efforts to correct and critique other views considered unacceptable, rather than primarily by an effort to explicitly or systematically develop a comprehensive view of the reign of God.

Given the circumstances of that time, this implicitly polemical approach is understandable. And given the lack of a systematic concept of the kingdom in the New Testament, any attempt to define the kingdom of God comprehensively would doubtless itself be a rather "uneschatological" act! Nevertheless, the Anabaptists' corrective effort may have caused them to overlook as well as emphasize some aspects of the kingdom which correspond to biblical perspectives.

For example, recent biblical studies have demonstrated that Jesus' proclamation of the kingdom includes a new economic practice in the community of the kingdom. Several scholars have shown how Jesus drew on the tradition of the Jubilee year to call for economic renewal in the community of the kingdom.[29] A recent study of the relation between Jesus' message on the reign of God and the economic conditions of first-century Palestine has also concluded that it had specific economic implications of a structural nature.[30] Although these interpretations vary in some details, they agree that Jesus' proclamation of the eschatological kingdom had immediate implications for economic renewal, both in relation to attitudes and to practice. These included the remission of debts and a new set of relationships between oppressors and oppressed in response to the coming of the kingdom.[31]

Anabaptist views on economics and the kingdom should doubtless be reassessed in the light of the gospel message. Such a reassessment would strengthen the Radical Reformation view that the presence of the kingdom has structural implications for the economic practice of the Christian community in the midst of the world. But it could also root that conviction more firmly in the biblical vision of the kingdom rather than in an attempt to separate it from the legacy of the "explicit protestation" type associated with Münster. Such a reassessment is also doubtless needed to correct tendencies among many contemporary Mennonites, who theoretically subscribe to the Anabaptist legacy while uncritically accepting dominant economic practices which contribute to injustice or limit Christian ethical concern to individual charity.

A second example in an Anabaptist understanding of the kingdom which needs clarification, for exegetical as well as theological and practical reasons, is the equation of the kingdom of God with the church. In Jesus' proclamation, God's reign is closely linked to the church as the community of disciples. Jan Lochmann quite rightly points out that: "Jesus' message of the coming kingdom is addressed primarily and unmistakably to the disciples."[32] Indeed, Jesus' public ministry and proclamation of the kingdom included calling together a circle of disciples, which called a new social reality, namely a community of disciples, into existence.[33] The kingdom is present not only in Jesus' person and ministry, but also in his calling together, creating, and commissioning a new community. "The kingdom of God is a category which presumes and creates a people."[34]

Nonetheless, the New Testament does not simply equate the church with the kingdom of God. The kingdom is always greater than the church, even though the life of the Christian community should never be less than a visible manifestation that the reign of God has "come near." Nor should the particular calling and mission of the church to be the people of the kingdom in the midst of the world be misconstrued as a claim to privilege or self-justification. Lochmann has observed that post-constantian Christendom has been full of attempts "to claim the kingdom for itself, to take over the management of the kingdom and even at the limit, to present itself as the realized kingdom of God over against the world."[35] Such attempts in fact amount to a denial rather than an acceptance of the reign of God, in the church as manifested in the life and ministry of Jesus.

Even though Menno and, others like him, spoke of the church as the kingdom of God, they hardly make the kind of false claims rightly rejected by Lochmann. As we have seen they rather critiqued Christendom churches as the Anti-Christ where they misrepresented and even contradicted the kingdom of God. They also rejected the Münsterite version of identifying the church with the kingdom and called for individual and corporate repentance. They sought to shape the life of the Christian community in the midst of the world according to the kingdom. In somehow identifying the church with the kingdom of God they had in mind the church insofar as it is faithful to its calling.

Nevertheless rather than equating the church with the kingdom it would be better theologically to speak about the church as the community of the kingdom in the midst of and in dynamic interaction with the world. This would correspond more closely to the biblical descriptions of the kingdom and its relation to the church and world. This distinction could also help correct the tendencies to misconstrue the primary role of the church in relation to the kingdom in ways which have been typical of constantinian Christendom. In addition, this clarification could also help correct tendencies which have often arisen among Christians to justify withdrawing from witness and ministry in the world by limiting the agenda of the kingdom to the internal concerns of the church.

This reformulation should however not weaken the direct relationship between the kingdom of God and the church as the community of the kingdom. As the community of the kingdom in the midst of the world the church is called to live by hope in the coming kingdom, and by the power of the Holy Spirit, to be a foretaste of the kind of peace and justice now which God shall one day establish in all its fullness. As the community of the kingdom in the midst of the world, the church is called to live as a forgiven and forgiving people, as a reconciled and reconciling people, as a justified and justice-making people, and as a peaceful and peacemaking people in practice as well as in attitude—because that both is and will be the reality of God's kingdom. In this sense, the church is to be closely identified with the kingdom of God.

The American Christian ethicist Stanley Hauerwas has observed that, unfortunately, theologians are reluctant to make "strong claims of some kind of identity between the church and the kingdom of God."[36] There have presumably been several reasons for this reluctance, some of ancient, some of recent vintage. The kinds of misuses to which Lochmann has referred have doubtless contributed to reservations about identifying the church too closely with the kingdom. The debacle of Münster and other such experiments have reinforced such reservations. Identifying the kingdom with the church in those ways has indeed been contrary to the reality of the Kingdon according to the New Testament. In addition, recent interpretations of eschatology have reinforced the reservations of many Christians and theologians toward understanding the kingdom of God as a category which presumes and creates the Christian community as a particular kind of people in the world.

A direct connection between the church and the kingdom of God is undermined by concepts of eschatology which separate ethics from eschatology. In an effort to correct concepts of the kingdom as an ideal which can be realized progressively through human moral action, some biblical interpreters and theologians since Johannes Weiss have emphasized a general discontinuity between eschatology and ethics. "Eschatological" then refers not only to the reign of God as the new reality of the end time which may also be present in some sense. "Eschatological" is taken to mean unilateral divine action which ends history in contrast to human action in history. Accordingly the kingdom is understood as having been present in some sense only in Jesus and as yet to come in a marvelous way through God's intervention in the future.

By thinking in the general categories of divine action and of history as the product of human action, such understandings of eschatology find it difficult if not impossible to acknowledge the church in the world as the focal expression of the reign of God. God not only initiates the kingdom in the proclamation, life, and ministry of Jesus. God not only will again initiate the kingdom in all its fullness. But God's initiative in Jesus Christ also calls forth repentance and response in actively living according to kingdom ways, both as individual believers and as the believing community in the midst of the world and in love and service to "neighbor" and "enemy" alike. The new reality of God's kingdom comprehends both divine initiative and the kind of obedient response which corresponds to the incarnation of God's reign in Jesus Christ. Because the Spirit has been given to the Christian community in a particular way, it is misleading to think only or primarily in terms of a contrast between human history in general and the kingdom of God as its ultimate goal. That too easily circumvents the church's calling to be the community of the kingdom in which human beings now confess God's reign and are committed to living now according to the standards of justice and peace which God shall one day bring to complete realization.

A direct connection between the church and the kingdom of God can also be undermined by concepts of eschatology which overemphasize temporal categories at the cost of spatial realities. I would suggest that this tendency surfaces in attempts to differentiate too sharply between "the rule of God" and the "kingdom of God" on the grounds that it means God's "kingship" or "reign" rather than "realm."[37] By implication, this tendency abstracts the kingdom of God from all spatial categories, until the new heaven and the new earth "at" (or "beyond") the end of history.

It is certainly the case that the kingdom of God does not refer to a particular territory in which God reigns, in analogy to human rulers in national states or territories in distinction to other territories where there are other rulers. God's reign is not constitutionally more distant from one place than any other place, nor is it mediated to all other places through one particular place (at least, after its coming in Jesus), either in a geographical or in an ecclesiastical sense. Nevertheless the New Testament "locates" the presence of the kingdom and speaks about it as having spatial as well as temporal dimensions. It has "come near"; people are invited to "enter the kingdom"; Jesus declares that it is "among" his hearers. Where people acknowledge the rule of God and respond to it in faith, obedience, and hope, there is the "place" of the kingdom in its present manifestation, regardless of geographical, national, social, or other such spatial boundaries. In this sense the church is called to be the "territory" of the kingdom, in which Christians have their primary citizenship.

Time does not permit us to review other examples in which some contemporary concepts of eschatology circumvent the concrete reality of the church as the community of the kingdom by an overemphasis on temporal categories.[38] In any case, it would appear that contemporary understandings of eschatology which seek to describe the present and future reality of the kingdom of God as the purpose and goal of history are both helpful and misleading from a Radical Reformation as well as from a biblical perspective.

On the one hand, there has been a "rediscovery" or at least a renewed interest in the kingdom of God, which was central to the preaching and ministry of Jesus. There has been a renewed appreciation that the kingdom of God is an "eschatological" reality as that qualitatively new order characterized by justice, peace, and communion with God. This qualitatively new order has already been proclaimed and exemplified in Jesus Christ and represents the redeeming purpose of God with humanity, which God shall accomplish as and when he wills.

On the other hand, this "rediscovery" has frequently been weakened and the eschatological reality of the kingdom misinterpreted by abstracting from the concrete reality of the church as the community of the kingdom in dynamic interaction with the world. The church is called to visibly manifest this qualitatively new order of justice, peace, and communion with God in its confession of faith and worship, in its own life and structures, in its ministry and witness in the world, and in its hope for the future. When and where it is the community of the kingdom in this sense, it also belongs to the eschatological reign of God and becomes a foretaste of kingdom in its fullness; where and when it does not live according to this vocation, it is called to repentance, just as Jesus called the people to repent because the kingdom has come near.

The kingdom of God thus represents both a comforting hope and a challenging call to the Christian community. The ways in which Christians may appropriately express this hope and respond to this challenge will doubtless vary in different historical settings. The Anabaptists of the sixteenth century lived in a context of sometimes intense apocalyptic awareness. In other historical contexts this kind of apocalyptic expectation may be considerably less intense or even largely absent. Similarly biblical scholars have suggested that Jesus and the earliest Christian congregations expected an imminent end to history and the imminent arrival of the kingdom of God in all its fullness.

However the present implications of the reign of God do not depend primarily upon the moods of the times (subjectively speaking) but upon a believing and hoping response to the qualitatively new order which has already come in Christ and shall come in its fullness. The question is therefore not whether we share with sixteenth-century Radical Reformers or first-century Christians the perception that time has almost run out. We may or may not share such a perception. The question is whether the church today acknowledges with them the eschatological priority of the reign of God and becomes a transformed and transforming community as the sign and prefiguration of the new age in the midst of, in solidarity with, and for the sake of the world.

If it does it may also in divine providence contribute "implicitly" and perhaps even directly to economic and social justice in the societies of the world, and to peace and justice in a warring world. To paraphrase Jürgen Moltmann: the churches are not only to talk about peace in heaven and on earth, but to be a sign and anticipation of the kingdom of shalom which God wills for humankind and creation. Indeed, the church already has spoken in fact by the way it lives, by its organization within society at large and by its policies and its politics, even before it talks about peace and justice.[39] This should not mean that the church remains silent about racial enmity and conflict economic injustice and the murderous violence of actual and potential wars. But it does mean that the church's speech about the God's kingdom of peace and justice should first be addressed to itself as the community of that kingdom and its speaking embodied in a practice which corresponds to and is sustained by the hope of that kingdom.

---

[1] See for example, Walter Klaassen, *Anabaptism in Outline: Selected Primary Sources* (Herald Press, 1981) items 17.2 (320); 17.21 (336); 17.24 (340f.).

[2] See, for example: "Chiliasm" in *The Mennonite Encylopedia* (Herald Press, 1955) vol. I, 557ff.; and "Eschatology," ibid., vol. II, 247f.

[3] Franklin Hamlin Littell, *The Anabaptist View of the Church* (Starr King Press, 1958) 129; compare Klasssen, ibid., 317.

[4] Examples in Klassen, ibid., 17.1 (Michael Sattler); 17.16 (Bernhard Rothmann, 1534); 17.23 (Dirk Philips, 1558).,17.25 (Menno Simons, 1539), and 17.26 (Menno Simons,1554).

[55] Klasssen, ibid., 319; see 331ff., 341 ff.

[6] Klaassen, ibid., 339f.

[7] Klasssen, ibid., 320.

[8] Klaassen, ibid., 325. For other examples, see Klaassen 17.8 (Schiemer), 17.11 (Hoffman), 17.23 (Philips), and 17. 24 (Menno).

[9] Christoph Bornhäuser, *Leben und Lehre Menno Simons* (Neukirchener Verlag, 1973) 140ff.

[10] Bornhäuser, 143.

[11] Klaassen, 341.

[12] Klaassen, 326; see other examples in Klaassen: 17.1 (Sattler); 17.15 (Hoffman); 17.16 (Rothmann); 17.23 (Philips).

[13] Littell, 135.

[14] Klaassen, 320.

[15] Klaassen, 334.

[16] Klaassen, 338.

[17] Klaassen, 320, 321.

[18] Klaassen, 17.21; see also 17.23 (Philips).

[19] "The Blasphemy of John of Leiden," in *The Complete Writings of Menno Simons* (Herald Press, 1956) 49. See Klaassen, 46-49.

[20] See, for example, Klaassen, 17.11; 17.13: and 17.14.

[21] Walter Klasssen, *Anabaptism: Neither Catholic Nor Protestant* (Conrad Press, 1973) 62f.

[22] Klaassen, *Anabaptism in Outline*, 11.8 (241); see also 11.5 (Schnabel), 11.7 (Marpeck), and 11.9 (Menno Simons).

[23] Klaassen, ibid., 11.6 (238).

[24] See, for example, the selections in Klaassen: 11.1 (Hubmaier) and 11.5 (Schnabel). Menno, Marpeck, and others had similar positions.

[25] Jean Séguy, "La Protestation Implicite," in *Archives de Sciences Sociales des Religions* 1979, 48/2 (octobre-decembre, 187-212; and "La Socialisation Utopique aux Valeurs," ibid., 1980, 50/1 (juillet-septembre), 7-21.

[26] See pp. 00 and 00 above.

[27] Bornhäuser, 144f. For references to kingdom of God/Christ in Menno's writings, see *The Complete Works of Menno Simons* 108, 119, 124, 128f, 140, 144, 175, 177, 181, 199f., 208, 217, 223, 554, 558, 832, 1031. See also Walter Klaassen, "Visions of the End in Reformation Europe," in *Visions and Realities* (Hyperion Press Limited, 1985) 56ff.

[28] This and the remaining quotes in this paragraph are taken from "The Foundation of Christian Doctrrine," in *The Complete Works of Menno Simons*, 217f.

[29] John Howard Yoder, *The Politics of Jesus* (Eerdmans, 1972); German translation: *Die Politik Jesu - Der Weg Des Kreuzes* (Agape Verlag, 1981); and Sharon H. Ringe, *Jesus, Liberation, and the Biblical Jubilee* (Fortress Press, 1985).

[30] Douglas E. Oakman, *Jesus and the Economic Questions of His Day: Studies in the Bible and Early Christianity*, vol. 8. (The Edwin Mellen Press, 1986).

[31] Oakman concludes that Jesus "did not speak of a redistribution of landed property, probably because of his aversion to self-sufficiency in any form... [but] he did advocate the other revolutionary agenda of antiquity—remission of debts.... With the expectation of the near advent of God's rule came several other constructive agendas. Oppressors could begin to behave toward the oppressed with generosity and magnanimity (Luke 16:6-7; Matthew 18:27; 20:9, 15; Luke 14:23). The oppressed themselves could find joy again in sharing (Matthew 6:33; Matthew 7:2, Luke 6:38; Luke 10:29-37; 15:9). Furthermore a new kinship (Mark 10:30) and new moral obligations based upon a "general reciprocity" (Matthew 5:38-42; Luke 6:29-30; Matthew 5:44; Luke 6:27; Matthew 7:2; Luke 6:38; Luke 7:41-42; 10:35) were coming into being with the proclamation of the kingdom" (168f.).

[32] Jan Milic Lochman, "Church and World in the Light of the Kingdom of God," in *Church, Kingdom, World: The Church as Mystery and Prophetic Sign*, edited by Gennadios Limouris, Faith and Order Paper No. 130. (Geneva: World Council of Churches, 1986) 68.

[33] Yoder, *Die Politik Jesu*, 38.

[34] Stanley Hauerwas, "The Reality of the Kingdom: An Ecclesial Space for Peace," in *Against the Nations: War and Survival in a Liberal Society* (Winston Press) 115.

[35] Lochmann, ibid., 69.

[36] Ibid., 118.

[37] For example, Karl Ludwig Schmidt, "Basileia," in *Theological Dictionary of the New Testament*, edited by Gerhard Kittel (Eerdmans, 1964), vol. I, 580.

[38] For example, Hauerwas, in his aricle already cited, criticizes Pannenberg's understanding of eschatology because it resorts to a "discussion of metaphysics" on the ontological priority of the future in ways which undermine the concrete ethical implications of the kingdom of God. I would suggest that, from a Radical Reformation perspective, Pannenberg's emphasis on the ontological priority of the future has similar (negative) consequences for the relation of the kingdom to the church. Demonstrating this thesis would however require a careful evaluation of Pannenberg's *Theologie Und Reich Gottes* (among other writings), which exceeds both the "time" and "space" available for this essay.

[39] "Bringing Peace to a Divided World," in *The Experiment Hope* (SCM Press, 1975) 176.

Chapter 8

Toward Acknowledging Together the Apostolic Character of the Church's Peace Witness

Reprinted by permission from *The Church's Peace Witness* edited by Marlin E. Miller & Barbara Nelson Gingerich (Eerdmans 1994), 196-207. In the original introduction to this essay, Marlin said the following about *The Church's Peace Witness:*

> Most of the essays in this volume laid the foundation for the second consultation on "The Apostolic Character of the Church's Peace Witness". Some of the essays have been revised on the basis of the conversations during that consultation, which was held in October 1991 in Douglaston, New York. In contrast, this chapter has been written after the fact and without being tempered by the discipline of that broader lively dialogue. Nonetheless, it presupposes the other chapters of this volume and the consultation itself as summarized in the Summary Statement.... It also provides additional analysis of the issues that figured implicitly or explicitly in the consultation and proposes several steps that may be taken toward acknowledging together the apostolic character of the church's peace witness.

Unless noted otherwise in footnotes, references in the text of this essay are to other essays and statements in *The Church's Peace Witness*.

Recent interest in the church's peace witness

What is required for movement of the diverse church communions toward acknowledging together the apostolic character of the church's peace witness? As the essays in *The Church's Peace Witness* by Howard Loewen (chapter 2: "An Analysis of the Use of Scripture in the Churches' Documents on Peace") and by Donald Durnbaugh and Charles Brockwell (chapter 8: "The Historic Peace Churches: From Sectarian Origins to Ecumenical Witness") indicate, some churches have taken a renewed interest in war and peace issues since World War II and especially during the last two decades, in the face of potential mass destruction by nuclear weapons. For other church bodies, rejecting participation in violence and war has long been part of their teaching, practice, and identity. For still others, neither a long tradition of pacifism nor international tensions and the devastating capabilities of modern weaponry have made the church's peace witness a matter of major theological and ethical concern.

Because of this wide diversity among the churches, any impetus toward common recognition that peace witness belongs to the faithful church's calling in the world encounters resistance even at the initial point of raising the question of the church's peace witness. For some communions, the first step would therefore be the discovery, or perhaps the rediscovery, of compelling reasons to give the matter serious attention. Those who have participated in the consultations on the apostolic character of the church's peace witness hope that this volume may plant some seeds that will bear fruit in such a discovery or rediscovery.

For the communions that, whether for a few years or for many centuries, have believed that this subject warrants both theological discernment and concerted action, movement toward acknowledging together the apostolic character of the church's peace witness presents several challenges (see Summary Statement, I). Particularly in North America, the historic peace churches have been tempted to accept their vision of the church's peace witness as a denominational peculiarity rather than as a legacy of the common faith to be commended to all Christians. Lack of ecumenical conversation and mutual correction between historic peace churches and other communions until the latter half of this century have no doubt increased this temptation.

Other communions' interest in the church's peace witness during this century has most frequently been aroused by devastating wars and the threat of nuclear annihilation. These churches have often been tempted to limit peace witness to a particular social-ethical issue or to Christians' action in the public arena, rather than grasping it as a matter that also strikes close to the heart of the church's faithfulness and unity. Both renewed concern for the churches' active contribution to peace in a world of violence and injustice and the continuing commitment to a distinctive heritage should be encouraged. But neither will suffice to bring us to acknowledge together the apostolic character of the church's peace witness. If the question of the church's peace witness is one day to be answered in concert rather than in cacophony, all groups will need to give more attention to critical reexamination of scriptural foundations, to historical relations among the church communions, and to theological justifications that inform contemporary ways of putting the question.

From historical divisions toward a common peace witness

Movement toward a common witness on peace calls into question not only the contemporary differences among the churches, but also the historical divisions that nurture and sustain these differences. Since the sixteenth century, the character of the church's peace witness has been a point not only of diversity but of explicit division among Christian communions. Latent differences over Christian participation in war and civil government, which had long existed and had sometimes surfaced within western Christendom, became matters of division and began to take on confessional status or its equivalent.

Among Anabaptist and Mennonite groups the principled rejection of violence and participation in war was given confessional status from their beginnings.[1] In response, both Lutheran and Reformed confessions explicitly affirmed Christian participation in civil government and in warfare, under certain conditions, and condemned the Anabaptists for their stance. For example, the Augsburg Confession (1530) states: "It is taught among us...that Christians may without sin occupy civil offices or serve as princes and judges, render decisions and pass sentence according to imperial and other existing laws, punish evildoers with the sword, engage in just wars, serve as soldiers.... Condemned here are the Anabaptists who teach that none of the things indicated above is Christian."[2] Similarly, the Thirty-Nine Articles of the Church of England affirm Christian participation in military service and war. Although this confession does not explicitly condemn other positions, Article XXXVII, on the power of civil magistrates, English Edition of 1571, asserts: "It is lawful for Christian men, at the commandment of the Magistrate, to weare weapons, and serue in the warres."[3] In later centuries, the Society of Friends and the Church of the Brethren explicitly and consistently rejected participation in violence and war. Although they did not express their conviction in formal confessional statements, its authority in their communions was comparable to that of the confessionally defined positions of other communions.

With an acute awareness of these historical divisions, participants in the consultations on the apostolic character of the church's peace witness recommended that "further attention be given to...conversation and reconciliation between the churches whose historical teaching and practice on war and peace have been an occasion for strife, division, condemnation, and persecution" (Summary Statement, VII.2). Fortunately, some attention has been given to conversation and reconciliation among some of these churches in recent years, after centuries of recrimination and silence.[4]

A summary and brief analysis of the salient points in the recent dialogue between Lutherans and Mennonites in Germany may illustrate what has been accomplished by such conversations and why we should invest more in such efforts.[5] The Lutheran participants in the conversations acknowledged that in general the Augsburg Confession's condemnations of the Anabaptists were frequently based on insufficient information and were indiscriminately and incorrectly applied to more people and more groups than was appropriate. They noted that condemnation language would not be used today and that in any case, identifying doctrinal differences and even false teachings should not become an occasion for inciting or justifying discrimination against people in either ecclesial or social arenas. Further, they believe persecuting the Anabaptists in the sixteenth and later centuries has left Lutherans with guilt that has encumbered their relations with Mennonites. For this they now ask forgiveness, in order to put these relations on a new spiritual level. Moreover, they commit themselves to additional conversations and encounters, which may help Lutheran and Mennonite Christians take more steps toward each other in the context of "reconciled diversity."

Both Mennonite and Lutheran conversation partners agreed that modern Mennonites do not characterize participation in civil government and in the police as un-Christian in the way that the sixteenth century Anabaptists who wrote the Schleitheim articles did.[6] Today, both Mennonites and Lutherans are ready to accept responsibility for public affairs and cooperate in shaping them. Both also agree that the church is to be the messenger of the kingdom of God in the world and is to be clearly differentiated from the state and from the broader society. Simultaneously, the church needs to maintain a critical stance in relation to the state in order to carry out its prophetic witness and service in the world. Within these broad lines of agreement, Mennonites continue to consider use of armed force problematic, even when it is authorized by the state. They remain convinced that Christians who exercise political responsibility do not need to follow standards that differ from those used by other Christians.[7]

Both the measure of convergence and the degree of divergence became more accentuated when conversation turned to military service. Lutheran and Mennonite representatives share the belief that the church is the fellowship of those who have received the gift of reconciliation and that Christians are therefore liberated from the way of violence and called to be ministers of peace and reconciliation, using and advocating nonviolent means of resolving conflicts. They diverge on the specific implications of this belief for military and peace service. The Mennonites continue in principle to reject military service and to accept the call to live as a peace church, rendering peace service. While respecting individual decisions of conscience, they recommend that members refuse military service and enter an alternative peace service. The Lutherans consider it possible for Christians under certain conditions to participate in armed conflict in order to reestablish peace, to preserve justice, and to protect those who have no weapons. They base this conviction on Article XVI of the Augsburg Confession and on the Lutheran two-kingdom doctrine. Simultaneously, they agree that Christians may refuse military service for reasons of conscience.

In spite of continuing disagreement on military service and service in civil government, participants in the conversations discovered that they agreed in their basic understanding of the gospel. They concluded that the differences remaining do not have church-dividing significance.[8]

Though the conclusions of the Lutheran-Mennonite dialogue in Germany have not yet resulted in a final agreement between the two church bodies,[9] they illustrate how such conversation can lead communions that have been divided toward acknowledging together the church's peace witness. This experience demonstrates how much we need this conversation and discernment. For example, participants came to recognize that both communions now view the once-divisive issues in ways that differ from their sixteenth-century forebears' approaches. The present shape of convergence and divergence has shifted since the sixteenth century, when conversation broke off. Participants needed to reassess the ways each communion has viewed the other's teachings and practices with regard to Christian faithfulness and unity. Further, the way toward reconciliation has been opened by confessing past wrongs, by extending forgiveness, and by praying together.

Nevertheless, these bilateral conversations stopped short (perhaps appropriately) of raising several basic questions that are implicit in the historical controversies and still crucial for faithfulness and unity in the church's peace witness. Is a Christian pacifist stance, together with participation in war and violence under certain conditions, compatible with the apostolic faith? Are communions that accept both Christian pacifism and Christians' participation in war and violence under certain conditions acting in harmony with or contrary to the apostolic faith (see the Summary Statement, VI, questions 6 and 7 in *The Church's Peace Witness*)? These questions raise the issue of *commonly accepted and appropriate criteria* for discerning the apostolic character of the church's peace witness and its faithful expression in a world of violence and war. This issue remains pertinent for all church bodies, irrespective of the measure of convergence some communions may reach on matters that have historically been explicitly church-dividing.

The Christology of the Nicene Creed and the church's peace witness

Through the initiative of the World Council of Churches, the Nicene Creed has been commended to the churches for study and recognition as a common expression of the apostolic faith and thus as a broadly ecumenical criterion for discerning what is in agreement with the apostolic faith. General questions about the sufficiency of the creed for expressing the Christian faith, about its relationship to Scripture, and about its relation to what should be included in a common expression of the apostolic faith today have figured prominently in Faith and Order discussions.[10]

More specific questions arise about using the Nicene Creed as a criterion for discerning apostolicity when we consider what steps we need to take toward acknowledging together the apostolic character of the church's peace witness. Apparently the church's earliest peace witness included a refusal to condone violence and war. Was there a major shift away from this position before the creed's formulation and widespread acceptance, a shift to church support for Christians' participation in warfare? If so, does the creed presuppose both theological and nontheological aspects of such a shift? Does the creed limit concern for apostolicity to specific points of doctrine while omitting reference to specific patterns of action and conduct (such as Christians' witness for peace) that may belong integrally to the apostolic faith? Finally, does the christology of the creed implicitly encourage or discourage the recognition that "the New Testament unambiguously calls the church to accept and proclaim the gospel of peace, to follow the way of Jesus in loving enemies and rejecting violence, to carry out a ministry of peacemaking and reconciliation, and to practice the justice of God's reign?" (Summary Statement, IV in *The Church's Peace Witness*).

It is hardly controversial to say that the church's peace witness underwent a significant shift between the second and fifth centuries. The extent of the shift, how it should be assessed, what brought it about, and what consequences it should have for Christian theology and ethics remain matters of debate. This is particularly true of understanding of the church's relation to the state and society and of matters such as the specific nature of Christian peace witness and response to violence.[11]

Some churches and Christians regard the shift as a deviation from the apostolic faith or even a betrayal of it; others regard it as an appropriate or even natural development in harmony with the Holy Spirit's leading in the changed context in which the church was to carry out its vocation. Those who see the shift as a departure from the apostolic faith usually appeal to Scripture and to the tradition of the first two or three centuries as the primary and secondary criteria of apostolicity (though they may not use that terminology).[12] Those who regard the shift as an acceptable development of the apostolic faith generally appeal to the relative weight of changed circumstances and the breadth of ecclesial consensus as additional criteria for the church's faithfulness and unity.

However this shift is understood, adopting a creedal statement from the late fourth century as the measure for common expression of the apostolic faith at least tends to render movement away from an earlier Christian stance less open to critical reassessment. At most, it excludes the possibility of regarding such changes as deviations from the apostolic faith. But it is precisely that possibility that needs to remain open to further examination if there is to be movement toward recognition of the apostolic character of the church's peace witness today sufficiently ecumenical to include the witness of the pre-Nicene church, the historic peace churches, and Christians of similar persuasion in other communions. The emphases of the creed and the ecclesial, social, and political contexts that influenced it and within which it functioned doubtless resolved particular controversies and provided a common reference for orthodox expression of apostolic beliefs. But the creed may also reflect questionable assumptions about the apostolicity of the church's peace message and the church's participation in the state, in military service, and in war.[13]

Perhaps the most serious questions raised about the Nicene Creed, with regard to theological criteria for the apostolic character of the church's peace witness, have to do with the creed's christological formulations. Are the terms of the creed in sufficient continuity with the New Testament's witness to the fully human as well as the fully divine Son of God? Do they ascribe fundamental importance to Jesus' life, teaching, and call to follow the way of the cross? Or do the categories of the creed discourage or perhaps even preclude acknowledging the normative significance for the church's peace witness today of Jesus' love for the enemy, his rejection of violence, and his proclamation of God's reign? Modern biblical scholarship has rediscovered the historical, social, and political significance—that is, in traditional terms, the fully human dimensions—of Jesus' messiahship, teaching, and example. This rediscovery has often been interpreted as a corrective, and sometimes as an alternative, to traditional christology.[14]

The essays in *The Church's Peace Witness* by Paul Anderson (chapter 5: "Jesus and Peace") and Richard Jeske (chapter 6: "War and Peace in the New Testament") draw heavily on the fruits of this rediscovery and on their potential significance for Christian life and the church's peace witness. Although Jeske and Anderson do not play the historical expressions of Jesus' messiahship off against traditional christological categories and emphases, the language and priorities of their portrayals differ significantly from the classical dogmatic concepts and concerns. If the directions of their interpretations are persuasive and stand up to further scrutiny and practice, then they will raise implicitly the question of the relationship between Scripture and the creed, specifically in relation to the theological basis for the church's peace witness. To be sure, the theological and biblical foundations for the church's peace witness are not limited to christological considerations. Nonetheless, these considerations are crucial. Movement toward recognizing together the apostolic character of the church's peace witness will thus require further conversation, clarification, and convergence on the basis for that witness in the churches' confession of Jesus Christ and in their christology.

Interpretation of Scripture and the church's peace witness

In addition to the diverging confessional traditions, differing appeals to Scripture have contributed to division among the churches on questions of peace and war. Authentic movement toward acknowledging together the apostolic character of the church's peace witness will thus also need to be measured by the criterion of Scripture. Indeed, the scriptural criterion for discerning apostolicity has been even more broadly acknowledged than the creedal standard in both the just war and the peace church traditions. Nevertheless, their respective interpretations of Scripture have all too frequently become captive to the traditional positions and have thus reinforced the divisions between church communions rather than encouraging movement toward a unity measured by Scripture as the primary common criterion of apostolicity.

For that reason, the consultation for which the essays in *The Church's Peace Witness* were originally prepared gave primary attention to clarifying the biblical bases for the church's peace witness.[15] Both the essays and the consultation demonstrate once again that bringing together disciplined biblical scholarship and sensitivity to the churches' differing traditions can lead us to reexamine our divergent traditions in the light of God's word as witnessed by Scripture. For example, consultation participants concluded that the New Testament poses specific problems for both the proponents of the just war tradition and adherents of the peace church tradition. In particular, it poses a major *confessional* problem for proponents of the just war tradition, and a problem of similar scope for the churches of pacifist persuasion.[16] Similarly the biblical scholars and other participants in the consultation concluded that the Old Testament renders problematic any *confessional* reading that claims to ground either a just war or crusade or pacifist position in it, though the problems posed differ in each case.[17]

It is one thing for interchurch consultations to draw on the resources of contemporary biblical scholarship to point to shortcomings or even errors in the divided traditions of scriptural interpretation. It is another matter to move toward a constructive articulation of the church's peace witness that meets the scriptural criterion of apostolicity. In addition to addressing the problems of divided confessional traditions and their use of Scripture, movement toward recognizing the apostolic character of the church's peace witness may also need to address critically the diverse hermeneutical and theological methods that permeate contemporary biblical scholarship and which are to some degree represented in this volume. Otherwise, instead of contributing to the formation of a broader consensus on the apostolic calling of the church to be a community of peace and of peacemaking in the world, we risk replacing traditional confessional divisions over the church's peace witness with reconfigured scholarly divisions.[18]

The Church's Peace Witness is thus intended to begin a conversation rather than to state conclusions of a finished debate. It will fulfill its purpose to the degree that it contributes to that ongoing conversation and to the churches' recognition of our common calling to be faithful witnesses in today's world to Christ's ministry of peace.

---

[1] See chapter 8 in *The Church's Peace Witness*. See also "The Schleitheim Confession (1527)" and "The Dordrecht Confession (1632),"in John Leith, ed., *Creeds of the Churches: A Reader in Christian Doctrine from the Bible to the Present* (3rd ed.; Atlanta: John Knox, 1982), 287-89, 303-5.

[2] "The Augsburg Confession," Article XVI, in Leith, *Creeds of the Churches,* 72-73. See also the "Second Helvetic Confession," Article XXX, in Leith, 190-91, and "The Attitudes of the Reformed Churches Today to the Condemnations of the Anabaptists in the Reformed Confessional Documents," in *Mennonites and Reformed in Dialogue: Studies from the World Alliance of Reformed Churches 7,* ed. Hans Georg vom Berg, Henk Kossen, Larry Miller, and Lukas Vischer (World Alliance of Reformed Churches, 1986).

[3] In Leith, *Creeds of the Churches,* 280. Not only Christians commanded by magistrates, but also magistrates as Christians are confessionally authorized to wage war, according to "The Westminster Confession (1646)," Chapter XXIII, in Leith, 219-20. This confession also asserts that it "is lawful for Christians to accept and execute the office of a magistrare"; in fulfillment of their duties magistrates "may lawfully, now under the New Testament, wage war upon just and necessary occasion" (220).

[4]Formal conversations between representatives of the Lutheran and Mennonite communions have taken place in both France and Germany. For the French conversations, see *Les Entretiens Luthero-Mennonites. Resultats du colloque de Strasbourg, 1981-1984, avec une préface de Pierre Widmer et une présentation de Marc Lienhard* (Christ Seul, 1984). For the German dialogues, see "Die lutherisch-mennonitischen Gespräche in der Bundesrepublik Deutschland 1989-1992," *Texte aus der VELKD* 53 (1993).

Conversations between Reformed and Mennonite groups have taken place in the Netherlands through the sponsorship of the World Alliance of Reformed Churches and Mennonite World Conference. See *Mennonites and Reformed in Dialogue* (note 2 above) and *Dopers-Calvinistisch Gesprek in Nederland* (Boekencentrum, 1982); *Mennonites and Reformed in Dialogue* contains a summary in English of the latter (pp. 61-71). See the select bibliography in *The Church's Peace Witness* for information on how to obtain these documents. See also Ross T. Bender and Alan P. F. Sell, eds., *Baptism, Peace, and the State in the Reformed and Mennonite Traditions* (Wilfrid Laurier University, 1991).

[5] The conversations covered several themes; here only points directly related to the church's peace witness are summarized.

[6] See chapter 8 in *The Church's Peace Witness,* "Anabaptists and Mennonites".

[7] In varying degrees and with differing emphases, other bilateral conversations have come to similar conclusions. See *Mennonites and Reformed in Dialogue,* 70-71; *Les Entretiens Luthero-Mennonites,* 45-46; *Baptism, Peace, and the State,* 235-37.

[8] This general conclusion applied to the other issues examined, not only to questions related to participation in civil government, the police, and military service.

[9] The report on the dialogue and the summary of convergence and divergence are being commended to the two church bodies for discussion and comment; the conclusions do not constitute a final statement of agreement between the two church groups.

[10] See, for example, the Odessa (1981) and Rome (1983) reports in *Apostolic Faith Today: A Handbook for Study* (Faith and Order Paper 124, ed. Hans-Georg Link; Geneva: World Council of Churches, 1985), 245-56 and 257-66.

[11] See chapter 8 in *The Church's Peace Witness* on the "Unity of Brethren, Anabaptists and Mennonites," and the "Religious Society of Friends"; compare the conclusions in chapter 7.

[12] For the Quakers, the active presence of Christ's Spirit in the community of believers is considered decisive, along with Scripture and the practices of the apostles. See Dean Freiday, "Apostolicity and Orthochristianity," *Apostolic Faith in America* (Grand Rapids: Eerdmans, 1988), 43-52. In "The Authority of Tradition" (*The Priestly Kingdom, Social Ethics as Gospel* [University of Notre Dame Press, 1984], 63-79), John Howard Yoder argues that the just war tradition as it developed in Christendom "is a fundamentally new political ethic, not organically evolved from the social stance of the early Christians, as that stance had been evolving up to and through Tertullian and Origen" (75). This ethic "rejects the privileged place of the enemy as the test of whether one loves one's neighbor. It rejects the norm of the cross and the life of Jesus Christ as the way of dealing with conflict" (75). In short, Yoder contends, "a change has taken place which must be described as a reversal" (76). He then draws out several implications of this assessment for current ecumenical discussion on the relation between Scripture, Tradition, and traditions (76-79).

[13] See Thomas Finger, "The Way to Nicea: Some Reflections from a Mennonite Perspective," *Journal of Ecumenical Studies* 24 (1987), 212-31. Note also Dean Freiday's survey of several communions and Christian movements that have emphasized the importance of faithful practice and authentic experience and his proposal that practice and experience be included in reciprocal relationship with right beliefs as dimensions of apostolicity ("Apostolicity and Orthochristianity").

[14] Liberal Protestant scholarship has frequently portrayed the Christ of the creed and the Jesus of the Gospels as reflecting radically different christologies. This posing of stark alternatives has also been attractive to some Christian pacifists, both in the historic peace churches and in other communions, because it seems to give increased normative ethical significance to Jesus' example and teaching. Others have argued that an emphasis on Jesus' teaching and example is a needed corrective but is also compatible with orthodox christology. See Thomas Finger, "The Way to Nicea"; John H. Yoder, *The Politics of Jesus* (Eerdmans, 1972), 106-7. Even more strongly, A. James Reimer claims that "trinitarian orthodoxy," as reflected in the Nicene Creed, is not only compatible with a Christian peace ethic based on the Jesus of the Gospels, but essential to it ("Trinitarian Orthodoxy, Constantinianism, and Theology from a Radical Protestant Perspective," in *Faith to Creed,* ed. S. Mark Heim [Eerdmans, 1991], 129-61; see especially 156-61).

[15] See the section entitled "A Biblical Study," in Jeffrey Gros's introduction to *The Church's Peace Witness* (pp. 10-11 in chapter 1); see also the Summary Statement, sections II, III, and IV.

[16] See the Summary Statement, IV.

[17] See the Summary Statement, III, and Ben C. Ollenburger's essay (chapter 3 in *The Church's Peace Witness*).

[18] On the promise and the limits of contemporary biblical scholarship for interchurch conversation and unity, see George Lindbeck, "Two Kinds of Ecumenism: Unitive and Interdenominational," *Gregoriarum* 70 (1989), 647-60.

II

Pastoral Leadership
and
Theological Education

Chapter 9

The Recasting of Authority:
A Biblical Model for Community Leadership

Reprinted with permission from *Sojourners*, 2401 15th St, N.W., 20009; (202) 328-8842 (800) 714-7474.

The various backgrounds out of which house church groups and Christian communities have come in the last 10 or 15 years often did not provide a clear basis for appropriate leadership. Some house church groups grew up in major Christian denominations. Whether Protestant or Catholic, these denominations assumed a focus on the pastor or the priest as the leader.

Very often there were those in the house churches who rejected the pastoral form of leadership. This reaction may have reflected adolescent growth syndromes, or bad experiences with authoritarian pastors. Whatever the reasons, that kind of reaction and response often did not lead to an alternate vision of what leadership should be.

House churches have also been influenced by student movements in the late 1960s and the early 1970s, where there were various cultural and sociological forces at work. For example, there was a sense of experiential immediacy: everyone wanted to experience truth and reality directly. Traditions, structures, authority patterns seemed distant, mediated ways of discovering reality. Stated more positively, the student movement wanted total and unmediated participation in all decision making, in the whole process.

Included in this mood was an egalitarian view of individuals. The biblical phrase that every person has a gift or a ministry was often interpreted in the context of this mood to mean that everyone takes a turn at doing everything. Everyone should take his or her turn at moderating, leading, preaching, teaching, speaking, dancing, or whatever else might be happening.

Another part of the student movement mood was a generational vision of the world in which everyone over 30 is compromised and everyone under 18 is unaware, leaving only those within a 10-year range as trustworthy. Because leaders had usually been over 30, and because they had ostensibly demonstrated both in church, political, and social life that they could not be trusted, the generational vision added to reactions against leadership.

Yet another element of the student mood was often an anti-institutional ideology which questioned leadership understood in terms of a particular office with particular status, and which used both office and status in order to accumulate power and manipulate others. Leadership looked like a child of the devil or one of his henchmen.

House churches which were influenced by these movements and moods discovered that groups which have no known and designated leadership have difficulty simply surviving and working together. Without clearly defined patterns of leadership, consensus was next to impossible. There were innumerable small groups and households that started with great vigor and broad vision, but completely folded within four to six months because they could not reach consensus on significant issues.

There was often lack of agreement on who should take initiative, or on who should follow through in the sometimes intense conflicts, arising often when people try to live and work together intensively. On the pragmatic level, it became evident that not everyone was equally gifted in all roles and functions of group life. Not everyone could lead singing, either by playing a guitar or carrying a tune; not everyone could moderate a meeting. Such experiences led to frustrations and confusion.

In the search for solutions to these frustrations, several of the house churches rediscovered that the Bible speaks about leadership authority and leadership roles. Throughout the book of Acts, the Apostles exercised significant leadership roles. In some English translations of the New Testament, terms such as "ruling" over the flock and of members "being subject" to those who are over them in Christ are used. That certainly didn't sound attractive to egalitarian-minded people, but the words offered reassurance and guidance in the context of confusion and frustration.

This rediscovery of biblical language in the midst of frustrating experiences with leaderlessness has often been used to reaffirm an hierarchical pattern of leadership. Because some house church groups organized their life by households, the "father of the household" image also reinforced this trend.

In some cases members of house churches drew on the traditions of their denominational origins. For example, persons coming out of the Episcopal Church or Roman Catholic Church had experienced subordination to the bishop as subordination to Christ's representative on earth. This tendency was further reinforced by the charismatic renewal movement, partly because the movement in the late 1960s arose in, and spread to, churches having an episcopal polity, and partly because strong individuals reinforced with qualifying experiences became "leader" of the charismatic movement.

In some of the house churches, the exercise of a therapeutic function in household settings reinforced the pattern. People who are troubled or weak, or whose families have disintegrated, need clearly designated structures for support and healing; hierarchical patterns of leadership have worked effectively in providing such structures.

A third way: the biblical model

Although the movement from egalitarianism and reaction against central leadership to a reinforcement of hierarchical patterns of leadership may be understandable and even partially justifiable, there is a third model which speaks to the situation of the house churches and which is intrinsically more biblical and more appropriate.

This model has four major characteristics.

First, all members in the church have a particular and identifiable gift or ministry. This is stated literally in two lists of ministries and gifts in the New Testament, found in 1 Corinthians 12:7 and Ephesians 4:7. These lists enumerate a series of gifts and ministries: apostles, prophets, teachers, miracle workers, healers, helpers, administrators, etc. In both of these passages it is clearly and unequivocally stated that everyone in the church has a gift.

First Corinthians 12 describes this universal ministry as characteristic of the Spirit's presence among the believers. Participating in the body of Christ means that everyone has a gift and that everyone has a part in the church's mission. There is no fundamental distinction between a clergy and a laity, however, that may be defined in various denominational patterns.

This universality of gifts and ministries does not therefore reflect a highly developed democratic society in a philosophical sense; it is rather living in the presence of the Spirit and participating in the body of Christ. A part of salvation in Christ means affirming and practicing this universality of ministry and gifts in the Christian church.

These key New Testament passages counter the general human trend to move away from the vision of a universal ministry toward religious specialization, where only one person in a particular religious community, or perhaps a few people, performs the necessary leadership functions, and where this person is given particular status.

Second, there is within the New Testament a particular gift or ministry which is leadership. One of the terms used for this kind of function is "elder." The term "elder" apparently derived from synagogue usage, where a group of older, experienced men provided the kind of oversight and leadership needed in a local synagogue. The "overseer" or the "bishop" terminology refers to a similar position, but from a more functional point of view.

The term "shepherd" is a figurative term which reflects the imagery of the flock and the shepherd. In the Old Testament, shepherd was one of the terms often used for the king. In the New Testament, because Jesus becomes the norm for shepherds, it no longer means ruling over others like a king, but giving one's life for others in service.

The overseer/shepherd function was sometimes linked with the teaching function. In Ephesians 4:11 and in 1 Timothy 5:17, some of the elders were also teachers. There was some overlap and some diversity in the way these roles were worked out.

It appears that there were several such persons in each local Christian fellowship. In the lists we have about the various ministries, they are almost always in the plural, referring to elders, apostles, prophets, teachers, etc. In Acts 20, Luke reports several elders for the congregation at Ephesus. Thus even though there is sometimes today a tendency to go toward the idea that in one house church there should be one elder (or equivalent), the New Testament pattern is constructed on plural eldership.

The Greek equivalent for our term "leader" is used only twice in the New Testament in referring to the church (Heb. 13:7, 17). The same term is used several times to refer to leaders in the Jewish community or in the Roman community.

It may be that the equivalents for our word "leader" in the first century culture were not used for the Christian church because of the shifts in understanding that took seriously Jesus' teaching that "among you there shall be servants and not rulers." The old language for leadership was linked with the language for ruling and domination. Jesus exemplified and taught the reality of leadership as serving.

This servant leadership in the house church takes initiative in helping the group form a consensus rooted in the Jesus tradition and moving in the direction of fullness in Christ. If we see that kind of servant leadership in the sociological context of the house church, it makes much sense. It can manifest itself more wholly in the context of small size and direct interrelationships.

Third, the New Testament describes the major characteristics of the elder/overseer/shepherd function. We learn from passages such as 1 Timothy and Titus that the kinds of persons who are equipped to be elders in a house church are the kinds of persons who demonstrate the qualities which encourage and build family solidarity.

The same qualities of leadership which inspire family solidarity will also help build solidarity in the family of God. These qualities, such as gentleness and a calm temperament, are generally antithetical to strong leadership as defined by secular society, but find their "home" in the house church setting.

Another characteristic of these leaders is that they already would have some Christian experience and maturity. Those who are "elders" are most readily agents and symbols of an internal and external group unity. People can point to them as, representative of group unity and solidarity, not because they impose their will upon the group, but because they have a way of bringing the group together.

In many cases, elders are described as those who can teach, meaning that they are the ones who, rooted in the Jesus tradition, have a discriminating judgment with respect to other influences that may come upon the group. They can help the group determine whether movement is in line with the Jesus tradition, or whether it deviates from it.

There is a natural spiritual authority in leaders/elders who demonstrate such characteristics. The naturalness means that they are persons who already have a certain kind of experience, a carry-over from broader family experience and responsibility in many contexts.

The house church context provides a congruity between these characteristics and a type of leadership which best reflects the biblical model. When the apostle Paul speaks of "managing" a household, he meant more than simply managing a nuclear family; the household may have included married and unmarried relatives, as well as slaves and visitors. In that context, the head of the household served as a host, supervised the budget, and represented the household in the public forum.

This functioning in the household context prepared elders to function in the Christian community. It also helped others discern who should fill the eldering function in the congregation.

For example, Priscilla and Aquila were such elders in the house church in Ephesus. They were naturally the hosts and leaders of the gatherings. This did not mean that they did all the preaching, teaching, and worship leading, but they symbolized the unity and continuity of the group and took initiative in helping to bring and weld that group together.

Stephen Clark, in the house church handbook edited by John Miller, refers to the environmental approach to leadership, over against a purely status understanding or function description. A status definition of leadership focuses on educational preparation, ordination, and the like. The functional one focuses on doing a particular job well.

The environmental perspective for discerning and affirming leadership asks primarily what happens to the total group when a given person leads it and how such a person functions in response to the whole group. This standard goes beyond status, because it attends to bringing out the gifts and the ministries of the whole group as well as the individual. It is more than an individual's effective functioning, because it extends to an ability to relate to the group and to encourage others in the group to relate to each other in such a way that the community life is enhanced.

According to Clark, "A good term for the type of leadership that is natural to community is elder. An elder has a position, he is one of the recognized heads and has an openly accepted responsibility for the order of community life. But he is chosen because he is really one of the elders and not only in name. He is chosen because he has the natural position of respect and leadership in that community."

He goes on to say: "If the church is going to be able to return to a community life, the position of elder has to be recaptured. Leaders are needed who can work with an environmental approach. They have to be the kind of people who have a spiritually natural authority. It is only as we have the kind of leadership which is appropriate to community life that we can have a successful community."

Fourth, the ministry of eldering should be exercised in the context of mutual subordination. The concept "mutual subordination" may help us in several ways: (1) by correcting the temptations to return to hierarchical models of leadership with a unilinear direction of subordination; (2) by correcting the tendencies to reject any kind of subordination and designated leadership; and (3) by correlating the domestic household language of the Pauline epistles with church structure in the house church.

In the "house tables" (for example, Eph. 4-5), the apostle Paul refers to those who made up the domestic households of the first century, describing the relationships between wives and husbands, servants and masters, parents and children in terms of "mutual subordination." This idea of mutual subordination brings together the concern for an authentic order in social relationships without adopting the hierarchical pattern of the surrounding pagan society.

In an analogous fashion, the eldering role is a specific gift or ministry exercised along with others. It would not be fitting to say that all other ministries are only subordinate to the eldering role. There is rather a more complex interrelationship in which the elders are subordinate, for example, to the apostles and prophets, just as they are subordinate in a specific sense to the elders.

There are several clues in the New Testament which point in this direction. Let us begin with the role of the apostle. In the various places where apostleship appears as a ministry or as a gift, it always comes first in the list. According to traditional Western ways of thinking, this should mean that the apostle would be at the top of a hierarchy in a structure of descending authority.

What it meant, however, was that in his apostolic ministry Paul provided a unique kind of leadership in founding and teaching churches. He was subordinate to other ministries and gifts in the church.

For example, in Acts 13 we see that Paul as apostle was commissioned and sent out by prophets and teachers together with the congregation and that he regularly reported back to that congregation. As an apostle, Paul exercised leadership and took initiative and moved forward in a dramatic kind of way: simultaneously he remained subordinate to others who were exercising their gifts and ministries in the church.

Another clue in the New Testament is found in 1 Corinthians 14. The prophets were expected to prophesy, admonish, and exhort the congregation. Other members of the fellowship at Corinth were subordinate to the prophets on these points.

But the prophets needed to be tested by the congregation which was to listen and discern. The authority of the prophets was exercised in the context of mutual subordination rather than in a unilinear structure of subordination. On the one hand, the prophets provided leadership in the prophetic ministry; on the other hand, they were accountable to the congregation for discriminating between true and false prophecy.

Yet another example would be 1 Timothy 5 which refers to the procedure for correcting elders. Even the elders who exercised a foundational ministry were themselves accountable to others in the church, and needed to be open to fraternal admonition and discipline, even by non-elders.

We have discovered a pattern of leadership in the New Testament house churches which provides both the model and the characteristics of what leadership should and can be in the house churches of our time. The recasting of authority, from the right to rule to the freedom to serve in a community of mutual subordination, is a biblical model which goes beyond both the restoration of hierarchical structures, on the one hand, and egalitarian individualism on the other.

Chapter 10

Priesthood of All Believers

Reprinted by permission from *Mennonite Encyclopedia V,* Cornelius J. Dyck and Dennis Martin, eds. (Herald Press, 1990) 721.

In contrast to the Old Testament, the New Testament does not use the term *priest* for a particular ministry among the people of God. "Priest" or "priesthood" is reserved either for the unique priesthood of Jesus Christ or for the priesthood of all Christians. The first epistle of Peter and the book of Revelation refer to the believers corporately as priests of God, as a kingdom of priests, or as a royal priesthood (1 Pet. 2:5, 9; Rev. 1:6; 5:10; 20:6).

This imagery builds on references in the Old Testament. According to Exodus 19:6 God has set the people of Israel apart, among the peoples of the world, to serve as priests. Isaiah 61:6 envisions the day when the other peoples will recognize Israel as God's priests and ministers as well as tend their flocks and cultivate their fields. First Peter specifies the believers' priestly functions: Christians offer spiritual sacrifices and declare God's wondrous deeds among the nations. According to the book of Revelation, the Christian community has been gathered from all the peoples of the earth, purified by Christ, and made a kingdom of priests to serve God and rule on earth with Christ.

During the early centuries of Christianity, the churches reverted to having a priesthood as a mediatorial class set apart from and over the laity. The Protestant Reformers reacted against this pattern and tried to correct it. Particularly Martin Luther articulated a doctrine of the priesthood of all believers and made it a popular Protestant motto by his early essays: *An Open Letter to the Christian Nobility of the German Nation, The Babylonian Captivity of the Church,* and *A Treatise on Christian Liberty,* all written in 1520.

According to Luther the priesthood of all believers has spiritual, ecclesiastical, and social implications. Socially he accepted the context of western Christianity, where temporal rulers belong to the body of Christendom. Within the Christian social order, the rulers are ordained of God to punish evildoers and protect those who do good. Luther argues against the medieval division between the temporal and the church authorities and their separate jurisdictions in all matters. Because the German nobles too are baptized and therefore belong to the priesthood of all believers, they should exercise their vocation by correcting wrong doing and reforming specific practices in the church without respect to pope, bishops, and priests.

Ecclesiastically, Luther rejects the clergy's monopoly on interpreting Scripture, determining correct doctrine, forgiving sins, and exercising discipline. Because all believers are priests, all are to participate in these functions of the Christian community. Properly understood, "priests" should be ministers of the Word, who are called by the congregation to preach the Word and administer the sacraments with the consent of and in the service of the congregation.

Finally, Luther applies the term "kingdom of priests" to all believers in a spiritual sense. As many as believe on Christ are kings and priests with him. All are kings because by faith all are exalted above all things which seek to harm them and because all things are compelled to work together for their salvation. And by faith all are priests, worthy to approach God in prayer for others and to teach one another the things of God.

Anabaptist writers in the sixteenth century rarely refer to the priesthood of all believers, although they have much to say in opposition to clericalism. Menno Simons does use the concept in *The Christian Faith* (1541). According to Menno, believers have been made kings and priests in order to be a chosen and holy people which serves God in love. As such, believers are to publish God's power and show by their life that God has called them out of darkness into light. As kings, Christians already reign, but with the sword of God's holy Word rather than with worldly weapons. And God's Word is more powerful than wealth, armies, persecution, death, or the devil.

All believers are also priests because they have been sanctified and are called to live as those sanctified by God. They are to sacrifice their own unrighteousness and evil lusts as well as admonish others to do the same. They are not priests who sacrifice bread and wine for the sins of the people or sing masses. Instead, they purify their own bodies daily, are willing to sacrifice themselves and to suffer for the Lord's truth, pray fervently, and give thanks joyfully (Menno Simons, *Writings,* 326-27).

In Menno's interpretation of the church as a royal priesthood he
thus emphasizes the spiritual and moral quality of its life, its missionary
witness, the self-discipline and mutual discipline of its members, its
dependence on the power of God's Word, and its willingness to suffer
for the gospel. He does not apply the priesthood of all believers to the
temporal authorities as did Luther. And apparently neither Menno nor
other Anabaptists and Mennonites of that time related the question of
Christian ministry or the appointment and ordination of ministers in the
church to the priesthood of all believers.

Since then Mennonites have usually agreed in theory, if not always
in practice, that the church should be a community of believers rather
than a combination of lay and clerical classes. They have usually agreed
in theory, if not always in practice, that all believers are called to
participate in the life and witness of the church, to share in mutual
discipline and forgiveness, and to test the interpretation of Scripture and
doctrine. And they have usually agreed in theory, if not always in
practice, that ministers are to be appointed by the community of
believers and to serve for its welfare. But these understandings have
been based on other New Testament teachings and examples rather than
linked with a doctrine of the priesthood of all believers.

In the twentieth century some Mennonites and non-Mennonites
have made passing references to "the priesthood of all believers" to
characterize some aspect of an Anabaptist (or presumably Anabaptist)
view of the church or Christian life. For some, it means that every
Christian is a minister (Kauffman/Harder, Yoder). For some, it signifies
a process of making decisions in the church (Littell, Yoder). For one, it
refers to the believer's access to God without the mediation of a priest
and to being a channel of grace for other Christians (Bender). For
another, it represents the Radical Reformation's rejection of dividing the
church into clergy and laity (Williams). So far, Mennonites have neither
developed a common understanding nor elaborated a particular view of
"the priesthood of all believers." [1]

---

[1]Works used or cited in this article: Franklin H. Littell, *The Origins of Sectarian
Protestantism* (Macmillan, 1964; originally published as *The Anabaptist View
of the Church,* 1952) 94; Kauffman/Harder, *Anabaptists Four Centuries Later*
(Herald Press, 1975) 184-85; Wim Kuipers, "Het priesterschap aller gelovigen,"
Doops. Bijd. n.r. 6 (1980) 65-77; John Howard Yoder, *The Priestly Kingdom*
(University of Notre Dame Press, 1984) 22-23; idem, *Fullness of Christ: Paul's*

Revolutionary Vision of Universal Ministry (Brethren Press, 1987); cf. *Concern* pamphlet no. 17 (1969) 33-93; George H. Williams, *The Radical Reformation* (Westminster, 1962); *Luther's Works,* vols. 31, 36, 44 (Fortress Press, 1955); Cyril Eastwood, *The Priesthood of All Believers: An Examination of the Doctrine From the Reformation to the Present* (Epworth Press, 1960) summarizes the doctrine according to various Protestant theologians and denominations, but does not refer to Anabaptists or Mennonites.

Chapter 11

Some Reflections on Pastoral Ministry and Pastoral Education[1]

Reprinted by permission from *Understanding Ministerial Leadership*, John A. Esau, ed. (Institute of Mennonite Studies, 1995) 57-69.

I need to start with a confession. Because of time constraints, I shall plagiarize parts of a presentation I made last January during Associated Mennonite Biblical Seminary Pastors' Week. Moreover, I would like to approach this presentation differently than I had originally intended and begin with some introductory remarks that are somewhat autobiographical. This part will be extemporaneous. It will either be the work of the Spirit or the foolishness of a human being! I shall then move to several points that I summarized last January in relation to the Pauline theology and understanding of pastoral ministry. Finally, I would like to close with three emphases for pastoral education.

An autobiographical introduction

I came to Goshen Biblical Seminary as a student in 1960-61. That preceded what later came to be called the "Dean's Seminar," a sort of foundational exercise for Mennonite Biblical Seminary and Goshen Biblical Seminary faculty to develop a new vision of theological education. I remained at Goshen Biblical Seminary (and on occasional days at Mennonite Biblical Seminary) for only one year, but over the years I kept in touch with developments at the seminaries. At the time that I came as a student, several faculty members criticized "pastoral ministry" and "pastoral office" on the basis of what was presumed to be a more biblical and a more radically Anabaptist vision of the "priesthood of all believers."

The memories that I have from those days and of what came out of the Dean's Seminar were that Anabaptists stood for the "priesthood of all believers." Protestants stood for a kind of pastoral ministry that undermined the priesthood of all believers and localized Christian ministry in the office of the pastor. In order to move away from the unfinished Protestant Reformation, we needed to recover the Anabaptist vision of the priesthood of all believers. We needed to recover the Pauline theology that teaches that the gifts of the Holy Spirit are given to everyone. We needed to develop a completely new understanding of ministry and to work out a completely new understanding of theological education. This understanding would not focus on pastoral ministry, but on an education for everyone to exercise their ministry in the congregation. Ministry would then depend upon the particular callings of particular people in particular contexts. It would not include some notion of a pattern of pastoral ministry or of an office of pastoral ministry that would be more or less constant in a variety of congregational settings.

That summarizes very rapidly an orientation that has been part of the legacy of Associated Mennonite Biblical Seminary and that has been for better or for worse, or for a combination of the two, something of the orientation in relation to the theology of pastoral ministry that has been nurtured here.

After a year at Goshen Biblical Seminary in 1960-61, I continued my study in two European settings. After completing graduate work, I ended up as part of a pastoral team in a small congregation in the suburbs of Paris, France. In the course of that period of time, about six years, I began to wonder more existentially and experientially about the notion of the priesthood of all believers interpreted in a way that seemed to undermine the specific characteristics of pastoral ministry. In the Paris congregation and in many other congregations among French Mennonites and among some Protestant churches, and to some degree in Roman Catholic parishes, it seemed to me that very much depended upon the quality of congregational leadership. The notion that if everyone got together and exercised their particular gift and the Holy Spirit would automatically make things comes out correctly became less credible. Simultaneously, it seemed like calling the "priesthood of all believers" into question would mean going against the Anabaptists and the Apostle Paul. They were rather formidable opponents!

After several years we returned to Elkhart County for a year's furlough. Instead of returning to Paris as planned, we remained here. And I began to work on matters of theological education and pastoral ministry from still other perspectives in the seminary setting.

In the last few years, and partially by request, I have needed to work further with notions about pastoral ministry and the priesthood of all believers. I discovered that some of the scholarship on which I was basing my earlier opinions was not well founded, that it was at least distorted. A couple of years ago C. J. Dyck asked me to write an article on the "priesthood of all believers" for the new volume of the Mennonite Encyclopedia (see chapter 10). So I went back through many of the Anabaptist sources looking for the understanding of the priesthood of all believers that I had heard about in the '60s and had read about from several Mennonite and other-than-Mennonite authors as being attributed to the Radical Reformation. I found only two pages in any of the Anabaptist and Mennonite sources in the sixteenth century explicitly on the "priesthood of all believers." Those two pages were in Menno Simons' *Complete Works*. They gave a fairly straightforward and simple interpretation of the concept of the priesthood of believers in 1 Peter and Revelation. Menno picked up on those passages and talked about Christians being a royal priesthood in terms of living a holy life and in terms of witnessing to the world. There was no whisper of anything in the priesthood of all believers having to do directly with a particular theology of ministry. There was nothing in Menno that would argue against the legitimacy of pastoral ministry as a specific ministry and as a specific gift in the church because of the priesthood of all believers.

Since I had not specialized in Anabaptist studies but had only made a hobby out of it, I assumed that I was probably overlooking something. After all, the people I had been reading were scholars of the sixteenth-century Anabaptist movement! So I checked with C. J. Dyck and asked whether he knew of anything I was missing. He couldn't think of anything else, and said my findings were probably correct. He had, in fact, suspected as much but had never checked it out. Rightly or wrongly, I thought that C. J. must know and so went on from there.

One place that I found something about the "priesthood of all believers" in the century was in Martin Luther's writings. And he interpreted it to say (among other things) that because everyone is a priest, and if the Pope and the clergy didn't reform the church, that the princes who had power in society could use their position to reform the church. That wasn't what Mennonites would tend to say! It hasn't occurred to most Mennonites so far to ask a Brian Mulroney or a George Bush to reform the church! But that is in nontechnical terms one sense in which Martin Luther was using the concept.

Then I began to wonder if recent Anabaptist scholarship had been trying to say that we are all called to be Christian ministers, and that in order to say that, had used the concept of the priesthood of all believers in ways that claimed to be from the Anabaptist movement but historically were not there. I further wondered whether something similar was going on with our understanding of Paul. Does Paul's theology of gifts eliminate the legitimacy of pastoral ministry as a particular calling, as a particular ministry, in the midst of other Christian ministries? That brings me to some of the background questions I had coming to the assignment that was given to me for Pastors' Week last January, to summarize the Pauline understandings of ministry.

To wrap up the autobiographical side, I would say that over a period of years, partly through a re-examination of both the theological and the exegetical sides of the question, and partly through needing to face the issues in terms of serving as a pastor and as a seminary educator, I have come out somewhat differently than where I was in 1960. Hopefully, that is a constructive sign! I would also solicit your perspective and your advice and counsel on these matters. I have come to the conclusion that pastoral ministry has been among the more controversial and significant debates and points of uncertainty among us in the last thirty years. I am concerned about how we can respond most faithfully in the coming years.

Pastoral ministry in the Pauline writings

Let us move now to some of the major points in the Pauline understanding of Christian ministry. I shall not try to summarize the biblical understanding of Christian ministry, but limit my remarks on the Pauline understanding. It is from interpretations of Paul's understanding of ministry that have most frequently come the sort of foundational criticisms that supposedly undermine the legitimacy of pastoral office or pastoral ministry.

First, on the place of Christian ministry within Paul's perspective: we need to remind ourselves that in Paul's perspective, the place of Christian ministry is within the community of believers, within the church, within the people of the future who are living in the present.

The diverse ministries (and there are many diverse ministries mentioned in the Pauline epistles) are all ministries of the church and in the church rather than being identified with jobs or activities in the broader society. Paul does not characterize his tent making as ministry. He does encourage Christians to work, says that work has dignity, that it is a means of caring for others, that it is a means of caring for one's family, and that it is a means of sharing resources with other believers. But he doesn't describe "work" as "ministry."

He does not describe "professions" that we exercise in the broader society as Christian ministry. Through Lutheran influences and through contemporary Mennonite efforts to enhance the relevance of what we as Christians do in the broader society, we have tended frequently to adopt the notion that what we do in our jobs is ministry. I think it is commendable to see what we do in the broader society as an expression of Christian discipleship. But there is in the New Testament perspective, particularly within the Pauline perspective and more broadly, a distinction between church and world, between the believing community and the surrounding world. And ministry is a concept that is particularly related to those things that are carried out within the church and in the church's mission in the broader world.

A second observation: in the Pauline epistles the source of Christian ministries is attributed variously to the Holy Spirit or to the exalted Lord at work in the church during the interim time between the resurrection of Christ and the return of Christ. Because the Spirit or the exalted Lord is the source of ministry, the normal situation of the church is one in which there is a rich variety and a great diversity of ministries and gifts given to the church for the common good. That much of the view and interpretation that I reported as a part of my own journey, I think, is a correct interpretation of the Pauline view of ministry. Paul encourages Christians to see that there are more rather than fewer ministries. But it seems to me that some in Mennonite circles have tended to push that view too far by insisting that everyone has an identifiable ministry, to make out of that thesis a kind of moral obligation, and further, to use that thesis as a way of undermining the distinctive calling of pastoral ministry.

I think the exegetical basis for this view is overdone or perhaps even nonexistent. More specifically, the exegetical basis for the combined notion that everyone has a ministry and that there are no significant differences between other ministries and pastoral ministry is based ostensibly on Romans 12:3, 1 Corinthians 7:7, and Ephesians 4:7. You find this interpretation especially in the writings of John Yoder. Those passages speak about everyone having a gift. But if you look a little more closely at the Pauline language, he uses a different kind of language to underscore "each and everyone" than he uses in these particular passages. In 1 Thessalonians 2:11 and 2 Thessalonians 1:3, for example, he uses "heis hekastos" to emphasize "each and every one." He does not use this phrase in Romans 12:3; he does not use it in 1 Corinthians 7:7. He uses another term that is more general and less insistent on "all" in the sense of "each and every one." Thus there is a nuanced difference in the language of the Pauline epistles. In Ephesians 4:7 the more specialized "each and every one" is used in the reference to "grace," but not directly for the specific ministries of verses 11ff. It seems to me that we should affirm, on the basis of the Pauline writings, that because the Spirit or the exalted Lord is the source of ministry, the normal situation in the church is a rich diversity and variety of ministries. But if we press that view in the direction of making a law out of "each and every one" having an identifiable ministry in the same sense as a pastoral ministry or a teaching ministry or an evangelistic ministry, we are going beyond the exegetical basis and overinterpreting the text.

A third point: what is pastoral ministry in a narrower sense against the backdrop of the diversity of ministries referred to in the Pauline epistles? Here I would like to make five points that I believe are the major points in the Pauline writings with regard to what we may call "pastoral ministry."

1. First, there are several terms that are used in the Pauline writings that seem to be synonymous. I would refer you to the document Leadership and Authority in the Church that was adopted in the Mennonite Church in 1981 for the details. The terms "overseer," "bishop," and "pastor" seem to be more or less synonymous in the Pauline epistles. And if one looks at all those passages, the terms apparently refer to a group of persons who are responsible for the community oversight, care, and leadership. Oversight, care, and leadership of the community as a whole would be the point of these different terms. Now why these different terms are used is not absolutely clear. It seems that they come from the different cultural contexts of the early Christians, with "elder" coming out of the synagogue context, and "bishop" and "overseer" being related more to the Roman or Hellenistic contexts. Essentially they tend to be synonymous in their point of reference. That means, however, that the use that churches have frequently made of those terms in church history or in the history of theology is rather different from the way they are used in Scripture.

2. Secondly, the "elders" responsible for community oversight are frequently linked with what is called "teaching," particularly Ephesians

4:11, 1 Timothy 5:17, and perhaps Romans 12:7. Perhaps it is implicit in Romans 12:7 that teaching is a part of this ministry. In any case, teaching is an important part of eldering and, apparently, judging from the Timothy reference, the overseers or bishops or pastors or elders could also frequently serve as teachers.

Teaching had to do with both transmitting the tradition and with addressing contemporary challenges. It focused on what we might call the normative beliefs and practices of the faith community. Scattered throughout the Pauline epistles, the apostle refers to the way we "teach in all the churches" or argues against people who are trying to deviate from normative convictions or develops some perspectives that others may not yet have understood. These efforts are always aimed at what should count as normative beliefs and practices, not just Paul's own opinions. When he is talking about his own opinions, he says so. But the teachers, the elders, are people who are to care particularly for the normative beliefs and practices of the faith community.

3. A third thing that relates to "pastoral ministry" (although not exclusively) is equipping others for ministry. The term "equip" is a direct quotation from Ephesians 4, and is not limited to the overseer-bishop-elder ministry. It probably also belongs to the prophetic and apostolic ministries. But the equipping of others seems to be a part of these particular ministries for the apostle Paul. Extrapolating from this observation, exercising these ministries should not discourage other ministries in the church, but encourage them, nurture them, call them forth, mentor them. It seems to me that this aspect is very important because we have sometimes gotten into the bind of thinking that if we call particular people to particular ministries, we more or less automatically discourage others from exercising their ministries. In the Pauline vision, people are called to a pastoral ministry to encourage others, to mentor others, and to build up others, not to exclude them from Christian ministries.

4. A fourth thing that comes out in these Pauline writings is that at least sometimes elders, and particularly teaching elders, are given financial support to provide the time that would otherwise be needed to earn a living. This is not necessarily a universal rule. We know well enough that the apostle Paul did not claim this kind of privilege. That had to do with his understanding of his particular mission and of his strategy of mission that really financial support would be justified, but unwise, under those circumstances. Thus there is biblical precedent for

providing financial support for people engaged in these types of ministries, even though it may also be better under some conditions to find other means of support.

5. Finally, the qualifications for an elder-bishop-overseer-pastor are phrased primarily in terms of attitudes, integrity between public and private life, conduct, and familiarity with Scriptures and traditions. This series of things may be lumped together in the term qualifications that have to do with the minister's "character." One's character is exemplified in the way one lives, in the way one conducts oneself in the family, in the way one conducts oneself with people outside the faith community. I have been involved in some conference debates in which "husbands of one wife" (1 Timothy 3:2) is interpreted to mean that women may not be "bishops" or pastors. That seems to me a little beside the main point. The point of the series in 1 Timothy 3 is to identify the quality of character, the fidelity of persons that is demonstrated by being monogamous rather than polygamous. Most other items in 1 Timothy 3 can also be generalized in terms of quality of character.

I really doubt that we can go much further than these five points in summarizing what the ministry of overseer-bishop-elder-pastor means in the Pauline epistles. Most other interpretations that we give to this ministry need to be considered theological extrapolations that may well be legitimate. But we should not over read what we find in the texts; and I don't think we find much more in the texts. If others of you have found more key characteristics of pastoral ministry, I would appreciate your sharing them.

Priorities for pastoral ministry

Based on these five observations of this particular ministry in the midst of many other ministries in the New Testament, I would like to make five suggestions on what might be the highest priorities of pastoral ministry. Here I am also introducing new terminology and speaking about a particular "role" or "office" in our context. "Office," of course, is not a biblical term. By this term, however, I mean a pattern of expectations about understandings and practices of ministry that fit together in a congruent way.

1. First of all, I suggest that a major aspect of pastoral ministry be based on the Pauline vision of congregational oversight in the sense of providing guidance for the welfare of the congregation as a whole. This particular ministry of bishop-overseer-pastor is oriented toward the

whole group, not only toward specific persons or specific parts of the group. It relates to the whole, tries to get a vision of the whole, tries to be concerned with the overall work of the church. This calls at least partially into question some of the emphases that have developed in our time and context on pastoral ministry. Some of these emphases have gone rather far in terms of focusing pastoral ministry on one-to-one care.

And at times in the past twenty to thirty years, seminaries have put a lot of emphasis on pastoral counseling in the sense of one-on-one care that can almost consume an entire week. When that happens, pastors lose out in terms of the vision of the church as a whole, of the congregation as a whole, of the group of believers as a whole. What this aspect means practically needs to be worked out. It doesn't mean that pastors should be unconcerned about the care of individuals. But it seems to me that addressing the care of the whole group, particularly through corporate decision making, through corporate worship, through corporate "administration," are major concerns; other things will then also need to find their proper place as well.

2. The second major aspect of the pastoral role is teaching, providing leadership in discerning, and passing on normative Christian beliefs and practices. This would include normative beliefs and practices in worship, piety, and ethics. What are the core beliefs; what are the core practices that really capture who we are as a faith community and that provide continuity for it? We live in a very pluralistic society, in a post enlightenment democratic society. Mennonites have tended frequently to be a little suspicious of normative beliefs and practices. We have even misused them and sometimes forced them down people's throats, so to speak. But unless we are able to develop, pass on, and articulate normative beliefs and practices, we are not really following out the teaching dimension of pastoral ministry, and, I think, we will be in serious trouble as faith communities.

George Lindbeck, Professor of Historical Theology at Yale Divinity School, has made a big point about the disintegration of Christian identity in American Protestantism. He feels that one of the basic problems is the loss of normative beliefs and practices. Based on a New Testament emphasis on the role of teaching, it seems we need to recapture something of a vision for teaching as a particular responsibility of pastoral ministry in order to cultivate and nurture Christian (and Mennonite) identity in our pluralistic society.

3. A third aspect would be the nurturing and empowering of other members ministries through mentoring and training. I know very few congregations that have written nurturing and mentoring others in their ministry into the pastoral job description. Practically, one person cannot do a lot of mentoring. But at least, it seems to me, if every pastor were mentoring and nurturing two or three other people every two or three years, developing others' gifts could be an important responsibility of pastoral ministry. Paul mentored Timothy and others as part of his apostolic and teaching ministry.

4. A fourth aspect is what we would normally call pastoral care and leadership in the faith community, walking with and helping others walk with members during crises or life transitions. Although that doesn't all need to be done by a pastor, general oversight in this area certainly would be a part of pastoral ministry.

5. A fifth aspect is something that can be extrapolated from the apparent plurality of such pastors in a local congregation. There has been a lot of discussion in recent years that the pastor or the pastors should work together with others in the congregation who are "co-ministers." We see in the Pauline writings and in many of the Mennonite traditions (with different terms) an understanding of pastoral ministry that is exercised by several people in a congregation. One or more of them may be full time; others may be less than full time. Some of our current patterns undermine this tradition in the sense that we may have "elders" who are elected for two or three years. When that happens, there isn't much continuity; they can't be a part of a team that provides longer-term support for a full-time pastor; and they can't provide the kind of eldering which demands continuity, shared vision, and longer-term service.

Implications for pastoral education

Finally, what are some implications for pastoral education? I would like to refer to three areas in general without developing them extensively. Perhaps the responses or discussion can push these issues out a bit more.

1. First, I suggest that an important part of pastoral education would be what may be called "character formation." I'm consciously not using the term "spiritual formation" (although we're using it at AMBS presently) because it seems to me that we need to look at this area a bit more broadly than only spiritual formation understood in the narrower

sense of encouraging the disciplines of prayer, Scripture, meditation, spiritual retreats, and the like. Those are all fine and wonderful and necessary, and there are many reasons they should be nurtured as a means of maintaining and strengthening one's relationship to God. But by "character" I mean something that includes the individual's relationship to God but also extends to interpersonal relations and to how we live within the faith community and in the larger society. The "formation" of "character" underscores the importance of community as well as the formation of my personal relationship with God.

It seems to me that we are in danger of taking a somewhat more individualistic approach if we buy uncritically into some of the things that are considered spiritual formation. In order to provide needed correctives, it may help to emphasize "character formation." To interpret and extrapolate from the passages in the Pauline epistles, to which I referred earlier, character was formed through the way one lived in the family, through the way one lived in the broader community, and through the expressions of life in these faith and other communities. Thus, what counts is not only praying a lot (although praying a lot is good); what counts is not only that we read the Scriptures a lot (although that is also very good); but what also counts is how we are formed by interacting with other people, by responsibility in family and in society.

I was struck several years ago while talking with Marcus Smucker, who directs the Spiritual Formation program here, with his comments on the "delayed adolescence" of many American young people. The period of adolescence has moved in many ways from the mid-teens to mid-twenties (or even later). We were speculating why that is so. Marcus suggested that part of the reason may be postponement of vocational decisions, of whether to remain single or to marry, of delaying children if one is married. A whole series of such things shape character by a participation in a broader community or in a broader social unit. Delaying these character-shaping events may also delay maturation. That's something of what I mean when speaking about character formation.

It seems to me that in pastoral education we need to give attention to character formation, a part of which includes what we are now calling spiritual formation, with some kind of corporate discipline, corporate responsibility, and corporate worship as well as the individual discipline, individual responsibility, and individual worship. Such an approach might well reinforce (or make plausible) an understanding of pastoral ministry as that ministry which gives particular attention to the congregation as a whole.

2. A second major component of pastoral education would be helping people who are to assume pastoral ministry develop clear understandings, acceptance, and interpretation of what we can call normative Christian beliefs and practices. What is "orthodoxy" and what is "orthopraxis," to use some of the contemporary terminology that is thrown around? I'm impressed by the fact that in the Protestant theological enterprise there is currently much discussion about the nature of theological education. One of the minority voices has come recently out of Andover-Newton Seminary in a book by Max Stackhouse called Apologia (apologetics). He is arguing that liberal Protestant seminaries need to find their way back to "defending" core Christian beliefs in the midst of our pluralistic age. To be sure, he only has four such core beliefs: sin and salvation, biblical revelation, trinity, and Christology. Nevertheless, these are some fairly foundational beliefs.

As Anabaptists and Mennonites, we would doubtless want to add some "core practices." It seems to me, in talking with students, seminary faculty members, and pastors these days, that as Mennonites engaged in pastoral education, we need to risk "promoting" normative beliefs and practices. We can't depend upon ethnic continuities without corporate conversation and discipline to nurture Mennonite identity. We should also spell out the importance of normative beliefs and practices in terms of biblical studies, historical studies, theological studies, and ethical studies in order to keep this agenda central in pastoral education.

3. Third, in addition to character formation and to nurturing normative beliefs and practices, pastoral education should include what we might call the "arts" of pastoral ministry. Some talk about "skills" or "competencies." That's fine, as long as those terms aren't taken too mechanically. I would prefer to use a term like the "arts" of pastoral ministry. I would suggest, at least for our discussion, four or five areas where the ministerial arts are critical for pastoral ministry and should, therefore, be emphasized in pastoral education.

One is good communication, whether publicly in preaching and teaching, or in more personal settings. The major tools of pastors are words. If we can't use words helpfully and constructively, we might as well hang up our shovel and hoe. Communication, of course, includes many things besides words. But if you stumble around as a pastor and say things like "Well, you know what I mean," most people won't. Communication is very crucial.

A second area of ministerial arts may be termed "representative events" of the faith community: worship, baptism, communion, funerals, and the like. Pastors, with the help of others, have a key role to play in focusing the life and practice of a community in and during these representative events. These representative events are very important.

They nurture the life of the community; they address the community as a whole; they communicate something of what the church is about to the broader society. The representational quality of these events is very important. The exercise of those ministerial arts is related to them and is also crucial.

Seminaries and other pastoral training programs generally work on these first two arts of ministry. A third one has not been developed very consciously in pastoral education. We haven't even lifted it up high enough to know whether we are succeeding or failing at it. I'm referring to the art of mentoring others in their ministries. Including the mentoring of others in their ministries as a key ministerial art would seem to be very important if we are trying to follow the Pauline vision and the Anabaptist vision of pastoral ministry. But we still need to work out what that may mean concretely for pastoral education.

A fourth area of pastoral education would be collaboration with co-ministers. One of the things that impressed me after having been away from the United States for several years (1961-1974) was learning that many congregations had moved from having several ministers (at least in the "Old" Mennonite tradition) to having one pastor. I kept asking people as I traveled to several congregations when and why that had happened. It didn't happen only because somebody went off to seminary and got formal training to be a pastor. It frequently happened because there were squabbles between the ministers. One pragmatic way of resolving the squabbles and of bringing peace to the congregation was to eliminate all pastors but one, on the assumption that one pastor could not fight with herself or himself. Since then (likely this was also known earlier!) we have also discovered that it's possible for congregations and pastors to squabble with each other.

I'm not proposing that having one (full-time) pastor in a congregation is wrong nor that having several ministers is always right. What I am suggesting is that if we want to develop pastoral ministry in ways that nurture and call out the gifts of others in the church, one way we might do that is to learn to develop the ministerial arts of collaborating with others who also exercise responsibility in the congregation.

Finally, the fifth major area of pastoral education would be in pastoral care, or as the longer-term Christian tradition would say, "care of souls." Pastoral education will certainly employ the disciplines of counseling, but do so in ways that include nurturing both the individual believer's and the whole community's relationship with God in the context of their life as a whole.

So those are several remarks, partly autobiographical and partly related to ongoing conversations over the years. I would be interested in your responses and perspectives.

-----

[1]The following was presented on November 3, 1991, to the annual Directors' meeting of Conference-Based Theological Education, an extension program related to Eastern Mennonite Seminary of Harrisonburg, Virginia, and Associated Mennonite Biblical Seminary of Elkhart, Indiana.

Chapter 12

The Seminary in a Believers Church

Reprinted by permission from *Gospel Herald*, vol. 68, no. 25 (June 24, 1975) 466-67.

The Mennonite Church in North America has only recently ventured into the area of seminary training. In 1946 the term "Biblical Seminary" was first used at Goshen, Indiana, for the training program for ministers; in 1965 the Eastern Mennonite Seminary was founded at Harrisonburg, Virginia. As a Mennonite Church, we have not yet reached a common mind on whether seminaries are a necessary or even helpful part of the life of the church.

On the more superficial level, this uncertainty extends to the lack of familiarity with the term "seminary." Sometimes it is unconsciously confused with the word "cemetery." Perhaps this mixing of terms expresses in a rather pointed way the feeling that a "seminary" may be characterized as a valley of dry bones. Even if a seminary were to become such a desert valley (something which has happened in church history), the prophet Ezekiel could teach us to pray for and expect that breath which infuses new life into dry bones and creates a new people from the scattered remnants of the old.

Before looking at the more important issues related to seminary education, let us clarify our terms. The term "cemetery" comes from a Greek word which originally meant "put to sleep" or "sleeping room" and has come to mean a "place for burying the dead." The word "seminary," however, comes from a Latin word related to the word "seed" and meant "a place where something is developed or nurtured," a place of cultivation. The word has come to mean particularly a "training school for priests, ministers, or rabbis." As used by Mennonite schools, "seminary" would therefore mean a place for training ministers, if we are to accept the simple dictionary definition. Such a description at least helps distinguish seminaries from cemeteries...though Mennonites have more of the latter than the former.

Ministry through diversity

We still need to clarify what we mean by "ministers," if the seminaries have the training of ministers as a significant part of their task. As a believers church which begins with the authority and example of the Bible as the basis and norm for teaching and life, we are committed to finding our models for ministry in the biblical vision and reality of the church.

One of the primary ways in which the New Testament view of the church breaks with non-Christian faiths and with general human tendencies of social organization is in the area of Christian ministry. The new creation in Christ includes a new ordering of life together in the Christian community. The richness of this new creation overflows into many gifts and ministries which Christ gives for the building up of the Christian church. This multiplicity and diversity of gifts shatters the traditional religious pattern of having a central religious person who performs the key religious functions for the total society, meditating between God and the rest of the community. This multiplicity and diversity of gifts sets a new pattern for leadership and ministry in the church.

This first means that a seminary with a believers church orientation will be committed to developing, nurturing, and cultivating the gifts of ministry which Christ has given to the church as a body through individual believers within the church. The task of the seminary begins with that which is *given* and provides a concentrated opportunity for its cultivation and development.

This means secondly that a seminary with a believers' church perspective will encourage a plurality and diversity of ministries rather than an all-inclusive office which moves toward training a clerical class in and for the church. Church planting, preaching, teaching, evangelizing, pastoring, administering, speaking the word of insight and discernment—these are some of the ministries necessary to the building up of the church—there are and will be others as well. A seminary provides the opportunity for training and equipping in these *diverse* ministries.

Attendance at and graduation from a seminary is not and should not be required for exercising these and other ministries in the Mennonite Church. But seminary attendance does commend itself as a significant means of becoming better equipped for such ministries. Both the seminaries and the congregations continually need to discern which ministries in the church are best helped by seminary training and how this training should happen.

Bible is normative

What, then, are the tasks of the seminaries in cultivating the gifts of ministry for the building up of the church? Or, to put it differently, what are the functions of theology in the church—and how can the seminary contribute to those tasks?

In the New Testament church, what we now call theology has a twofold role. On the one hand, it recalls and maintains the tradition or the heritage of faith. On the other hand, it continually needs to face new issues and different ways of speaking as the church moves and finds itself in new historical situations. The one function is a looking back to and maintaining clarity concerning the foundations of the faith. The other is a testing and discerning of faithfulness in the midst of new challenges.

Within the believers church orientation, the normative "tradition" is the Bible rather than a particular stream of church history or a special system of doctrines. The Bible is that "which has been handed down" (1 Cor. 15:3) and the treasure put into our charge (2 Tim. 1:14). For that reason Mennonite seminaries are biblical seminaries, focusing on careful study and teaching of the Scriptures and on examination of practical and theoretical issues in light of the biblical standard.

But the commitment to biblical authority goes further to include those who interpret the Bible and the context in which they interpret it. Who interprets the Scriptures? To say only that the Bible interprets itself is a half-truth, since people also interpret Scripture. In one church tradition the final authority in biblical interpretation is the pope; in most Protestant church traditions, the final authority of interpretation is the biblical scholar, seminary professor, or perhaps the trained pastor.

Within the believers church tradition, the person who has acquired tools of study and language has a significant contribution to make, but cannot alone be considered the final authority on biblical interpretation. The context of biblical interpretation is rather the congregation of believers where those who have specialized biblical tools as well as who have other gifts of discernment seek together to faithfully interpret the words and obey the Word.

This means that a biblical seminary must focus not only on the careful study and teaching of the Bible, but also must train persons to contribute to the interpretation of scripture in the congregation of believers—which is the primary place where God's Word is heard and obedience tested.

Seminaries cultivate heritage

Mennonite seminaries are also committed to cultivating the heritage of those groups and churches which can be called "believers churches." The sixteenth-century Anabaptists were most radical precisely because their call for church renewal extended to the example and life as well as the doctrines of the New Testament church. Similar groups (in some respects) have been the Waldensians, the Czech Brethren, the early Quakers, Church of the Brethren, some Pentecostal groups in North America, some Independent church groups in Africa, and several contemporary renewal movements.

Reading the Bible in the context of the believers churches means a foundational commitment to have our theology and church life shaped by the biblical vision rather than trying to adjust the Bible to a theology and church life formed primarily by other sources. This commitment requires a good measure of critical self-awareness on our part so that we do not simply read our own prejudices back into the Bible.

Finally, the theological task in a believers church and therefore in a Mennonite seminary also includes testing for faithfulness of life and thought in new situations. In some respects the most crucial issue is not only what the Bible says (there is more agreement on this than we often realize), but what it means to live by biblical faith.

Again, this is a task which the seminaries cannot carry out single-handedly. They have a particular responsibility, nevertheless, to carefully test the cultural and social forces which influence us, sometimes consciously, sometimes unconsciously—as well as to test the different religious voices calling for Christians' loyalty.

For these reasons, a seminary education includes a careful examination of past history and how the churches have responded faithfully, or less than faithfully, to the challenges of past times and places. Seminary training for these reasons also includes a careful study of the contemporary issues the churches face, both internally and in their missionary and witness outreach. Some of this training takes the form of theory; some of it takes the form of experience and practice.

In both cases, the primary issue remains the faithfulness of God's people in our time. And in both cases the seminaries do not have and do not claim a monopoly on this function. They rather remain a resource for the churches in helping train for ministry and in discerning the signs of the times. Sometimes the seminaries reflect the state of the congregations; sometimes they challenge them to greater clarity and faithfulness. And sometimes the seminaries are challenged by the congregations to greater clarity and faithfulness.

The difference between a cemetery and a seminary will depend upon the degree to which the seminaries, together with the congregations, cultivate the "treasure put into our charge," perceptively and faithfully respond to the challenges of our time—and help to develop the diverse ministries which are needed for the building up of the church.

III

Theology in a Believers Church Perspective

Chapter 13

America's Anabaptists:
What They Believe

Reprinted by permission from *Christianity Today*, vol. 34, no. 15 (October 22, 1990) 30-33.

Ask 20 Anabaptists what they believe and you will probably get 20 different answers. This diversity stems from differences among the earliest Anabaptists, from the varied countries that played host to the Anabaptists before their migrations to North America, and from recent developments on the American scene. In addition, Mennonites and other Anabaptist groups have usually stressed *living* the faith, giving more weight to Christian practice than to standardized doctrinal formulations.

All Anabaptists, nevertheless, share a number of Christian convictions about belief and practice:

• Believing in Jesus as Son of God and Savior can never be separated from following him in everyday behavior.

• Baptism is reserved for those who confess their faith in Jesus Christ and commit themselves to live as his disciples.

• The Scriptures, not creeds or traditions, provide the primary standard for faith and life.

• God's saving grace in Christ results not only in newness of life for the individual but also creates and sustains the church, a community called to radical discipleship and service.

• Discipleship in the new community obligates members to invite unbelievers to accept the Christian faith, love the enemy, reject war and violence, and seek peace in the church and in the world.

The Bible in practical terms

From their earliest days, Anabaptists have sought earnestly to be a biblical people. They have tended to understand biblical authority more in practical than in dogmatic terms, however, placing the emphasis on *applying* the message of Scripture. While the largest Mennonite and Brethren denominations in North America have all in recent decades adopted statements that acknowledge and reaffirm the Bible as inspired and authoritative for the church, Anabaptists hesitate to fasten on one set of theological concepts as the decisive test for a correct doctrine of biblical inspiration.

Anabaptists also place great stress on the church body as the locus for biblical interpretation. Scripture is not to be interpreted so much by the individual as by the body of believers. They emphasize that it is as the gathered community listens together to Scripture that God makes his purposes clear and his will known.

Therefore, Anabaptists stress that answers to questions about women pastors, Christ's nature, the church's response to charismatic renewal, or Christians' social responsibility must be based on biblical truth that is tested in congregational meetings and regional conferences. Recent Mennonite meetings provide a good example. Variously called "Conversations on Faith" or "Dialogues on Faith," these assemblies have over the years brought together persons representing different views on controversial matters to study and interpret Scripture's teachings on concrete issues.

At its best, this pragmatic approach to scriptural authority has nurtured a broadly based love of and familiarity with the Bible among Anabaptists. At its worst, it has turned disagreements about relatively insignificant matters into church divisions, and reinforced tendencies toward legalism. Early in the twentieth century, for example, some Mennonite groups considered radios "unbiblical" and "worldly." By mid-century, they sponsored their own radio programs and spots.

Reactions against this "shadow side" of Mennonite biblicism have more recently contributed to a growing biblical illiteracy, which increasingly concerns church leaders and teachers.

The church's one foundation

Menno Simons, the sixteenth-century Dutch Anabaptist leader, chose 1 Corinthians 3:11 as a key verse and theological motto: "For no one can lay any foundation other than the one already laid, which is Jesus Christ" (NIV). Most of Menno's essays and his other writings carried this verse on the title page. It became the basis for the Anabaptists' growing convictions about the centrality of the life, death, and resurrection of Jesus Christ for understanding salvation, the church, Christian ethics, and eschatology.

Anabaptists like to stress that Jesus is both the Son of God by whom we are saved through faith, and the Lord who has exemplified in his earthly life and ministry the way Christians are called to live in this world. This emphasis on Jesus Christ as both Savior and Lord has usually included efforts to interpret his saving work in terms that provide the basis for both salvation and ethics.

Among several North American Mennonite groups, discussions on Christology have come center stage in the last two decades. These have produced sometimes lively debates about the continuing relevance of the Chalcedonian two-nature doctrine and its theological and ethical implications. For example, these and other issues fed into a conjoint inter-Mennonite and Brethren in Christ consultation on Christology in August 1989. Rather characteristically, the 1989 consultation focused on the relation between Christology and mission, church and ethics.

Members of the household of God

Since their beginnings, Anabaptists have understood the church as the "called-out" community of believers in the midst of an unbelieving world. The church is not a mixture of nominal and serious Christians, but the visible body of those who have voluntarily confessed their faith in Jesus Christ and have committed themselves to follow him in life. This view of the church as the community of committed believers includes strong emphases upon believers (rather than infant) baptism, mutual admonition and correction, sharing material resources, and all members' active involvement in the church's ministry, witness, and service.

The emphasis upon mutual admonition and correction has traditionally been based on Matthew 18:15-18 ("If your brother sins against you, go and tell him his fault..."). Such correction is usually seen as essential for church renewal and congregational life. Beyond these general areas of agreement, Mennonite and Mennonite-related groups (such as Hutterites, Amish, and others) have diverged on which matters should appropriately become the subject of mutual admonition.

The Amish, and some Mennonite groups, for example, have taken clothing styles to be a matter of church discipline. Most have made the peace position a matter of mutual admonition and correction. All have considered issues such as fidelity in marriage and divorce to be important subjects of church discipline.

Anabaptists historically have practiced church discipline in different ways. At times it has been implemented almost exclusively by ministers. Recently the Anabaptist view of congregational involvement has been regaining importance. While ministers traditionally administered the standard that made divorce—and particularly remarriage—incompatible with church membership, some congregations are developing other patterns. They may appoint a small group of members to work with the pastor and the persons concerned to provide discernment, counsel, and support to both the individuals and the congregation.

Anabaptists have also understood the purposes of church discipline in different ways. Some have considered the primary goal to be restoring the erring member through forgiveness and reconciliation; others have emphasized maintaining "a church without spot or wrinkle." Groups differ on the rigor with which they have suspended relations with unrepentant members. The Amish, for example, have maintained the practice of breaking off all social relationships ("shunning"), as dramatized in the television portrayal *Silence at Bethany.*

Most contemporary North American Mennonites, however, would hold up accountability and restoration rather than sanctioning as the primary purposes. Consequently, church discipline may lead in extreme cases to suspending fellowship in relation to Communion until there is reconciliation and restoration, but not to breaking off all relations. In the case of ministers, it would include suspension of ministerial privileges.

Church discipline among Mennonites is now being complemented—sometimes replaced—by pastoral counseling. The influences of individualism and reactions against past misuses in congregations or conferences have contributed to an erosion of the practice.

Mutual aid and the sharing of material resources are also expressions of Christian community among Anabaptists. Most Mennonites have not followed the Hutterite pattern of establishing and maintaining communal life (Reba Place Church in Evanston, Illinois, and Plow Creek Fellowship in Tiskilwa, Illinois, are exceptions). But they have emphasized sharing their material resources with sisters and brothers as needed. Organizing barn raisings, harvesting together, sewing quilts, making loans with little or no interest, and giving money outright have been characteristics of mutual aid, especially in rural settings.

With rapidly increasing urbanization and professionalization, mutual aid is taking on more institutional forms. The Mennonite Central Committee (MCC) is an example. Begun during the 1920s to provide food for Russian Mennonites in the wake of revolution and civil war, MCC has since become the major relief, service, and development agency of North American Mennonite-related groups. Started with three volunteers who were sent to Russia to provide assistance to other Mennonites, the agency today has 964 volunteers in over 50 countries around the world, working in programs and projects serving both Christians and non-Christians.

Believers baptism represents a third aspect of understanding the church as the community of committed believers. For early sixteenth-century Anabaptists and Mennonites, rejecting infant baptism in favor of believers baptism amounted to an act of civil disobedience. For centuries everyone (except the Jews) had been baptized as infants and were therefore presumed to be Christians even, in many cases, when what they believed or how they lived violated the church's norms.

Furthermore, in that context of widespread nominal Christianity ("Christendom"), believers baptism meant the faithful church is necessarily a missionary community that lives by inviting people to a personal commitment of faith, baptizing them upon their confession of faith. In contrast to the mainstream Protestant Reformation, the Radical Reformation thereby unleashed a strong missionary movement.

Since the end of the nineteenth century, North American Mennonite groups have sought to regain something of the vision of the church as a missionary community. In doing so they have also borrowed in varying degrees from the modern missionary, revival, and church growth movements. As a result, most groups sponsor mission and church planting efforts both in North America and in other countries. The Mennonite Church in particular has adopted several far-reaching evangelistic and church-planting goals under the rubric of "Vision 95." The General Conference Mennonite Church has included mission and witness concerns in its current set of priorities known as the "Call to Kingdom Commitments." The Church of the Brethren's "Goals for the Nineties" places high priorities on enlarging the community of faith through evangelism as well.

Jesus' "hard sayings"

Mennonites believe that Christian faith should therefore be understood and expressed as discipleship, as following Jesus Christ in all of life. Coming to faith includes both accepting Jesus Christ as Savior and committing oneself to follow him as Lord of one's life.

This vision of discipleship focuses particularly on the "hard sayings" of the Sermon on the Mount. Dispensationalists interpret them as a blueprint for conduct in a future dispensation; Lutherans as a mirror to magnify human sinfulness and the need for justification by faith alone. Anabaptists take them as standards for Christian conduct here and now. Because the "hard sayings" of Jesus frequently run counter to sinful human tendencies and to the structures of society in general, the call to follow him in life includes the call to take up our cross—that is, to accept suffering readily when faithfulness to his way leads to conflict with social structures.

Other expressions of discipleship are less visible to the broader society: prayer and worship, almsgiving and benevolence, fasting and voluntary poverty. According to Matthew 6, these things are to be done "in secret." More visible expressions of discipleship stressed include being reconciled to an offended sister or brother before offering one's gift, on the altar, lifelong faithfulness in marriage, simplicity of language and refusal to take oaths, doing good to evildoers rather than resisting them with violence, and loving the enemy. According to Matthew 5, these things represent ways in which followers of Jesus Christ are called to be the salt of the earth and light of the world.

Conscientious objection to participation in war and military service and the commitment to a biblically based peace position have been characteristic implications of an Anabaptist view of discipleship. At its best, this position does not depend primarily on an isolated reading of the Sermon on the Mount, but also draws on a "reading" of Jesus' life, and especially his death, where the Cross both redeems human beings from sin and reveals the way followers of Christ are called to live.

The peace stance has in recent times contributed to concerns for peace and justice that go beyond conscientious objection to military service. Questions about appropriate ways of witnessing to and participating in the larger political and social institutions for the sake of justice and peace continue to be vigorously debated among Anabaptists in their conversations with other Christians.

Searching for commonalities

Anabaptists' concern for radical faithfulness sometimes has made their cooperation with other Christians and even other Anabaptist groups a thorny issue. Mennonite history includes both cooperative efforts and divisions among various Mennonite groups. Some American Mennonite groups are themselves the products of mergers between previously divided groups. The two largest bodies, the General Conference Mennonite Church and the Mennonite Church, decided last year to give serious consideration to eventual merger.

Several Mennonite groups also work cooperatively in various ways with the other "historic peace churches" (the Church of the Brethren and the Friends [Quakers]) on peace and voluntary-service concerns.

Mennonites have occasionally been open to cooperation with interchurch and interdenominational bodies. No North American Mennonite group is a member of the National or World Councils of Churches. The Church of the Brethren is a member of both, and individual Mennonites have been consultants or observers at conferences and study projects sponsored by these bodies. Only two groups, the Mennonite Brethren and the Brethren in Christ, are members of the National Association of Evangelicals (NAE). Individuals from other Mennonite groups have participated at conferences and study projects sponsored by NAE and Lausanne.

For the most part, Mennonites think of Christian unity like they think of the Christian life in general: it is found in following Christ, in joining hands with others in discipleship and service.

As the Anabaptist denominations share their accent on living as Christ taught and modeled, the wider church can stand to learn from the Reformation's "radicals." Whatever their deficiencies, the Anabaptists remind us that the church must get on with the radical, risky business of being Christ's disciples.

Chapter 14
The Mennonite Practice of Baptism

Originally published as "The Mennonites" in *Baptism and Church: A Believers' Church Vision*, Merle D. Strege, ed. (Sagamore Books, 1986) 15-28. Reprinted by permission.

The conference planners have asked me to summarize the Mennonite understanding and practice of baptism both in their historical development and in their contemporary realities. Given the diversity of groups as well as the chronological and geographic spread of Mennonites, the scope of this presentation will need to be drastically limited. Rather than attempting a balanced survey of the entire history, I shall concentrate on the Anabaptist-Mennonite origins in sixteenth-century Europe. And rather than tracing the understandings and practices represented by all Mennonite groups, I shall focus on the strands claimed by two Mennonite groups in twentieth-century North America. These two groups, the Mennonite Church and the General Conference Mennonite Church, are numerically the two largest Mennonite bodies in the United States and Canada; they are also the two groups being represented in this conference by the Associated Mennonite Biblical Seminaries.

My remarks will consequently be divided into two major sections. The first part of this presentation will review understandings and practice during the beginnings of the Anabaptist-Mennonite groups in the early and mid-sixteenth century. The second part will report on the results of an impressionistic survey on contemporary understandings and practices among Mennonites in the midwestern United States and Ontario.[1]

The Anabaptists and baptism

The formative significance of the 1527 Schleitheim Articles for the consolidation of the early Swiss and South German streams of the Anabaptist movement has been rediscovered in contemporary historical scholarship. Moreover the Schleitheim Articles have found their way into recent North American Mennonite catechetical materials. At least one major Mennonite group, the Mennonite Church in North America has included it in the denominational constitution as one of the confessional statements which provide a standard for membership. We may therefore appropriately begin with the Schleitheim Articles as a benchmark in an Anabaptist-Mennonite understanding of baptism and church membership. By comparison and contrast we will also be able to note some similarities and differences between sixteenth-century understandings and current North American Mennonite tendencies.

The Schleitheim Articles begin with the baptism theme. Article One reads as follows:

> Baptism shall be given to all those who have been taught repentance and the amendment of life and who truly believe that their sins are taken away through Christ and to all those who desire to walk in the resurrection of Jesus Christ and be buried with him in death so that they might rise with Him; to all those who with such an understanding themselves desire and request it from us; hereby is excluded all infant baptism the greatest and first abomination of the Pope. For this you have the reasons and the testimony of the writings and the practice of the apostles.[2]

This article offers in rather concentrated form an order for understanding the baptism which characterizes a formative stream of Anabaptist life and thought. Note particularly that baptism shall be given to those:

1. who have been taught repentance and the amendment of life;
2. who believe that their sins have been removed through Jesus Christ;
3. who express their desire to walk in newness of life, namely to take up what came to be called discipleship or following Christ in life;
4. who so understand baptism, desire it, and ask for it.

This pattern repeats itself in the writings of major sixteenth-century Anabaptists such as Balthasar Hubmaier, Menno Simons, and Pilgram Marpeck. Focusing particularly on the Great Commission in both its Matthean and Markan forms, they reiterate the priority of preaching/teaching, followed by a response of faith, inner regeneration, a commitment to discipleship, and baptism and a public confession of faith, or as Menno puts it, as a sign of obedience to the command of Christ. This sequence necessarily excludes the baptism of infants, who can neither respond to God's Word in faith, nor commit themselves to a life of discipleship, nor request baptism.

Article Two of Schleitheim deals with the "ban," that is the exercise of congregational admonition and discipline according to Matthew 18. The ban is to be employed "with those who have been baptized into the one body of Christ...and still somehow slip and fall into error and sin. . . ."[3] The next article concerns "the breaking of bread," and stipulates that those who desire to participate "must beforehand be united in the one body of Christ, that is the congregation of God...and that by baptism."[4] Baptism as understood in Article One is thus directly linked to entry into the Christian church. Membership in the church is furthermore indissolubly tied to the exercise of church discipline and sharing in the Lord's Supper. Baptism on confession of faith and with the commitment to discipleship thus includes becoming a member in the church and beginning to participate in its discipline as well as to partake in communion. Baptism as a public confession of faith and a sign of obedience to Christ simultaneously means entry into a congregation of believers characterized by separateness from the evil and wickedness in the world, by sharing in a unity of spirit and love maintained by a common discipline, and by a common remembrance of Christ's broken body and shed blood.

Hubmaier tied the authority to bind and loose to the baptismal pledge perhaps more explicitly and systematically than Menno, Marpeck, or other sixteenth-century Anabaptist writers or church leaders after Schleitheim.[5] Nevertheless, the linkage of baptism with entry into church membership, mutual submission in congregational discipline, and access to communion are broadly assumed and practiced in some fashion. We shall return later to this connection between baptism and church membership, which has often undergone significant modifications and has sometimes been challenged in more recent Mennonite practice.

The Anabaptist-Mennonite emphasis on baptism as a visible testimony to faith and as a sign of obedience implies a departure from sacramental views of baptism which consider it a means of grace. Mennonites often refer to baptism as a symbol to distinguish their view from sacramental views. If sacramentalist views unduly emphasize baptism as God's action and gift at the expense of prior faith and commitment, Mennonite views may frequently tend toward a "moderate spiritualism" or excessive "subjectivism." Both these tendencies and

attempts to correct them in ways consistent with believers' baptism
accompany both the historical and the contemporary discussion and
practice among Mennonites.

In his study on *Anabaptist Baptism*, Rollin Armour has described
the varying emphases among several sixteenth century Anabaptists,
ranging from the moderate spiritualism of a Hubmaier to the later, more
"objective" view of Marpeck. In addition to focusing on the sequence of
teaching, faith response, and baptism, Hubmaier, as many others then
and now, emphasized that baptism represents the pledge of a good
conscience before God, citing 1 Peter 3:20ff. in this regard. Marpeck
however moved beyond grounding baptism only in the dominical
command or describing it simply as the sign of a good conscience before
God in his search to avoid both the spiritualist and the sacramental
pitfalls. Marpeck shared with other Anabaptists the view that
regeneration began prior to baptism and that baptism was an outer sign
of the new birth. However, Marpeck went on to contend that the sign
participated in the reality of regeneration.

> As in all other matters, the reality must precede its own
> witness, so that the sign can be rightly taken or given. When
> otherwise, the sign is false and a vain mockery. If the reality is
> there and is known, then the sign is truly and wholly useful,
> and everything signified by the sign is [then] to be given to the
> sign, for it is no more a sign, but a reality.[6]

This means that even though forgiveness of sin precedes baptism in
that the Holy Spirit was already at work creating a good conscience,
forgiveness is also given "in" baptism. Conceptually, Marpeck
elaborated the concept of a "co-witness" in which the inner witness of
the Holy Spirit is matched by an outer witness which complements it.
The co-witness is by implication as valid as the inner action itself, even
though it corresponds to it rather than mediating it. In addition to the
notion of a co-witness, Marpeck also described the unity of baptism in
terms of the action of the Trinity. According to this view, the unity of
inner and outer baptism is founded in the nature of God whose inner
spiritual actions in human beings are always complemented by the
outward actions of Christ, or the Christian church as His successor. And
finally, he offered an anthropological rationale, interpreting baptism as
including both the inner and the outer aspects of the human individual.

Armour concludes that Marpeck thus understood baptism to transmit God's grace to the baptizand in a limited sense, namely as a divine word assuring the one being baptized of forgiveness and regeneration through faith. The "objective" character of the baptismal action thus means that the baptizand receives the testimony from the baptizing church that they have recognized in him or her the inner gift of the Spirit, of forgiveness, and regeneration. Because this external co-witness of the church follows and completes the inner witness of the Spirit, infant baptism is by definition excluded, as well as exegetically unfounded.

Although Marpeck sought to articulate a theology of baptism which integrated both "subjective" and "objective" dimensions, another strand has, on the whole, more broadly influenced Mennonite thought and practice over the centuries. Menno Simons may be taken as the representative voice for a more "subjective" tendency, formulated in large measure as a corrective to pedobaptist and sacramentalist views. In his *Foundation of Christian Doctrine* (1539), Menno emphasizes baptism as a "covenant of a good conscience with God."[7] In his essay on "Christian Baptism" (1539), he describes baptism as a sign of obedience which proceeds from faith, emphasizes that regeneration comes by faith in God's Word rather than by receiving the sacrament, and reiterates that baptism follows regeneration rather than effecting it.[8] Those so baptized become members of the Christian church understood as the "communion of the saints," in which a disciplined life of faith, worship, and Christian obedience—as well as suffering—are the hallmarks. In comparison to Schleitheim or Marpeck, Menno's view focuses more on the individual believer than on the corporate reality of the believing community. In his emphasis on baptism as a symbol of obedience to Christ's command, Menno gives very little attention to the "objective" side of baptism, which Marpeck also articulated in his debate with spiritualistic tendencies.

This strand took confessional shape in the Dordrecht articles of 1632.[9] It has significantly informed North American Mennonite confessional and catechetical statements, at least until recent decades. The renaissance in Anabaptist studies and the more recent use of "believers church" typology have documented the range of views among early Anabaptists, and have sought to rehabilitate the ecclesiological, hence the corporate dimensions of baptism. The same tendencies are seeking to recapture something of the social-ethical context of Christian baptism and its "objective" as well as "subjective" aspects.

In both strands of baptismal theology, Mennonites have emphasized the corollary doctrines of "free will" and "discipleship." Sinful human beings have sufficient free will to respond to the Gospel—or to reject it. And those who confess Jesus as Lord and declare their intention to follow him in life are enabled by the Holy Spirit to live as disciples. This ethical capacity enabled by the Spirit has not been perceived as a capacity for leading a sinless life. Practically speaking, the strong emphasis on "fraternal admonition" and church discipline presupposes the continuing lack of perfection in the sense of sinlessness. Theologically, the dialectic between discipleship and the disciples' shortcomings has been articulated in several ways. Already Menno Simons phrased this tension in a manner which reflected both a certain confidence about the reality of regeneration and a measured sobriety about baptized believers: we are "not cleansed...of our inherited sinful nature...so that it is entirely destroyed, but in baptism we declare that we desire to die to it and to destroy it, so that it will no longer be master" (Romans 6:12).[10]

These understandings of baptism excluded infant baptism and implied baptizing those who have reached an age of moral awareness, who ask for baptism out of their response to Jesus Christ in faith, who commit themselves to follow Christ in faith, who commit themselves to follow Christ in life, and so become members of the Christian church. Among the Anabaptists and Mennonites in the sixteenth century, proposals on an appropriate age for baptism, assuming the faith-response and the commitment to discipleship, ranged from 7 to 30 years.[11] In the historical context of European Christendom where all had been baptized as infants, the question of age was not phrased primarily in terms of integrating a younger generation into the faith community. The experiential frame of reference was shaped by a missionary and persecuted minority which had challenged a major supporting axiom of the *Volkskirche.*

As to the mode of baptism, pouring water on the head most likely has been most broadly used, both in the early years and at the present time. However some early Anabaptist and Mennonite leaders apparently practiced baptism both by pouring and by immersion. One major Mennonite group, the Mennonite Brethren Church, practices baptism by immersion. Others either prefer and practice baptism by pouring or accept both forms, particularly in recent decades.

Historical developments

Within the constraints of this presentation, I cannot trace the historical developments of baptism among Mennonites between the sixteenth and twentieth centuries. Painting with very broad strokes, one can perceive both similarities and changes. Generally speaking, Mennonites have sought to maintain "believers baptism" in thought and practice. Numerous influences and challenges have however inflected both the significance and the exercise of baptism among Mennonites in North America since their coming to this continent in 1683.

One set of changes may be characterized as the routinization of baptism in the preservation of a predominantly ethnic religious community. Through a variety of expectations and practices, there was a movement toward considering the years from 15-18 as appropriate for baptism. Baptism became one among several landmarks on the way from adolescence to adulthood and marriage as well as church membership.

In more recent history, American revivalism has in part reinforced the emphasis upon believers baptism and in part introduced new emphases into Mennonite understandings and practice. Revivalism's emphasis on conversion and a voluntary response to the Gospel renewed the view that baptism as a public sign should be preceded by a voluntary and personal faith. Revivalism's preoccupation with an individual's crisis conversion has however diminished both the direct relation between baptism and church membership and the understanding of faith as a commitment to Christian discipleship in all areas of life, both personal and social.

Together with the broader stream of revivalism, child evangelism has made some inroads into Mennonite groups in the mid-twentieth century. These influences have been most perceptible in the Mennonite Church, where young children of 4 or 5 years have been baptized. The neo-Anabaptist renaissance beginning in the late 1920s and more careful attention to children's development and nurture particularly since the 1950s have gradually raised the average baptismal age somewhat.[12] A survey taken during the 1970s pegged the average age for baptism in the Mennonite Church at 11; and in the General Conference Mennonite and Mennonite Brethren churches at 16 years of age.[13] Mennonites have most likely done rather well in maintaining a form of believers—or at least youth—rather than infant baptism. Voluntary response, the obedience of faith, and "joining the church" are somehow related to the "symbol" of baptism. However Mennonites also lack a comprehensive reformulation of baptismal theology and practice in view of several historical tendencies and contemporary challenges. And the linkage between baptism and church membership may have eroded in some instances.

These tentative impressions are partly informed by a resent non-scientific survey of several Mennonite conference, congregational, and educational leaders.[14] These tentative impressions may be summarized in six major points.

First, fourteen of twenty-two respondents to the questionnaire understood baptism primarily as a symbol of conversion, pardoning, and cleansing. Only one-third see baptism primarily in terms of a public commitment to Christian discipleship. The relative weight of these responses may reflect the revivalist emphasis on personal conversion with less attention to Anabaptist concerns about a commitment to walk in newness of life. Half of the respondents linked baptism to entry into the church.

Secondly, the relation between water baptism and the gift of the Holy Spirit apparently constitutes a major problem area in present understanding and practice. Only two of the twenty-two persons explicitly view baptism as a symbol for the gift of the Holy Spirit. Sixteen of the twenty-two or over two-thirds of the respondents favored or practiced and taught baptism by pouring, the mode which in traditional Mennonite doctrine symbolized the gift of the Spirit; only one explicitly expressed this relation. A separate question on water baptism as related to the anointing by the Holy Spirit was understood and answered primarily in reference to neo-pentecostal and charismatic currents among Mennonites. Approximately one-third (8) thought that the relation is a very close one but an equal number considered the question a non-issue. Four persons answered that the Holy Spirit is given with conversion and three that the gift of the Spirit and water baptism are completely separate.

Thirdly, the majority (16) of the respondents continue to connect baptism directly with the beginning of church membership. That is hardly surprising; more significant may be the finding that the remaining seven did not postulate a direct link. The reasons for loosening this connection vary and are not always clear. In some cases where baptism has been understood as a public confession of faith the need for baptism after a public confession during revival meetings has seemed less pressing. On the other hand baptism may be understood as related to the universal body of Christ without direct relationship to membership in the local congregation. Or in still other instances baptism may be practiced in other than congregational settings, thus effectively diminishing the visible connection between membership in a gathered congregation and baptism. In one instance young people see little need for becoming church members and hence for requesting baptism, because it appears to make little practical difference. They perceive church membership to differ from regular participation in Sunday services and other church activities only in two ways, namely voting at church business meetings and tithing—neither of which exercise great attraction as reasons for requesting baptism! Finally, in some congregations, baptism as the prerequisite to participation in the Lord's Supper is also being questioned. This may also effectively make baptism itself less meaningful as incorporation into the Christian church.

Fourthly, the average age for baptizing young people who have grown up as children of Christian parents in the church seems to be rising somewhat. Some reasons for this trend are most likely indebted to a renewal of Anabaptist perspectives on a voluntary faith response, commitment to discipleship, and mutual accountability in congregational life. Many ministers are encouraging this direction. Some reasons for this trend are more problematic. Postponing baptism because church membership seems less than meaningful may demonstrate a measure of integrity, but also points to serious problems in the nature of church life. The increased mobility of youth and young adults is also a factor in postponing baptism for extended periods of time after coming to faith. If baptism signifies entry into the church, some new believers hesitate to identify with a local congregation and hence to request baptism while they are pursuing their education, accepting service assignments, or beginning careers in settings other than the congregations of their parents.

Fifthly, current practices vary with respect to nurture and baptism. In some congregations, pastors schedule instructional classes for specific age groups, usually during the early teen years, as a routine teaching instrument. Those completing the period of instruction may choose whether or not to request baptism, although peer and familial pressures favor baptism as the normal outcome. In the last two or three decades however, a majority of ministers have begun to schedule the instructional classes when specific individuals request them and express interest in considering or readiness for baptism. A comprehensive reflection on and approach to nurture in the church consistent with believers church perspective, continues as a matter of discussion and debate rather than as a clear consensus.

Sixthly, and finally re-baptism is being understood somewhat less consistently and practiced somewhat less rigorously among contemporary Mennonites than four centuries ago. In the sixteenth century, Anabaptists and Mennonites rejected the charge of rebaptism because they considered infant baptism to be in fact no baptism. Most Mennonite groups have continued this view through the centuries. Some extended the criteria of valid baptism to include the mode as well as the faith-response of the believer. Most recently however, and as reflected in our impressionistic survey some are more reluctant to insist that those baptized as infants need to be (re-)baptized upon confession of faith.

Five of the twenty-two respondents require baptism on confession of faith, and between nine and twelve strongly prefer it with very rare exceptions. The remainder however would give significant weight in the candidates preference particularly if they "resist rebaptism." In such cases there would be greater openness to ask what confirmation or baptism as an infant means to the candidate. Or there would be greater openness to receiving such persons into church membership if they have been living as Christians and participating actively in another congregation for some time. In situations where these persons have been received without re-baptism other congregational members may or may not be of a common mind on the matter.

I shall attempt no clear conclusions—particularly the impressionistic and non-scientific character of our survey would caution against conclusive statements on current Mennonite understandings and practices of baptism. Nonetheless, my impression remains that Mennonites would do well to seriously address, in a renewed and serious fashion, the whole issue of baptism. It may be that those things which ostensibly belong most obviously to our legacy of faith are in danger of erosion or of failing in part to meet present-day challenges. My hope would be that such a review and reconsideration may occur in dialogue particularly with others of the "believers church" and with all churches who confess Jesus as Messiah, Savior, and Lord. Something like that dialogical context sparked the rediscovery of believers baptism in sixteenth-century Europe, although "disputation" and "argument" backed by governmental authorities would be more appropriate terms than "dialogue." Something similar may contribute to parallel renewal in our time.

---

[1] Lynn Miller, departmental assistant at AMBS, interviewed over twenty conference and congregational leaders in midwestern United States and in Ontario on the basis of a questionnaire which I prepared. See Appendix A.

[2] John H. Yoder, *The Legacy of Michael Sattler* (Herald Press, 1972) 36.

[3] Ibid., 37.

[4] Ibid.

[5] See Rollin S. Armour, *Anabaptist Baptism: A Representative Study* (Herald Press, 1966) 46ff.

[6] Ibid., 121ff.

[7] In J. C. Wenger, ed., *Complete Writings of Menno Simons* (Herald Press, 1974) 103ff.

[8] Ibid., 227ff.

[9] In Thieleman J. van Braght, *Martyr's Mirror* (Mennonite Publishing House, 1951) 38ff. The "Dordrecht Confession" has been printed, translated into German and English for use among North American Mennonites, frequently reprinted, and broadly used as a catechetical piece until very recently. Article VIII is on baptism.

[10] "Christian Baptism," in Wenger, *Complete Writings*, 244.

[11] See Armour, 55, 95.

[12] For example, see Gideon Yoder, *The Nurture and Evangelism of Children* (Herald Press, 1959); more recently, see especially Marlin Jeschke, *Believers' Baptism for Children of the Church* (Herald Press, 1983), and Maurice Martin and Helen Reusser, *In the Midst of the Congregation* (Mennonite Publishing House, 1983).

[13] J. Howard Kauffman and Leland Harder, *Anabaptists Four Centuries Later* (Herald, 1975) 71.

[14] See footnote 1.

APPENDIX A
Random and Impressionistic Survey on Present Baptismal Teaching and Practices:

A Checklist

1. The primary theological understanding of baptism, is it seen and taught as:
    a. participation in the cross and resurrection of Jesus Christ;
    b. a symbol of conversion, pardoning, and cleansing;
    c. a symbol of the gift of the Holy Spirit;
    d. a symbol of commitment to a life of discipleship;
    e. something else?

2. How does the congregation work with the whole matter of Christian nurture in relation to baptism (cf. paragraph 12 in the WCC "Baptism" document)?

3. Is there a teaching and/or practice of child dedication? Is this understood and practiced primarily as the blessing or dedication of children or as the dedication and commitment of parents?

4. Does the congregation and/or conference recommend or require "rebaptism" of those who may join Mennonite churches after having been baptized in pedobaptist churches?

5. How is the relation between water baptism and baptism of the Spirit understood?

6. What form of baptism is usually used?

7. What is the relationship between baptism and church membership?

8. Are there any trends in the average age at which children of Christian parents are baptized? Do people need to request baptism? Is there a regular instructional class after which young people are more or less "automatically" baptized?

Chapter 15

Baptism in the Mennonite Tradition

This article was originally presented at the conference on "Baptism, Peace, and the State in Reformed and Mennonite Traditions" at the University of Calgary, Alberta, October 12-14, 1989. It appeared in *Mennonite Quarterly Review*, vol. LXIV, no. 3 (July 1990) 230-258 and in *Baptism, Peace and the State in the Reformed and Mennonite Traditions*, Ross T. Bender and Alan P.F. Sell, editors (Wilfrid Laurier University Press, 1991) 37-67. Reprinted by permission.

The topic of this article is misleading if taken at a simple and straightforward surface reading. The title refers to "baptism in the Mennonite tradition" as if baptism were a univocal and coherent concept among Mennonites. The topic further implies that "the Mennonite tradition" with respect to baptism is like a single river that has remained within the same well-worn riverbed and flowed continuously in one direction through the surrounding ecclesial and theological landscapes for the past four and a half centuries. Neither apparent implication would be correct. There have been and continue to be several Mennonite traditions with regard to baptism. And both the understanding and practice of baptism have varied not insignificantly among Mennonites in North America, and even more among Mennonites around the world.[1]

Both differing theological understandings and various practices of baptism itself have comprised the somewhat diverse Mennonite traditions of baptism. The understandings include but are not necessarily limited to (1) variations in focusing upon the divine initiative or upon the believer's response as decisive for baptism; (2) the ways in which the "internal" baptism of the Holy Spirit and the "external" baptism with water relate to each other; (3) the relative emphasis placed upon the individual believer's or the Christian community's role and significance in baptism; (4) whether baptism is by the Holy Spirit, water, and "blood," or primarily by the Holy Spirit and water; (5) the theological connection between baptism and church discipline; and (6) both varied and changing interpretations of "rebirth" or "regeneration" or "conversion" as the presupposition of baptism in Mennonite history. In addition, influences from the contemporary charismatic movement and occasional and scattered tendencies to distinguish between being baptized and becoming a member of the church have further varied understandings of baptism.

The practices among Mennonites with regard to baptism have also varied. Such differences have included (1) whether the preferred or even normative mode of baptism should be immersion, pouring, or sprinkling; (2) the average age at which children born into and nurtured in Christian families may be expected to come to faith and receive baptism;[2] (3) whether being "baptized upon confession of faith" means publicly affirming one's faith in Jesus Christ as Lord and Savior, giving public assent to the faith of the church as articulated in a corporate confessional statement, or writing out one's own faith statement; and (4) the specific content of baptismal liturgies and vows (e.g., whether the baptismal vow includes a commitment to participate in church discipline, the readiness to serve in pastoral ministry if called by the church, etc.). To this list could be added the differing degrees of routinization among some Mennonite groups during different periods of their history, that is, of "instruction" (catechism) of children of the church during their early teen years with the expectation that they would more or less automatically request baptism upon completion of instruction. In other settings such classes have not been formalized but are convened only when young people express personal interest in beginning such instruction with a view toward being baptized.

Reasons for the varieties in baptismal understanding and practice are doubtless multiple. Simple biblicism, the lack of an explicit dogmatic tradition, the consistent ambivalence toward formally binding corporate confessions of faith, the congregationalist-oriented polity, and influences from numerous revival and church renewal movements among Mennonites in several religious, cultural, and national settings have doubtless contributed to these differences. For whatever reason, there are more differences and variations among Mennonites on this presumably distinguishing cardinal practice and doctrine than might be expected on first glance. The closer one looks at varieties of baptism in Mennonite traditions, the more problematic the assumption becomes that *the* Mennonite tradition on baptism has been passed on without spot or wrinkle and can easily be located and summarized for the purposes of ecumenical and theological conversation. These variations would only increase if their implications for other doctrines, such as original sin and free will, were listed in the catalog already assembled.

Nevertheless, Mennonites over the centuries and in many countries have shared a set of common convictions about Christian baptism. These common convictions regarding baptism have, in fact, counted as a distinguishing doctrine and practice for Mennonites, particularly when compared to many, if not most, major Christian traditions. These common convictions have focused on several central understandings and practices. They particularly include both the acceptance of believers baptism as the only valid Christian baptism and the consequent rejection of infant baptism, either a fundamental reinterpretation of or a rejection of a sacramental view of baptism (and the implications of such a view), and the close connection between baptism and beginning a life of Christian discipleship.

Mennonites in one way or another have also usually emphasized "regeneration" as a presupposition of baptism. The several Mennonite traditions have further agreed that unbaptized infants are saved rather than eternally condemned and have frequently commended some pattern of child and/or parent dedication as a alternative to infant baptism for children of Christian parents. And at least until rather recently, Mennonites have generally insisted that persons baptized as infants may become members of a congregation only by being "baptized upon confession of faith" (called "rebaptism" by most major Christian traditions).[3] Finally, Mennonites, like most Christian groups, have traditionally grounded water baptism in the ordinance and institution of Jesus Christ. Simultaneously they have understood its significance in ways which have undergirded believers baptism rather than pedobaptism.

In light of the convictions shared by most Mennonites regarding baptism and in view of the not insignificant variations in baptismal understandings and practices among them, this paper will attempt to represent "the best" regarding baptism in the Mennonite traditions. I have selected the major cues from several sixteenth-century Anabaptist writers, from a few Anabaptist and Mennonite confessional statements (ranging from the sixteenth to the twentieth century), from the results of contemporary "neo-Anabaptist" thought and scholarship, and from some formal as well as informal discussions regarding baptism among Mennonites. In addition to and because of the context of conversation between Reformed and Mennonite traditions for which it has been prepared, this attempt will seek to address several issues that have arisen in the traditional controversies and disputations as well as in more recent ecumenical dialogue between spokespersons of these two ecclesiastical and theological streams.[4]

I consider Balthasar Hubmaier, Pilgram Marpeck, and Dirk Philips the most helpful sixteenth-century Anabaptist and Mennonite writers on baptism. The first book-length treatment on Anabaptist baptism was Rollin S. Armour's *Anabaptist Baptism: A Representative Study* in 1966. Other scholars, including A. J. Beachy, Christof Windhorst, and Wayne Pipkin have since provided insightful interpretations of Anabaptist thought and practice. Further, from among the many Mennonite confessional statements, this article gives primary attention to the traditions represented by the Schleitheim Articles of 1527, the Dordrecht Confession of 1632, the Mennonite Articles of Faith (Ris) of 1766, the Mennonite Confession of Faith of 1963, the Mennonite Brethren Confession of Faith of 1975, and the Confession of Faith in a Mennonite Perspective currently being drafted.[5] And finally, other than several article- or essay-length treatments, Marlin Jeschke's *Believers Baptism for Children of the Church* provides the most comprehensive constructive interpretation of baptism in a "neo-Anabaptist" vein among contemporary North American Mennonites.

Even within this selective reading of baptism in Mennonite traditions, I shall further limit this paper to five specific themes: the scriptural order of baptism, baptism as "sign" or "sacrament" (and in what sense), the relation between baptism and the church, the relation between baptism and discipleship or ethics, and the recipients of baptism. These topics are either of foundational significance for baptism in the Mennonite traditions or of particular relevance for conversation between the Reformed and the Mennonite traditions.

The scriptural order of Christian baptism

In his *On the Christian Baptism of Believers*, completed on June 11, 1525, Balthasar Hubmaier sounded a theme that has recurred with variations throughout Anabaptist and Mennonite annals of baptismal thought and practice.[6] Written in part as a response to Zwingli's *On Baptism, Rebaptism, and Infant Baptism*, Hubmaier's booklet underscored a specific biblical order of Christian baptism "both in regard to the words and the meaning," namely, "(1) word, (2) hearing, (3) faith, (4) baptism, (5) work."[7] Hubmaier contended that this order of baptism appears consistently both in Jesus Christ's institution of baptism according to Matthew 28:18ff. and Mark 16:15ff. as well as in apostolic teaching and practice according to the book of Acts and the Epistles. Baptism follows the proclamation of the gospel, the hearing of the gospel, and the response to it in faith. Moreover, baptism is to be followed by a life of Christian discipleship sustained and encouraged by the community of believers.

This understanding of the scriptural order of baptism from the very beginnings of the Anabaptist movement subsequently gained the broad consensus of Anabaptist and Mennonite groups. Its normative significance was echoed also by Marpeck and Philips in the third and fifth decades of the Anabaptist movement. After commenting on Matthew 28:18ff. Marpeck summarized this view as follows:

> Thus, briefly concerning the order: first, to learn; we are instructed to know the will of God and to believe Christ. When we have been taught that we can know Christ and believe in Him, then it it is time to be baptized, to take off our old fleshly lusts and to put on Christ, a new spiritual life. After that, just as we have agreed, in being baptized, to complete the will of God, we learn, or are instructed, to be obedient in all things, and not again return to sin, as a dog does to his vomit or as a washed sow again to its dirt (2 Pet. 2:22). Let each Christian judge what we say, and especially consider Romans 6, Galatians 3, Ephesians 5, Hebrews 6, 1 Peter 4, 2 Peter 2, John 3, 1 John 5, and other passages of Scripture....[8]

Although the nuances of Marpeck's terminology ("teaching" or "instruction") may differ somewhat from Hubmaier's vocabulary ("proclamation of the gospel" and "teaching"), the foundational order remains the same. In both cases one kind of "teaching" (or preaching) precedes baptism, and another kind of "teaching" follows it. Baptism properly comes in the "middle," between the initial proclamation of the gospel and the instruction in Christian discipleship.

Philips similarly based the order of baptism particularly upon the "ordinance and institution" of Jesus Christ as recorded in Matthew 28 and Mark 16 and confirmed and maintained by the apostles. In his *Concerning the Baptism of Our Lord Jesus Christ* of 1564 he asserted:

> This is the true unalterable ordinance and institution of
> the Lord with respect to baptism just as the words of
> Christ above, quoted out of both Gospels (Matt. 28:19;
> Mark 16:15), clearly bring together and testify. The
> teaching of the gospel before and after baptism must be
> pursued, so that everyone may come to a genuine faith
> through the grace of God and may be baptized, manifest
> his remorse over sin and prove his faith therewith (Acts
> 2:38; 3:19). Thereafter, he must still hear God's word at
> all times and dedicate himself to maintain all the
> commandments of Jesus Christ.[9]

As did Marpeck, Philips thus emphasized that the biblical order of
baptism includes the initial preaching of the gospel, a faith response to
it, the reception of baptism, and continuing instruction in the Christian
life within the context of the believing community.

In grounding their understanding of baptism on the ordinance and
institution of Jesus Christ, these early Anabaptist and Mennonite writers
agreed with the Roman Catholic and Protestant theologians who taught
that Christian baptism had been instituted by the resurrected Lord on the
basis of Matthew 28 and Mark 16. The Anabaptist and Mennonite
teachers, however, interpreted the term "making disciples" in Matthew
28:19 as meaning "preaching" the gospel (and synonymous with
"preach" in Mark 16:15) or "teaching" salvation through Jesus Christ to
nonbelievers, as the necessary precondition to their hearing the word of
salvation and responding to it in faith (or rejecting it). The word in
Matthew 28:20, "teaching," was then interpreted to mean the ongoing
and comprehensive instruction in all of Jesus' teachings and
commandments, within the context of the Christian church, for those
who respond in faith to the gospel and are baptized and thus
incorporated into the believing community. This particular passage,
broadly adopted as a classical baptismal text in the mainstream Christian
traditions, thus provided the incipient Mennonite traditions not only with
a major building block in the theological foundation for baptism, but
also with an essential component of the brief for an order of baptism
which considers believers baptism to be the normative and only
scriptural pattern of valid Christian baptism.

This order of baptism, in which the proclamation of the gospel and
a faith response issue in the request for and the reception of baptism as

incorporation into the church and the beginning of a life of Christian discipleship, represents the foundational consensus of the Mennonite traditions from their origins in the sixteenth century to the present.[10] To be sure, this consensus has been articulated in various ways and has been made more or less explicit in churchly statements and theological writings.

The diversity of formulation has doubtless been conditioned in part by somewhat differing theological perspectives among the Mennonite traditions as well as by the varieties of polemical situations which have contributed to the shaping of these traditions. For example, the importance of having come to faith in Jesus Christ as the prior condition of baptism has at times been emphasized to such a degree that it has overshadowed other dimensions of the biblical order of baptism. Such overstatements have frequently arisen as attempted correctives to what have been perceived to be unacceptable understandings and practices of baptism in the pedobaptist traditions. Furthermore, the influences of pietist, revivalist, and charismatic renewal movements, as well as of more recent cultural influences, have frequently contributed to what sometimes amounts to an overemphasis on the subjective and individual dimensions of Christian baptism in Mennonite teaching and practice."[11] (Nor should one rule out the possibility of an occasional lack of theological balance among Mennonites!) The foundational consensus of the Mennonite traditions regarding the normative scriptural order of Christian baptism thus remains at least as much a challenge to many contemporary Mennonites as to other Christian traditions and communities.

Within the limitations and specific purposes of this presentation, I shall not weigh the detailed exegetical basis for the order of Christian baptism in a believers baptist perspective as outlined above.[12] The basis for this pattern of baptism does not depend only on a particular reading of an isolated text, but is the most clearly attested view generally in the New Testament. Moreover, both the current ecumenical consensus as reflected in the *Baptism, Eucharist, and Ministry* document and the conclusions of the Mennonite-Reformed dialogue in the Netherlands either agree with or are compatible with the view that this order of baptism comes closest to the scriptural pattern.[13]

I would, however, like to make several additional comments on the concept of a normative biblical order of baptism and its potential significance for the understanding and practice of Christian baptism.

Some of these comments will develop the concept as articulated in Mennonite traditions without attempting to further document it in the literature. Some of these comments will unfold several implications that have not necessarily been explicitly articulated in Mennonite writings.

First, the emphasis upon a normative order of baptism means that a specific temporal sequence of events, decisions, and actions belongs to a correct understanding and practice of Christian baptism. The proclamation of and the hearing of the gospel precede water baptism. The baptizand's having come to faith and a request for baptism precede that individual's baptism and incorporation into the Christian church. Participation in the life of the church and walking in the way of Jesus Christ are to follow the commitment made in that direction during the ceremony of baptism.[14]

Second, the emphasis upon a specific order of baptism includes the claim that this order is normative because it is the New Testament order. According to the New Testament, this order has been established and commanded by Jesus Christ and maintained by the apostles. Hubmaier, Marpeck, and Philips as well as more recent representatives of this tradition have based this order on the "ordinance" and "command" of the risen Lord and apostolic practice. "Order" thus connotes not only temporal sequence but also the authoritative pattern. Varieties of experience and diversity of traditions outside and beyond the New Testament should therefore be judged by this pattern rather than fundamentally modify or supplant it. This claim should not be construed to mean that every instance of baptism in the Scriptures explicitly reflects precisely the same experience of baptism or an identical sequence of events in all accompanying details. But the claim does contend that the variations in individual cases tend to reinforce rather than significantly modify or contradict the normative scriptural order.

Third, this emphasis upon the biblical order of baptism presupposes what may be called the structure of baptismal reality. This emphasis thus assumes that the various "images" of baptism in the New Testament are posited upon and reflect this pattern of baptism.[15] Any theological interpretation of Christian baptism should therefore correspond to the baptismal reality embedded in this order rather than seek to provide the rationale for a significantly different order of baptism.

For example, a theological understanding of the priority of divine grace that would issue in an order of baptism in which water baptism may precede the baptizand's faith response to the proclamation of the gospel would, from this perspective, be seen to reflect both a different baptismal reality and a qualitatively different interpretation of divine grace than those reflected in the New Testament. Similarly, an interpretation of baptism as the incorporation of persons into the Christian church in such a way that baptism may precede the baptizand's declared intention to begin a life of discipleship and to begin participation in the church as the body of Christ would imply both a fundamentally different baptismal reality and a qualitatively different ecclesiology and understanding of Christian life and ethics than those presupposed and articulated in the New Testament. In either case, theological interpretations of the priority of divine grace, the nature of the Christian church, and Christian ethics which may claim scriptural foundations should also be consistent with the biblical order of baptism as the normative structure of baptismal reality.

Fourth and finally, the biblical order of baptism points to an appropriate relation between the "objective" and "subjective" dimensions of Christian baptism.[16] Mennonite traditions have frequently given considerable—and most likely excessive—attention to the subjective aspects of baptism. This emphasis has sought to maintain the biblical order of baptism and to correct what have been seen as the deviant and excessive emphases upon the so-called objective side of baptism by the mainstream traditions since the fourth and fifth centuries. But the influences of Zwingli and some mystic traditions upon sixteenth-century Anabaptists and Mennonites, the traditional believers baptist insistence upon personally coming to faith and confessing faith prior to being baptized, the reactions to and suspicions of sacramentalism in all forms, and the subsequent influences of pietism, revivalism, and modern Western individualism have doubtless contributed to an all-too-frequent exaggerated preoccupation with the subjective, and an all-too-frequent neglect of the objective, aspects of baptism. The concept of a normative biblical order of baptism, however, is here meant to connote a certain "objectivity" and to include both objective and subjective as well as individual and corporate dimensions.

I have so far spoken somewhat vaguely in terms of a "normative structure of baptismal reality" and of "an appropriate balance between the objective and subjective dimensions of Christian baptism" in order to temporarily avoid such concepts as sacrament, sign, and symbol. In the following sections I shall seek to summarize and develop the further aspects of believers baptism according to Mennonite traditions in ways which join the issues implied by sacramental and other-than-sacramental understandings of baptism.

Baptism as sacrament or sign

Although the various Mennonite traditions have frequently differed on the theological categories which they have used to speak about baptism, they have shared a common rejection of traditional sacramental understandings and practice. During the last three centuries this common stance has usually included a strong preference for an alternative theological vocabulary as well. Terms such as "ordinance," "sign," and "symbol" have become commonplace and have almost entirely replaced the concept of sacrament. Particularly the concept of mystery in the theological sense remains an almost incomprehensible and unknown "mystery" in the ordinary sense among Mennonite and broader believers church groups.

In the early decades of the Anabaptist and Mennonite movements, however, the term "sacrament" was sometimes reinterpreted as well as avoided. The early reinterpretation of sacrament is instructive for understanding the core convictions regarding baptism in the Mennonite traditions and for evaluating the theological validity of their formulations.

The early Anabaptist and Mennonite teachers and groups who did refer to baptism as a sacrament explicitly rejected the understanding of sacrament as a means of grace *ex opere operato*, which can take place quite independently of faith. They interpreted sacrament rather in the sense of a covenant or a solemn pledge of loyalty on the basis of the term's classical meaning in Latin.[17] Thus understood, the term underscored their view of the biblical order of baptism, which includes a public commitment to follow Jesus Christ in life as a consequence of having come to and confessed faith in him. In addition, they found confirmation for this concept of sacrament as a pledge or covenant in the words of a widely used baptismal text among them, namely, 1 Peter 3:21, which refers to baptism as the "pledge of a good conscience to God."

Among those who reinterpreted the traditional concept of baptism as a sacrament, Pilgram Marpeck was perhaps the one who gave it the most substantive theological meaning. He also sought to incorporate both the subjective and the objective dimensions of Christian baptism into his reinterpretation of sacrament.[18]

Marpeck acknowledged that the term is never used in the Scriptures to refer to baptism. But he proposed that it can be used correctly in relation to baptism if taken in its ancient and natural meaning, namely, as an oath or pledge that "...refers to an event that is special and holy or a work that has that kind of connotation...."

The relation between the perceptible expression of the pledge and that to which it refers can be illustrated by the example of a knight who commits himself to serve his lord in battle and raises his finger in making this oath. The raising of the finger is not the fighting nor the endurance during the battle nor the victorious outcome of the battle. The "action" is rather the "...covenant, made in the firm hope that, according to the command and the desire of his Lord, he will diligently attack the enemy of his Lord, even risking his life until death." Marpeck thus suggested that baptism is a sacrament in the sense that it is the visible expression of the believer's pledge or covenant of faithfulness to Jesus Christ in life.

But baptism as a sacrament refers not only to the believer's part in this covenant of faith. Baptism also refers to the divine initiative of grace which initiates and establishes this covenant. Marpeck illustrated this aspect of baptism with an analogy between the covenantal transaction of which baptism is a sign and the way in which friends give and receive gifts. When this happens,

> ...all that is done thereby is to indicate the friendliness, love, and faithfulness of those who give them toward those who receive them. In the same way, love and faithfulness are not the gifts themselves but are, rather, the heart which the gifts indicate. Unity and trust are indicated to the receiver of the gifts, and all goodness, love, friendliness, and faithfulness to the one who gives it. Similarly, the word sacrament has no other meaning.... He who receives the gift receives that for which it was given: sanctification.... The gift must come spontaneously [*auss freier herligkeyt*] as an act of love and an inclined will, and it must come from one who could very well neglect it without any shame or disrespect.... He who receives the gift reciprocates in turn with his whole heart and being, and that is called sanctification.[19]

The "covenant of a good conscience with God" is thus established by the grace of God, which is grounded purely in itself. The believer's commitment and pledge is the grateful acceptance of this divine gift and the desire to use it according to the intention for which it has been given. Water baptism as a sign of the believer's commitment to this covenantal transaction thus presupposes the action of divine grace in initiating the covenant, forgiving the sinner and enabling the believer to respond by committing him- or herself to the purpose for which God has given the covenant.

This emphasis upon both the prior action of divine grace and the necessity of a personal faith commitment in relation to the baptismal covenant has generally been shared in the Anabaptist and Mennonite traditions. To be sure, the usual insistence upon repentance, confession, and the commitment of faith has not infrequently overshadowed the emphasis upon the priority of grace. Sometimes repentance as belonging to the beginning of the saving process and discipleship to its continuance was stressed so much that it sounded to Protestant ears as if repentance and good works were being made the necessary means for meriting God's grace.

Nevertheless, contemporary scholarship has shown that the early Mennonite and Anabaptist traditions usually acknowledged that the ability and the will to turn to God in faith are a gift of God in Christ rather than an ability resident in human beings apart from divine grace.[20] This traditional view has continued to be affirmed by Mennonite teachers and theologians. For example, Marlin Jeschke reiterates the point in his recent *Believers Baptism for Children of the Church*:

> In the New Testament baptism is...always considered the work of divine grace. Baptism represents the activity of God's Word and Spirit in creating spiritual life. And baptism is the church's overt recognition of this prior work of God, this act of prevenient grace.[21]

Even though both the Mennonite and Protestant traditions can therefore generally agree on the priority and the gift-quality of divine grace in the relationship between grace and the response of faith, the nature of God's grace and its effects in the lives of Christian believers have usually been understood differently by these traditions.

The preceding quote from Jeschke reflects the understanding broadly shared by the Anabaptist and Mennonite traditions that God's grace is not only expressed in a declaration of forgiveness but is primarily a creative and transforming power which regenerates and renews sinful human beings (and will one day issue in the "creation of a new heaven and a new earth"). This view has provided the basis for expecting grace to produce a significant and even visible transformation of character, conduct, and relationships in the believers and in the church as a community in the midst of the unbelieving world. In this regard they have differed from the Protestant traditions that have understood grace primarily in terms of God's forgiveness and acceptance, granted through justification, which restores fallen human nature.

The interpretation of baptism as a sacrament in the Anabaptist tradition thus shares with the majority Protestant traditions the assumption that God's graceful initiative precedes and calls forth the believer's faith and commitment. Because divine grace is primarily a power which restores fallen human nature and enables the response of obedient faith, the sacramental significance of baptism focuses upon the believer's confession of faith and pledge. Any understanding of baptism which can be enacted not only independently of the believing response of faith and commitment, but even without emphasizing that the believing response and commitment is an essential part of the divinely initiated covenantal transaction of which baptism is the sign, represents a different understanding of both divine grace and sacramental reality. Baptism is thus a sign of God's new creation and new order, not only of God's restoration of a fallen creation and a fallen order. Because baptism witnesses to the renewal of human nature through divine grace, the concept of baptism as a sacrament focuses on the believer's commitment and pledge to live according to God's new creation in Christ as the effect of divine grace.[22]

The Anabaptist/Mennonite rejection of sacraments in the traditional sense and the reinterpretation of sacrament has led to somewhat diverse ways of theologically understanding and formulating how the grace made available in Jesus Christ is communicated to the believers. Sometimes this communication has been formulated primarily in terms of the believers being baptized by Christ "inwardly" with the Holy Spirit. Sometimes it has been couched primarily in terms of the believers hearing the Word of God, which was made incarnate in Jesus and is proclaimed to us.[23]

In either case, however, the Anabaptist and Mennonite traditions did not intend to separate Word and Spirit any more than the mainstream Protestant traditions, even though there have doubtless been differences of emphases between them. According to the Reformed tradition, the Spirit is understood particularly as the interpreter of the Word. This orientation accordingly stresses the relation of baptism to the proclaimed Word of forgiveness as the means of communicating divine grace to the believer, which is confirmed by the Holy Spirit. According to the Mennnonite and Anabaptist traditions, the Spirit, above all, "makes the Word become reality in the life of the believer and in that of the congregation."[24] This emphasis is quite consistent with their concept of grace as a creative and transforming power at work in the lives of the believers and the believing community. This emphasis accordingly focuses—after presupposing the dimension of forgiveness—on the relation of baptism to the transforming action of the Holy Spirit in the believing community and in the believer in both the community's and the believer's response to the grace of God incarnate in Jesus Christ the Word as known in the Scriptures.

Baptism may thus be understood as the visible sign and witness of that covenantal transaction which is initiated and established by God's grace in Jesus Christ and issues in the believer's confession of faith in and commitment to Jesus Christ and incorporation into the Christian church. Baptism does not effect the communication of this covenantal transaction apart from the individual's faith and commitment. But baptism does witness to, correspond to, and participate in this covenantal transaction when the baptismal candidate's faith and commitment are expressed and confirmed by the baptizing church.[25]

Baptism as incorporation and entry into the church

As the visible mark of entry and incorporation into the Christian community, baptism can be properly understood only in relation to the reality of the Christian church. Or to phrase the point somewhat differently, the theology and practice of baptism should be consistent with a corresponding ecclesiology—and a given ecclesiology implies and brings with it a corresponding practice and view of baptism. The believers baptist tradition in a Mennonite perspective corresponds to an identifiable understanding of the church and proposes that this understanding of the church is consistent with the order and reality of baptism as summarized in the two previous sections of this essay.

In particular, believers baptism corresponds to an understanding of the church in which the church is by definition a missionary community in the midst of a still-unbelieving world. Furthermore, by virtue of its existence as a missionary community the church is grounded upon the work of the Holy Spirit, who has called it into being and sustains it, rather than built upon the continuities of familial or ethnic or national peoplehood. This means that baptism signals the incorporation and entry into the society of those who are being redeemed through the power of the Holy Spirit and through faith in Christ, and in which the divisions of family and race and gender and class are relativized and reconciled in him. The churchly reality which coincides with the normative order and reality of baptism therefore represents a qualitatively different society than the communities which extend and reinforce familial, national, class, and other such bonds.

In contemporary ecumenical theology it has become more or less commonplace to refer to the church as a missionary community. This emphasis doubtless derives from the renewal of a biblical vision of God's people, from the rise of the modern missionary movement, from the dechristianization of the West, and from the legal disengagement of church and state in post-Enlightenment, Western societies.

With respect to the question of Christian baptism, the broader ecumenical emphasis upon the church as a missionary community has meant a growing awareness and theological articulation of the missionary dimension of baptism in the sense that baptism marks the boundaries of the faith community in distinction to those of the entire society or national body and in the sense that the continuing existence of the Christian church depends upon inviting nonbelievers to faith in Jesus Christ. This emphasis has also meant a growing awareness and appreciation of the minority and missionary stance of the Christian churches in many countries which have never been nominally Christian and in some cases are avowedly non- or even anti-Christian. Traces of this growing appreciation for the church as a missionary community have shown up in ecumenical conversations on baptism and contributed to some measure of convergence between believers baptist and pedobaptist perspectives.[26]

The sociological referent for baptism which remains controversial between the pedobaptist and believers baptist traditions, however, is the situation of the Christian family in relation to the church as a community of believers. The current practice of infant baptism finds a major theological justification in the argument that a child of Christian parents is surrounded by the faith of the parents (and that of the Christian community) in a way which significantly differs from the situation of a child born to non-Christian parents. Up to this point the believers baptist traditions would doubtless agree. From their perspective, however, the move from acknowledging a significant difference in the two situations to justifying infant baptism on the basis of that difference amounts to the shift from one concept of the Christian church to a qualitatively different ecclesiology, namely, from the church as a faith community to the church as an ethnic community (or at best a confusing mixture of the two). Even the commendable reservations about the frequent "apparently indiscriminate" baptismal practice of many large majority churches in North America and Europe and the laudable call to "rediscover" the "continuing call of Christian nurture" do not fundamentally alter this ecclesiological issue.[27] The missionary character of the church necessarily implies that the church is a faith community rather than an ethnic community, and calls for an ecclesiology and an accompanying baptismal practice that witnesses to and reinforces rather than undermines this reality.[28]

In addition to signaling the missionary character of the Christian community, baptism marks the candidate's entry and incorporation into the Christian church. As Jeschke observes:

> The believer is baptized by the church, not self-baptized. To begin with, he receives the invitation of the gospel from someone who is already a member of the body of Christ. And then it is the church that hears and recognizes the authenticity of the confession of faith. And finally baptism according to biblical thought entails binding oneself to the regenerate assembly.[29]

Baptism as the sign of the covenantal transaction which issues in the identification of a believer with Christ necessarily includes entry and incorporation into the Christian community as the concrete and visible expression of the body of Christ.

Although generally agreeing on the linking of baptism with church membership, Mennonite traditions have differed in the emphasis they have placed upon this connection and the ways in which it has been theologically articulated. One line of thought has emphasized the spiritual and individual aspects of the connection between baptism and the church by stressing the fundamental significance of the believer's identification with Christ. Another has stressed the visible and corporate dimensions of this connection by emphasizing the incorporation of the believer into the Christian community as the visible church.

Dirk Philips was an early representative voice of the first view. Although he assumed, and occasionally explicitly asserted, that entry into the visible church is through baptism, he loosened this connection to some degree by repeatedly emphasizing the importance of the individual and spiritual dimensions in the relation of the believer to the body of Christ. In his *Concerning the Baptism of Our Lord Jesus Christ*, for example, he stressed that

> ...faith is a gift of the Holy Spirit through which all believers
> are gathered into one body, and thereupon they are baptized as
> a sign and proof of the true inner being and the spiritual
> fellowship they have with Christ and all the holy ones.[30]

This orientation has been at home primarily in the Dutch Mennonite tradition and extensions of it into other Mennonite groups over the centuries. Within the North American and European contexts it has been reinforced and at times distorted by the influences of revivalism and pietism as well as Western individualisn.[31]

Pilgram Marpek is a representative early spokesperson for the line of thought which stresses the corporate and visible aspects of the connnection between baptism and becoming a member of the church. In his *Admonition of 1542* he concluded his summary of baptism as follows:

> Therefore, whoever wants to be a member of Christ's church
> must first enter through baptism, through faith in Christ, and
> must lead a new life in obedience to the Word, shunning and
> avoiding all evil through the true ban of Christ. This,
> summarized, is the true church of Christ, no matter where it is
> in the world, no matter how many or how few members there
> are in the world. They lead an external life, that is, in baptism,

teaching, the ban, and communion of Christ, and they walk in
righteousness and truth.[32]

Similar understandings have been at home primarily among the
Swiss and South German traditions and their extensions into other
Mennonite groups. In the North American context this orientation has
been aided and abetted by the use of the Dordrecht Confession of 1632
(Dutch!) among these groups. In its articles on baptism and the church
the Dordrecht Confession also underscores the significance of baptism
as incorporation into the visible church. This stance has doubtless been
both reinforced and distorted by the frequently strong ethnic character of
European and North American Mennonite groups.

Neither of these traditional emphases has intended to divorce the
individual from the corporate, nor the spiritual from the visible, aspects
of the connection between baptism and church membership. And even
though the link between church membership and baptism has been
couched in different theological terms and weighted differently by the
various Mennonite traditions, the primary concerns in this regard would
have been to affirm baptism as the sign of the believer's becoming a
member of the church and to strike a proper theological and practical
balance between the individual and corporate aspects of baptism. In any
case, baptism as incorporation and entry into the church upon the
baptizand's confession of faith remains a constitutive dimension of
baptism in a believers baptist perspective as represented, however well
or poorly, by the Mennonite traditions.[33]

In addition to marking the entry and incorporation of believers into
the church and corresponding to the missionary character of the church
as a faith community, baptism in a believers baptist perspective focuses
on the constitutive importance of the individual believer's faith in
relation to the faith of the believing community. For this reason
Mennonites and others have consistently emphasized that the "faith of
the church" should be interpreted in ways which invite, encourage, and
support the individual's coming to faith and requesting baptism rather
than in ways which amount to having the "faith of the church" stand in
for an individual's baptism prior to his or her coming to faith.

The baptism section of the *Baptism, Eucharist, and Ministry*
document states that the "practice of infant baptism emphasizes the
corporate faith and the faith which the child shares with its parents...."[34]
From a believers baptist perspective the justification of this practice on

the grounds that the faith of the church surrounds the child of Christian parents obscures beyond recognition how it is that the child may come to "share" the faith of the church and the faith of its parents. Furthermore, this rationale appears not to acknowledge, other than by default, that the baptized child may not come to actually share the faith of the church and its parents.[35] Simultaneously, the *Baptism, Eucharist, and Ministry* document's emphasis on the Christian nurture of children born to Christian parents in both the home and the church, and on the "constant requirement of a continuing growth of personal response in faith," can only be affirmed from a Mennonite perspective. But the Christian nurture of children takes place in the hope that they will themselves appropriate the faith of the believing community and receive baptism on that basis. In this sense the faith of the church precedes and encourages the faith of the individual but cannot substitute for it.[36]

The emphasis upon the faith of the individual believer in contrast to the faith of the church has sometimes been exaggerated among believers baptist groups. This happens when a believer's confession of faith is taken to be almost exclusively a confession of individual faith rather than including, at least in significant measure, the appropriation of the faith stance of the believing community.

For a variety of reasons (or even lack of reasons) Mennonites sometimes have also been susceptible to emphasizing the individual's faith at the cost of the faith of the church in relation to baptism. Among the Dutch Mennonites this has taken the form of individuals writing and making their own personal confession of faith on the occasion of being baptized. Among some North American Mennonite groups there are currently tendencies for baptismal candidates to "say something about" their faith during the ceremony without necessarily including any explicit references to the corporate faith of the believing community. Such tendencies should, however, hardly be considered endemic to a believers baptist orientation rightly understood and practiced. They do not correspond well either to the missionary character of the church or to becoming a member of the faith community . And they tend to replace a personal confession of faith which the believing community also acknowledges as an appropriation of its corporate faith, with a predominantly individual expression of faith the community is asked to ratify.

The theology and practice of valid Christian baptism thus corresponds to an ecclesiology which includes the understanding of the church as a missionary community, according to which baptism marks the entry and incorporation into the church, and in which the individual believer's coming to faith includes an appropriation of the faith of the church.

Baptism and the pledge to mutual support and discipline

By now it will have become evident that the various Anabaptist and Mennonite understandings of baptism have consistently included an ethical orientation. The normative order of baptism concludes with the believer's declared intention to begin a life of discipleship as enabled by the Holy Spirit. The reinterpretation of sacrament sees baptism as the sign in which the believer makes a holy commitment in response to God's transforming grace in Jesus Christ. The view of baptism as entry and incorporation into the Christian church as a faith community in which believers are called to live out their new humanity in Christ implies an ethical orientation in which the divisions of ethnic and racial and national bonds lose the status of primary moral obligations. As we have seen, this ethical orientation is certainly not the entire story of baptism. But the commitment to "follow Christ in life" has been linked with baptism among Mennonites since the beginnings of the Anabaptist movement in the sixteenth century.

In his paper on "The Baptismal Theology of Balthasar Hubmaier" Wayne Pipkin suggests that the Anabaptist "emphasis on discipleship may well be the distinctive element in believers baptism."[37] Whether or not it is *the* distinctive element, discipleship certainly constitutes a significant dimension of Christian baptism in a believers baptist perspective. Indeed, any attempt to describe and evaluate the common convictions of the Anabaptist and Mennonite traditions on Christian baptism without attention to discipleship as foundational for both the understanding and practice of baptism would be seriously remiss. Discipleship presupposes the forgiveness of sin and the transforming power of grace in the believer. Discipleship unfolds the ethical implications of baptism as a sign of new life in Christ. And discipleship links both of these dimensions with an understanding of the church as the community of mutual support and discipline for those whose sins have been forgiven and who have committed themselves to walk in newness of life.[38]

Of the ways in which baptism is linked to Christian ethical concerns, perhaps the most significant is the connection between baptism and discipline. The early Anabaptist and Mennonite vocabularies referred to congregational discipline as "fraternal admonition" or "the ban" on the basis of Matthew 18:15ff., a classical text for church discipline. The practical and theological connection between baptism and mutual discipline goes back to the origins (and even "pre-origins") of the Anabaptist movement.

Several months before the first believers baptisms took place in Zurich, Conrad Grebel and his associates contended in their letter to Thomas Müntzer that

> ...without Christ's rule of binding and loosing, even an adult should not be baptized. The Scriptures describe baptism for us, that it signifies the washing away of sins by faith and the blood of Christ (that the nature of the baptized and believing one is changing before and after), that it signifies one has died and shall (die) to sin and walks in newness of life and Spirit and one will surely be saved if one through the inward baptism lives the faith according to this meaning....[39]

By "Christ's rule of binding and loosing" Grebel meant the procedure outlined in Matthew 18:15-18 for accountability and mutual discipline among the followers of Christ. He had doubtless learned from Zwingli to understand this "rule of binding and loosing" as the basis for the congregation's authority to make binding decisions in doctrinal and ethical matters. Making—or at least maintaining—the connection between baptism and discipline appears, however, to have arisen among the radical reformers like Grebel and his circle.

For the early Anabaptist and Mennonite movements, congregational discipline became an essential means of renewing the church and encouraging a life of Christian discipleship in both its corporate and individual expressions. Furthermore, the "rule of Christ" was understood as the alternative to the rule of the sword used to maintain and enforce the standards of the "world." As the rule of Christ's love, congregational discipline constitutes among believers the alternative to the rule of coercion and violence in the civil community.[40]

For these reasons, mutual address and discipline constituted a key mark of the true church and took on an importance equal to or at least similar to baptism and the Lord's Supper. The Schleitheim Articles of 1527 exemplify this significance of discipline and its relation to baptism (as well as to the Lord's Supper). The first three articles record consensus on baptism, congregational discipline, and the Lord's Supper, in that order. Using the term "ban" for congregational discipline, Article 11 states:

> The ban shall be employed with all those who have given themselves over to the Lord, to walk after [Him] in His commandments; those who have been baptized into the one body of Christ, and let themselves be called brothers or sisters, and still somehow slip and fall into error and sin.... The same [shall] be warned twice privately and the third time be publicly admonished before the entire congregation according to the command of Christ (Mt. 18).[41]

Balthasar Hubmaier was the first to give the relationship between baptism and mutual discipline liturgical shape by including a pledge to participate in mutual accountability and support in the actual baptismal ceremony. According to his "A Form for Water Baptism," the minister should first ask the baptismal candidate to confess his or her faith in question-and-answer form and in terms of the Apostles' Creed. After the candidate has responded affirmatively to each of the three articles in the creed, the minister should ask whether he or she renounces the devil. After an affirmative response to this question the minister should inquire about the candidate's commitment to walk in newness of life and to give and receive counsel:

> "Will you henceforth lead your life and walk according to the Word of Christ, as he gives you grace: So speak":
> "I will."
> "If now you should sin and your brother knows it, will you let him admonish you once, twice, and the third time before the church, and willingly and obediently accept fraternal admonition, if so speak":
> "I will."
> "Do you desire now upon this faith and pledge to be baptized in water according to the institution of Christ, incorporated and thereby counted in the visible Christian church, for the forgiveness of your sins, if so speak":
> "I desire it in the power of God."[42]

Although Mennonites have never adopted a uniform liturgical order, traces of a pledge to walk in Christian obedience and to participate in mutual discipline have persisted in their understandings and practice of baptism. In a recent *Minister's Manual* jointly published and recommended by the two largest North American Mennonite groups, two of the three suggested forms of baptism solicit, among other things, a response to the question of whether the believer is "willing to give and receive counsel" in the congregation.[43] In both cases the candidate is baptized after his or her affirmative response to this question.

According to Hubmaier, the theological rationale for linking with baptism the commitment to participate in mutual discipline and support is related both to the nature of the church and to sin. The church is the body of those who have been forgiven and who have committed themselves to live as disciples of Christ. Living according to the way of Christ includes adopting his "rule" for mutual correction in the body of believers. Baptism as the sign of entering into and being incorporated into the body of believers therefore includes declaring one's intention to accept this "rule." The "authority" of one member to "admonish another" comes from the "baptismal commitment" in which a person "subjected" him- or herself "to the church and all her members."[44] In this sense the entering into mutual support and discipline shares in the voluntary character of believers baptism in response to the divine initiative of grace which creates the church as the new community of the redeemed. In addition to this ecclesiological basis for connecting discipline and baptism, discipline is an essential means by which sin is addressed, ongoing forgiveness and reconciliation are experienced, and mutual support and correction are implemented in the community of believers.

Although congregational discipline in one form or another has remained a major concern for Mennonite understandings and practice among most groups, at least until recent decades, relatively little attention has been given to its theological and liturgical significance for baptism and to baptism's connection to it beyond what had already been articulated by Hubmaier.[45] As a consequence, baptism and discipline have not infrequently been understood and practiced as two basic, but separate, characteristics of the church. In such instances the loss of a substantive theological vision for including the commitment to participate in a process of mutual discipline and support in the congregation has most likely contributed either to excessively individualistic understandings of baptism or to legalistic practices of discipline or to both.

Regaining and elaborating something of this vision could be crucial for the churches in today's world. Individualism and secularism are making their inroads among Mennonite and other believers church groups in which baptism is not explicitly linked to mutual support and address. In addition to facing similar challenges, the majority churches can no longer assume an identity between themselves and the surrounding society. If our churches are to be characterized by a missionary and an ethical orientation in today's pluralistic societies, they may very well need to rediscover and regain a theology and practice of supportive congregational accountability and discipline, including its connection to Christian baptism.

The recipients of baptism

To say that believers baptism and the rejection of infant baptism have been common tenets of Anabaptist and Mennonite baptismal understandings and practice would be to state the obvious. But to assume that the justification for this twofold consensus hinges *only* upon a narrowly defined understanding of baptizing those who can "make a personal confession of faith" should, by now, be considerably less obvious.

According to the biblical order, valid baptism follows the response of faith to the proclamation of the gospel and the renewing work of the Holy Spirit in the person who requests baptism. The biblical order is grounded in the reality of the covenantal transaction which issues in the beginning of Christian life. This covenantal transaction has been initiated and established by the grace of God, which in turn enables the free response of the person coming to faith. Moreover, divine grace is expressed not only by God's forgiving and accepting the person for Christ's sake, but also in transforming the person into a member of Christ's body and enabling the person to live as a follower of Christ. For that reason, baptism includes both the believer's confession of faith and a commitment to a life of discipleship.

The confession of faith and the commitment to a life of discipleship include both individual and corporate dimensions. Baptism is therefore the sign of entry and incorporation into the church as the body of Christ. The character of the church as a missionary and faith community rather than an ethnic or national community means that the church baptizes those who have come to faith in Jesus Christ irrespective of their familial, social, or national adherence. And the nature of the church as the community which is called to extend forgiveness and reconciliation as well as to provide mutual address and discipline in the name of Christ means that baptism includes the readiness and commitment to participate in that calling. The acceptance of believers baptism and the rejection of infant baptism in the Mennonite traditions has been based upon several foundational characteristics of the Christian church as well as upon the reality of God's grace and human response of obedient faith.

The issue of who may receive baptism has been answered among Mennonites primarily on the basis of the foregoing considerations. The question of what constitutes valid or spurious Christian baptism has therefore not usually been answered by stipulating criteria having to do with ministerial office, mode of water baptism, or baptismal liturgy.[46]

Whether to acknowledge the baptism of infants as a valid baptism has been raised among contemporary Mennonites primarily in the practical terms of whether to accept persons baptized as infants by other churches into the membership of Mennonite congregations. North American Mennonite congregations, at least until recently, have generally assumed the resolution of this matter to be an open-and-shut case: because infant baptism does not meet the normative biblical and theological criteria for Christian baptism, the candidate may become a member only upon "confession of faith" *and baptism*. Strictly speaking, this has not been understood as amounting to requiring rebaptism, because infant baptism by definition would not be considered a valid baptism.

More recently a number of congregations have begun to differentiate between persons who were baptized as infants but did not subsequently confess their faith in a public way and persons who, though baptized as infants, have at some point publicly confessed their faith and have continued to lead a Christian life. Some congregations have left it to individuals in the latter category to decide whether they wish to request baptism in becoming members or whether they desire to become members without baptism by publicly acknowledging that they are in harmony with Mennonite teachings and church practices.[47]

The present draft for a new Confession of Faith in Mennonite Perspective also suggests that congregations "may consider transfer of membership unaccompanied by baptism" for persons in this category.[48]

This suggestion has thus far proven to be quite controversial. Some pastors and church leaders see in the proposal an unwelcome compromise of a foundational principle, for which many early Anabaptists and Mennonites suffered persecution and death. Others have expressed support for the proposal on the basis of both historical and theological reasons. In any case, from a Mennonite perspective the major problem amounts to breaking apart the various elements of baptism, which belong together in a particular way. Neither baptizing infants fifteen years before they come to faith and begin to participate in the life and work of the church nor baptizing believers ten years after they have appropriated the Christian faith and been participating in the witness and service of the church clearly put together all the pieces of Christian baptism which belong together.

This brokenness may itself suggest that the baptismal issue is no longer as divisive as it was when it contributed to divisions in the sixteenth-century reformation movements that have persisted until the present time. Nevertheless, this brokenness will doubtless remain until the further reformation of the churches' baptismal traditions has again brought them into agreement with the apostolic tradition. Karl Barth was most likely correct in not expecting "the full healing of the Church from advances in the matter of infant baptism." Simultaneously, he was most likely also correct with what appear to be a series of rhetorical questions in the preface to his volume on baptism:

> ...how can the church be or become again...an essentially missionary and mature rather than immature Church, so long as it...continues to dispense the water of baptism with the same undiscriminating generosity as it has now done for centuries? How can it be credible to the rest of the world so long as it persists in thinking that it can pacify its concern for recruitment of personnel in this way which is responsible neither to God, to its own message, nor to those who live either externally or internally *extra muros*? Of what help will the best ecclesiology be to us so long as there is obstinate evasion of long overdue reform at this small but practically decisive point?[49]

[1] See, e g., "Baptism," *ME*, 1, 224-28; and my article "The Mennonites," *In Baptism and Church: A Believers' Church Vision*, ed. Merle D. Strege (Sagamore Books, 1986), 151ff. The following bibliographies list approximately 280 entries on baptism: *A Bibliography of Anabaptism, 1520-1630*, comp. Hans J. Hillerbrand (Institute of Mennonite Studies, 1962); and *Mennonite Bibliography*, 1631-1961, comp. Nelson P. Springer and A. J. Klassen, 2 vols. (Herald Press, 1977).

[2] This age has varied among Mennonite groups, from five or six years of age among some North American Mennonites influenced by the "child evangelism" movement before the mid-twentieth century, to the thirties and forties among the Dutch Mennonites. For the most part, the ages of those baptized in their youth in North American congregations have gone up during the last few decades. The median age of baptism in the major North American Mennonite groups in the early 1970s was 14.9. See J. Howard Kauffman and Leland Harder, *Anabaptists Four Centuries Later* (Herald Press, 1975) 70-72.

[3] Because of its significance for ecumenical conversation and interchurch relations, I will return to this issue later. A *few* congregations and church leaders have either made exceptions to this general rule, left the matter up to the candidate for baptism, or proposed reconsideration of the traditional practice. A preliminary draft of a commentary to the article on baptism in a confession of faith being developed cooperatively by the General Conference Mennonite Church and the Mennonite Church in North America suggests: "If applicants for membership who were baptized as infants have since publicly confessed or confirmed faith in Jesus Christ, have long been living a life of faith and Christian witness, have been actively participating in a Christian congregation, and commit themselves henceforth to teach and practice baptism for those of an age of accountability who freely request it, churches may consider the transfer of membership unaccompanied by baptism. These exceptions tend, however, to confirm the current status of this expectation as a common conviction among Mennonites." (Editor's note: This "exceptional" statement was dropped during the testing phase of this confession of faith.)

[4] See *Mennonites and Reformed in Dialogue*, ed. Hans Georg vom Berg et. al., Studies from the World Alliance of Reformed Churches, Vll (Mennonite World Conference, 1986).

[5] These statements, except the confession currently being drafted, are reprinted in Howard John Loewen, *One Lord, One Church, One Hope, and One God: Mennonite Confessions of Faith* (Institute of Mennonite Studies, 1985). Schleitheim and Dordrecht are also included in *Creeds of the Church*, ed. John Leith, 3rd ed. (John Knox Press, 1982) 281ff.

[6] In *Balthasar Hubmaier: Theologian of Anabaptism*, trans. and ed. H. Wayne Pipkin and John H. Yoder (Herald Press, 1989) 95-145. See also Rollin Stely Armour, *Anabaptist Baptism: A Representative Study* (Herald Press, 1966), 19-

57; Christof Windhorst, *Täuferisches Taufverständnis: Balthasar Hubmaiers Lehre zwischen traditioneller und reformatorischer Theologie*, (E. J. Brill, 1976); and H. Wayne Pipkin, "The Baptismal Theology of Balthasar Hubmaier," *Mennonite Quarterly Review* VLXV (January 1991) 34-53.

[7] Hubmaier, *On the Christian Baptism of Believers*, in Pipkin and Yoder, 129.

[8] The Admonition of 1542, in *The Writings of Pilgram Marpeck*, trans. and ed. William Klassen and Walter Klasssen, Classics of the Radical Reformation, II (Herald Press, 1978) 183.

[9] Dirk Philips, *Concerning the Baptism of Our Lord Jesus Christ*, in *Bibliotheca Reformatoria Neerlandica, ed.* S. Cramer and F. Pijper, X (The Hague: Martinus Nijhoff, 1914), 69ff.; translation according to a forthcoming book by C. J. Dyck, Associated Mennonite Biblical Seminaries, p. 3.

[10] See, e.g., the Schleitheim Articles of 1527, Article I; the Dordrecht Confession of 1632, Articles V and Vll; the Mennonite Articles of Faith (Ris) of 1766, Article XXV; the Glaubensbekenntnis der Mennoniten in Canada of 1930, Article IX, The Mennonite Confession of Faith of 1963, Articles VIII and XI; and the Mennonite Brethren Confession of Faith of 1975, Articles Vll and IX— all in Loewen, 79, 64f., 97f., 306, 75f, 176f. The same order is reflected in Marlin Jeschke, *Believers Baptism for Children of the Church* (Herald Press, 1983) 41ff.

[11] The Reformed expressions of concern for giving the "faith of the Church" its appropriate weight and for avoiding an excessively "individualistic faith" merit the serious attention of believers baptist traditions. *Mennonites and Reformed in Dialogue,* 69. See *Baptists and Reformed in Dialogue* (World Alliance of Reformed Churches, 1983) 18f.; and the section of this essay below on "Baptism as Incorporation and Entry into the Church."

[12] For example, contemporary biblical scholarship would suggest that some aspects of traditional Roman Catholic, Protestant, and Mennonite interpretations of Matthew 28:18f. may require revision and even correction. Karl Barth, among others, notes the reservations which should be brought to bear upon the traditional interpretations of the passage. Barth, *Church Dogmatics*, IV, pt. 4, trans. G. W. Bromiley (T. & T. Clark, 1969) 51f. The 1982 *Baptism, Eucharist,, and Ministry* document of the World Council of Churches presupposes some modification of traditional interpretations (§1). With respect to the Mennonite traditions in particular, the participial forms of "going," "baptizing," and "teaching," in verses 19 and 20, together with the imperative form of "make disciples," do not unambiguously reinforce the simple sequence of preaching, hearing, responding in faith, receiving baptism. Nor do they, depending on the meaning of "make disciples" and "baptizing," necessarily contradict that order.

[13] *Baptism, Eucharist,, and Ministry,* §11: "…baptism upon personal profession of faith is the most clearly attested pattern in the New Testament documents." See also *Mennonites and Reformed in Dialogue,* 67ff.

[14] Alan P. F. Sell suggests that the "process of Christian initiation as comprising several moments–baptism, nurture, conversion, confession of faith, reception as a member–be reexamined with a view to determining whether baptism need any longer be a church-dividing issue" between the Reformed and the Mennonites. Sell, "Anabbaptists and English Independents," *MQR,* vol. LXI (1987) 333. If Sell's initial phrasing were to follow the sequence "preaching and/or nurture and instruction," it would be recognized as synonymous with a believers baptist perspective.

[15] The term "images" is borrowed from *Baptism, Eucharist, and Ministry,* §2 in the baptism section. Theses images include participation in Christ's death and resurrection, a washing away of sin, a new birth, an enlightenment by Christ, a reclothing in Christ, a renewal by the Spirit, the experience of salvation from the flood, an exodus from bondage, and a liberation into a humanity.

[16] Armour, 139f., correctly notes that "…there were objective elements in Anabaptist baptism as well as subjective elements."

[17] See Hubmaier, "A Form for Water Baptism," in Pipkin and Yoder, 391; Marpeck, *Admonition of 1542,* in Klassen and Klaassen, 168ff.; and Armour, 56 and 185, n. 132. On sacraments among sixteenth-century Anabaptists and Mennonites, see Alvin J. Beachy, *The Concept of Grace in the Radical Reformation* (B. de Graaf, 1977) 99ff. Karl Barth, 109, refers to this possible interpretation in a passing note on Zwingli but does not employ it constructively in his rejection of the sacramentalist theological tradition and for his interpretation of water baptism in ethical terms.

[18] Armour has demonstrated that there were objective as well as subjective elements in Anabaptist baptism. This objective character was, however, not located simply in the ordinance of baptism, "for behind the baptismal action stood the church of the regenerate, which administered the ordinance. The action, therefore, …was the testimony of the very people of God, which people would give the signs of Christ only to those in whom they recognized His Spirit" (140).

[19] Marpeck, *Admonition of 1542,* in Klassen and Klaassen, 169f. Although Marpeck's *Admonition of 1542* borrows heavily from B. Rothmann's *Bekenntnisse van beyden Sacramenten,* the citation comes almost entirely from Marpeck and his circle.

[20] See Beachy, J. A. Oosterbaan, "Grace in Dutch Mennonite Theology," in *A Legacy of Faith,* ed. C. J. Dyck (Faith and Life Press, 1962) 69-85; John R. Loeschen, *The Divine Community: Trinity, Church, and Ethics in Reformation Theologies* (Sixteenth Century Journal Publishers, 1981) 79ff. (on Menno Simons); *Mennonites and Reformed in Dialogue,* 69; and Thomas N. Finger,

"Grace," *Mennonite Encyclopedia* V. In Anabaptist and Mennonite traditions this prevenient grace has sometimes been grounded more in Christ's atonement, sometimes more in God's original creative activity. Marpeck and Hubmaier tended toward the latter view, Menno Simons and Dirk Philips toward the former. Contemporary Mennonite theologians have not yet devoted major attention to clarifying this issue or to working toward theological consensus on it.

[21] P. 54.

[22] Karl Barth's rejection of baptism as a sacrament also seeks to emphasize both the priority of divine grace and the free and obedient response of the believer. As a consequence, Barth limits sacramental reality to Jesus Christ, i.e., interprets sacrament in strictly Christological terms. "Baptism takes place in active recognition of the grace of God which justifies, sanctifies, and calls. It is not itself, however, the bearer, means, or instrument of grace. Baptism responds to a mystery, the sacrament of the history of Jesus Christ, of His resurrection, of the outpouring of the Holy Spirit. It is not itself, however, a mystery or sacrament" (Barth, 102). Similar formulations may be found among some early Anabaptist writers—e.g., Dirk Philips: "...Jesus Christ alone ...is the only and true sign of grace.... Christ is and remains the true and only sign of grace, and all external signs direct us from themselves to him...." (Philips, *Concerning the Baptism of Our Lord Jesus Christ*, trans. C. J. Dyck, 45f.) However, the reinterpretaion of sacrament in the Anabaptist and Mennonite traditions has apparently included ecclesiological and anthropological/soteriological dimensions rather than being limited strictly to a Christological reference as in Barth's case.

[23] For example, Menno Simons and Dirk Philips strongly emphasized the role of the Holy Spirit in this regard; Hubmaier, on the other hand, spoke more in terms of the proclaimed Word. See also Windhorst, 185ff. The above quotation from Jeschke simply refers to the activity of both God's Word and Spriit in creating spiritual life.

[24] *Mennonites and Reformed in Dialogue*, 63.

[25] Within the limits of this essay I shall not seek to summarize—or to constructively formulate—more precisely the relation between baptism and the "covenantal transaction" (my term) of which it is the sign or sacrament in a way consistent with the Anabaptist and Mennonite traditions. Here again, attempts to counter and correct the majority churches' sacramentalist views, the Mennonites lack of a consistent teaching tradition, and various church renewal and cultural influences have all contributed to some diversity and most likely to some confusing and theologically problematic views which tend either toward making arbitrary the relation between baptism and that to which it refers or toward overemphasizing the individual believer's confession as the referent of baptism at the expense of divine grace and the confirming testimony of the church.

[26] For example, the Dutch Reformed-Mennonite dialogue noted that "the period of the 'nation-church' and of the Christian society is past." *Mennonites and Reformed in Dialogue*, 69. See also Faith and Order Paper #97 on the 1979 Louisville Consultation on Believers' Baptism, reprinted as the Winter 1980 issue of *Review and Expositor*, vol. LXXVII, no. 1, 103, 106, 108; and *Baptists and Reformed in Dialogue*, 16, 32.

[27] In the baptism section of *Baptism, Eucharist, and Ministry*, the commentaries to paragraphs 13 and 14. Jeschke, 27ff., agrees that children of believers "have always had the best exposure to the appeal of the covenant of faith." Nonetheless this does not theologically and practically justify a baptismal practice which cannot avoid an ecclesiology that mixes—or confuses—ethnic community and faith community. Jeschke notes that two conceptions of the people of God (Israel)—namely, as ethnic nation versus community of faith— came into tension long before the rise of the church. This tension was resolved in the New Testament in favor of the faith community.

[28] Franklin H. Littell underscored the significance of the Great Commission and missionary witness for the early Anabaptist and Mennnonite understanding of the church: *The Origins of Sectarian Protestantism: A Study of the Anabaptist View of the Church* (Macmillan, 1964) 109ff. See also Donald F. Durnbaugh, *The Believers Church: The History and Character of Radical Protestantism* (1968; reprint, Herald Press, 1985) 226ff. Later Mennonites have unfortunately all too frequently in their own ways undermined the missionary nature of the church by adopting an understanding of the church and a routinization of catechetical and baptismal practice which have in effect reinforced the notion of the church as an ethnic group at the expense of the church as a faith community.

[29] Jeschke, 47.

[30] Translation by C. J. Dyck, 43.

[31] The Ris Confession, e.g., in the very lengthy Article XXV, "Of Water Baptism," notes only in passing that believers were "added to the church" according to the book of Acts, but does not further develop this observation. In Loewen, 97ff. The bilateral conversations between the Reformed and the Mennonites in the Netherlands during the 1970s reflect this orientation among the Mennonites. See *Mennonites and Reformed in Dialogue*, 64ff. In the North American context similar emphases have—perhaps oddly—found expression not only among the groups which derive from the Dutch stream, but also among some groups whose traditions originated with the other major strand, namely, the Swiss and German movements. In such cases, such as the 1963 Mennonite Confession of Faith, revivalism has presumably played a major role. This confessional statement omits any reference to baptism as entry/incorporation into the church in its article on baptism: "We regard water baptism as an ordinance of Christ which symbolizes the baptism of the Holy Spirit, divine cleansing from sin and its guilt, identification with Christ in his death and

resurrection, and the commitment to follow him in a life of faithful
discipleship." Nor does the confession make any such reference in its article on
the church. In Loewen, 76, 75.

[32] In Pipkin and Yoder, 300. The entire paragraph is original to Marpeck and
his circle rather than having been adopted or adapted from Rothmann.

[33] Morris West observes that "there would be a number of Baptists who would
also say that it [the point at which a person is brought into the community of the
church] is really at the point of a believing response to the fact of the Gospel by
the individual...." Faith and Order Paper #97, 19. There may also be individual
Mennonites who entertain a similar view. But this would be in conflict with the
generally strong emphasis upon becoming a member of the church with baptism
in the Mennonite traditions.

[34] In the commentary to par. 12.

[35] To be sure, the document assumes that when an infant is baptized "the
personal response will be offered at a later moment in life" (par. 12). And it also
suggests that "the personal faith of the recipient" is essential for "the full fruit of
baptism" (commentary to par. 12). For these assumptions regarding the relation
between the individual's and the church's faith to be credible and theologically
consistent, at least from the position represented by this essay, would, however,
minimally seem to require a practice and theological justification for something
like a ceremony of "disavowal" as well as of "confirmation." Note also the
measure of convergence as well as basic divergence on this matter in
Mennonites and Reformed in Dialogue, 69.

[36] See esp. Jeschke, 66-80. In the baptism both "of an adult convert from
paganism and of someone nurtured within the church," the common
denominator is that baptism calls for the "appropriation of faith."

[37] P. 12.

[38] Larry Miller has noted that the theme of mutual support and congregational
discipline was "most conspicuous by its absence" in reports of the Reformed-
Baptist bilateral conversations, in spite of the presumption that such concerns
were historically an important element in both the Reformed and Baptist
traditions. *Baptists and Reformed in Dialogue*, 53. Nor did the relation between
baptism and discipleship, including mutual support and discipline, apparently
figure prominently in the dialogues between the Mennonites and the Reformed
in the Netherlands, even though discipline was mentioned as one of the
distinguishing marks of the church. Cf. *Mennonites and Reformed in Dialogue*,
65-71. Miller suggested that Mennonites and Reformed (and Baptists) might, in
future exchanges, do well to listen to Schleitheim and Hubmaier, and to Bucer
and Calvin on communitarian discernment and congregational discipline. I have
accepted that "fraternal admonition" with respect to Schleitheim and Hubmaier
in the hope that others will do the same with regard to Bucer and Calvin.

[39] In *The Sources of Swiss Anabaptism: The Grebel Letters and Related Documents*, ed. Leland Harder (Herald Press, 1985) 290.

[40] For further information on congregational discipline among Mennonites in general, see "Discipline," *ME*, II 69f.; and Walter Klasssen, ed., *Anabaptism in Outline: Selected Primary Sources* (Herald Press, 1981) 211-31. Contemporary interpretations have been developed primarily by John Howard Yoder and Marlin Jeschke: Yoder, "Binding and Loosing," *The Concern Pamphlet* Series, #14 (Feb. 1967); Jeschke, *Discipling the Brother: Congregational Discipline According to the Gospel* (Herald Press, 1972).

[41] In Loewen, 79.

[42] In Pipkin and Yoder, 389. See also Hubmaier's "On Fraternal Admonition," in *ibid.*, 386ff.

[43] *Minister's Manual*, ed. Heinz and Dorothea Janzen (Faith and Life Press; Mennonite Publishing House, 1983).

[44] Hubmaier, "On Fraternal Admonition," in Pipkin and Yoder, 383.

[45] In their interpretations of discipline neither Jeschke nor Yoder makes constructive use of this connection, which has ecclesiological and ethical as well as liturgical dimensions.

[46]This statement would need to be qualified with respect to the mode of baptism. The Mennonite Brethren consider baptism by immersion to be normative and have historically not considered other modes of baptism to constitute valid baptism. According to the 1975 confession, however, "local congregations may receive into fellowship those who have been baptized by another mode on their confession of faith." In Loewen, 177. That means that decisions on the matter have been left in the hands of the congregations rather than being binding on the entire group of Mennonite Brethren congregations.

[47] Jeschke, 139, argues for this position: "On the cardinal principle that baptism signifies the act of accountable entrance upon the way of faith, we must decide that baptism is out of place here, for the individual in question is not now coming to faith but has been a practicing Christian for possibly many years and is merely transferring church membership."

[48] See footnote 4 of this essay.

[49] Barth, xi.

Chapter 16

Is the Bible a Relevant Resource?

"Is the Bible a Relevant Resource?" *Perils of Professionalism,* Donald B. Kraybill and Phyllis Pellman Good, eds. (Herald Press, 1982) 176-184.

The gap between yesterday and today

Many Christian professionals perceive a fundamental discontinuity between the Bible and today's world. The realities of which the Scriptures speak appear shrouded in the gathering mists of an antiquated past. Complex contemporary social organizations have replaced the apparently simple social organization of biblical times. Modern urban values and lifestyles have superseded the agrarian lifestyles and values of Jesus' day. Technological advances have fundamentally diminished fearful dependency on overpowering forces of nature. Scientific analysis of the world and human experience have challenged and ostensibly rendered traditional belief systems obsolete. If today's world seemingly shares so little with the world of the Bible, can the Scriptures remain the unique guide and foundational resource for Christian faith and life in our time?

Mennonite professionals in particular may sense an even greater distance between the New Testament and contemporary society. The Anabaptist emphasis on following Christ in all of life has depended on biblical standards of discipleship and moral judgment. But how does biblical nonresistance apply to the exercise of power in legal and business professions? What guidance do the Scriptures offer on whether and under what conditions medical doctors should discontinue medical support systems for dying patients? Are there biblical perspectives which can or should inform the decisions and priorities of Mennonite social workers? Besides participating in the broader movement from rural to urban society and from traditional to modern ways of thinking, Mennonite professionals face choices and challenges for which there often seem to be few or no relevant biblical answers.

For Mennonite professionals, this apparent distance and discontinuity between the Bible and today's world is reinforced by the presumed synthesis between the ethnic Mennonitism of the last generation and the Bible. The traditional Mennonite way supposedly fit the biblical standards like a well-tailored coat. Church discipline and minimal involvement in the broader society made litigation irrelevant as well as morally prohibited. Rural, general practitioners didn't face the complex ethical issues of technological medical care. But as Mennonites move into the professions and urban society, the previously experienced harmony between a Mennonite subculture and the Bible has been at least threatened, if not stymied. The distance and discontinuity between modern professional life and traditional Mennonite mores has thus been projected onto the difference between contemporary urban society and the biblical world. The cultural and ethical irrelevance of traditional ethnic Mennonitism to contemporary professional life has been transferred to the Bible.

The question of whether the Bible is a foundational resource and guide for Mennonite professionals can be looked at fairly only by simultaneously distinguishing between rural ethnic Mennonitism and a renewed biblical vision of discipleship. We first need to differentiate between our perceptions of traditional Mennonitism and our approach to biblical discipleship. In other words, leaving ethnic Mennonitism "back on the farm" doesn't necessarily confirm the "irrelevance" of the Bible for Christian professionals.

The overlap of subculture and biblical interpretation

We have often identified traditional Mennonitism with biblical discipleship. That skews our perception of the Bible as a unique guide for Christians in modern professions.

Traditional Mennonitism often became a provincial subculture which imposed its standards by an authoritarian appeal to the Scriptures. Attempts to debate or deviate were, on occasion, squelched by a contrived appeal to favorite proof texts. This uncritical identification of the subculture with the biblical standards also implied that the Bible offered little or no guidance for living "outside" the Mennonite subculture "in the world." When some left for a career in nontraditional Mennonite professions, they quite logically expected little biblical direction. They had learned their lesson well and they accepted the message: The Scriptures are largely "irrelevant" to living in the "world" outside a Mennonite subculture.

Moreover, identifying biblical discipleship with traditional Mennonite mores often contributed to the belief that the Bible is a unique guide and foundational resource, giving explicit directives and universally applicable principles for all of life. If, however, the

Scriptures offer no explicit instructions for many issues in modern medical technology, in financial management, or in legal practice, can they remain the normative guide for Christian discipleship? Certain forms of traditional Mennonitism may assume that the Bible's authority and relevance is diminished if it does not provide explicit answers or an obvious consensus on complex contemporary questions. This assumption has more to do with a style of biblical interpretation than with the Bible as a foundational resource. It points toward the need for an alternate method and context of interpretation which allows the Bible to function as a critical norm and ordering principle of Christian professional life.

The failure to distinguish between a Mennonite subculture and the biblical context may also contribute to a sense of distance between the Bible and contemporary issues. Many Mennonite professionals perceive a discontinuity between ethnic Mennonites and life in the late twentieth century. And that may affect how they see the historical context of the Bible in relation to the modern world. On the other hand, instead of diminishing the relevance of the Scriptures, that distance can be a critical instrument to distinguish ethnic Mennonitism from formative biblical perspectives. It can also be an interpretative instrument for discerning analogous patterns of belief and life in today's setting without rationalizing our thoughts and actions as unquestionably biblical and therefore in no need of continuing discernment and prayer.

Modern professionals may feel that as contemporary Christians they have more in common with the modern world than with the church throughout history. The Bible is hardly the book of contemporary Western society. Seen in the perspective of general historical consciousness, the Bible belongs to a past period in human history. The discontinuity between the modern and the ancient world would in this view supersede the continuity of the Christian church through the ages. The question is, however, whether those who confess Jesus as Messiah and Lord find their primary historical identity in the Christian community, which reaches back to the New Testament churches, or primarily in the communities of modern professional guilds.

Thus, traditionalistic Mennonite biblical interpretation has likely contributed as much to the assumption that the Scriptures offer little guidance for Christians in modern professions as has contemporary society's disregard for the Bible. The lack of explicit biblical directives for all significant ethical decisions does not in itself make the Bible less relevant for Christian professionals, unless relevancy is defined primarily in terms of explicit moral rules and policies. That the biblical writings were first addressed to Christians of other cultures can enhance their use for discerning the direction of Christian life and witness in our time, rather than making them less relevant. The Christian church as the confessing community, rather than a particular cultural epoch, should constitute the primary frame of reference for Christian identity and the primary context in which the Bible is interpreted and contemporary issues confronted. An authentic biblical authority becomes useful as the Scriptures provide the foundation for responding to the values, insights, and practices of the modern world as well as of traditional subcultures.

The archive of our witness

The Bible constitutes the normative guide and foundational resource for Christian faith and life because it is the primary and unique witness to Jesus Christ. Throughout the history of the Christian churches, the Bible has been the standard which has preserved the Christian confession of Jesus as the Christ from fragmentation on the one hand and embellishment on the other. Where the Bible has functioned this way in the churches, we find keener moral and spiritual discernment, more authentic church renewal, more vigorous Christian witness, and more significant contributions to the broader culture and society.

As the primary and unique witness to Jesus as the Christ, the Bible becomes the normative guide for Christian life and ethical discernment. This implies that constant recourse to the biblical witness itself rather than to particular theological constructs about the Scriptures remains of primary importance for Christians in general and for Christian professionals in particular. Our theological constructs as well as particular issues need to be tested by continuing to wrestle with the texts themselves. For example, Christian ethical thought has often assumed that the biblical image of Jesus as the Christ is "apolitical" and that therefore the New Testament offers little or no guidance for "political" life. Taking the biblical witness to Jesus Christ as the guide for ethical discernment on its own terms, André Trocmé in *Jesus and the Nonviolent Revolution*, John Howard Yoder in *The Politics of Jesus*, and others have demonstrated its relevance for developing a Christian perspective on politics and an alternate style of political action.

Affirming the Bible as the normative guide and foundational resource for Christian life and thought does not blind Christians to truth and insight from other sources. Indeed, it should encourage Christian professionals in particular to engage in discriminating dialogue and debate with the understandings, values, and practices of modern society. Recent biblical studies have shown that many themes in the Scripture reflect their historical origins but simultaneously reshape those elements as carriers of the biblical message. Biblical scholars have shown, for example, that a variety of legal materials is reflected in Exodus 20 to 23. Some of the legal materials reflect prevailing customs and social differentiation of the time; others a distinctive standard of equality and compassion. In contrast to the ancient Mesopotamian culture which separated civil, moral, and religious codes, the book of the covenant in Exodus brought together moral, cultic, and civil prescriptions. Moreover, God's saving activity was the central dynamic which shaped and reshaped these legal materials into a distinctive code for ordering anew the life of God's people. In a similar fashion, the Bible can function as the normative guide as Christians confront, critique, adapt, and reshape concepts, values, and practices which communicate the distinctiveness of Christian faith and practice in our time.

Jacques Ellul illustrates in some measure this effort in a French Protestant setting. His writings seek to articulate a distinctively Christian witness in the modern world. The Scriptures function as the normative guide for his dialogue and debate with contemporary culture and society. In this way Ellul avoids both a strictly intra-church monologue as well as a benign adaptation to the spirit of the age. In *The Presence of the Kingdom*, he outlines what he considers the unique tasks of Christian intellectuals and professionals in the modern world. Many of his writings are set in tandem: for example, his sociological diagnosis of *The Technological Society* is the companion volume to his biblical interpretation of contemporary society in *The Meaning of the City*. Those of Anabaptist persuasion will miss the constitutive reality of Christian community in Ellul's vision. And his ethics may reflect his radical Calvinist heritage more than a consistently Anabaptist stance. Nevertheless he offers a significant model as an intellectual and a professional who takes the Bible seriously as normative guide and foundational resource.

Finally, accepting the Scriptures as normative also implies remembering that the Bible is a missionary document rather than the charter of a professional guild. As such, it has a particular bias. Mennonite professionals who are moving from agrarian and traditional to urban and cosmopolitan settings may tend to forget this bias. But the New Testament writings in particular arose in the context of mission. They don't speak to maintaining the self-interest of a particular group nor to smooth adaptations from rural to urban culture. They focus rather on the ever renewed call of God's people in a variety of historical and cultural contexts to witness in word and deed to salvation, justice, and reconciliation in Jesus Christ. They reflect the bias that "being his witness" constitutes the primary vocation of Christians in the world. This can hardly be construed to mean that Christian professionals in general, or Mennonite professionals in particular, will have "all the right answers" for their specific professions. But it should mean an ordering of priorities in which the vocation of Christian witness takes precedence over professional demands, values' and role expectation.

Interpretation in community

If the Bible is to function as the foundational resource and unique guide for Christian professionals, they will need the context of a Christian community devoted to biblical interpretation and moral discernment on at least two levels. A local congregation constitutes the primary expression of this process. Second, networks and gatherings of Christian professionals beyond the usual professional organizations provide an additional Christian community.

Boyd Reese rightly proposes that

> as professionals, it is crucial that we address the issues with fellow professionals who share our Christian vision.... We need a forum for this. We need to be able to reflect together on issues with our brothers and sisters and seek to break the sovereignty of the powers. In talking with people who understand the profession, we must discern the issues that the profession faces, the issues the profession should face but does not because of its sovereignty, and the issues that face us directly in our practice as professionals....[1]

This kind of common discernment among Christian professionals would provide a setting for dialogue about professional issues and ongoing biblical interpretation. Biblical scholars, theologians, and ethicists could also commit themselves to longer-term dialogue and discernment with such groups of Christians in other professions, rather than remaining within their own boundaries.

Such common discernment among Christian professionals where the Bible functions as a foundational resource need not replace membership in the usual professional organizations and societies. The question is rather one of priorities, namely, that the Christian community takes precedence over other communities in shaping the values, commitments, and actions of those who seek to follow Christ in all of life. The participation or nonparticipation—or the degree of participation in the guild associations—depends on its compatibility with the prior claim of the confessing community.

The other context in which the Bible can function as a normative guide and foundational resource for Christian professionals is the local congregation. Citing Reese (1979:53) again, "Even if our congregation does not have the inside, expert knowledge of the profession, most of us are caught up in involvement in the world in such a way that our experience can throw light on the perplexing decisions our brothers and sisters must face. Again, while we won't be able to share from the perspective of people who have been socialized into the profession, this very fact can be helpful because of the possibility of the input of a perspective that is not bound by the conventional wisdom of our profession." The continuing task of interpreting the Scriptures in the encounter with the contemporary world belongs to this type of moral discernment in a local congregation. But the style of congregational life may need to undergo significant changes in order to function as a community of moral judgment and discriminating biblical interpretation.

In the Assembly congregation (Goshen, IN), such a beginning attempt has been made in two ways. In the longer-range worship planning, a series of Sunday services were focused on the issues faced by members of the congregation in several different professions. During this series, the two-and-one-half hour services included open forums, dialogue between persons of various professions, dramatic portrayals of crucial issues, biblical studies related to the themes, and congregational discussion. In addition to the extended series, professionals have been encouraged to share and reflect on their concerns, questions, and insights during the "open sharing time" each Sunday service.

In addition to participating in the Sunday services, all members of the congregation, including "professionals," belong to house meetings which usually meet on a weekly basis. These settings provide a context where members can seek guidance in a continuing manner, where common discernment and scriptural interpretation takes place, and where accountability to discipleship priorities can be combined with mutual support and understanding. On occasion, the "findings" in the house meetings, whether with regard to specific issues or in biblical interpretation in relation to such issues, become a part of the broader congregational agenda.

The Bible can thus function as a foundational resource for Christian professionals to the extent that they allow it to become their normative guide. Moral discernment will be a process in the Christian community as it encounters the contemporary world. For Mennonite professionals in particular, the creation and strengthening of alternate styles of church life may be necessary to enable this interpretive process to happen. And for Mennonite professionals, a "renewing of our minds" may also be needed, lest we assume that the disintegration of rural, ethnic Mennonitism diminishes the relevance of the Scriptures for Christian life in contemporary society.

---

[1] Boyd Reese, "Within or Outside the System: An Anabaptist Perspective," in *Conflict in the World of Professions* (Elkhart, Ind.: Mennonite Student and Young Adult Services) 52.

Chapter 17

Criticism and Analogy in Historical-critical Interpretation

"Criticism and Analogy in Historical-Critical Interpretation," *Essays on Biblical Interpretation: Anabaptist-Mennonite Perspectives,* Text-Reader Series no. 1, Willard M. Swartley, ed. (Institute of Mennonite Studies, 1984) 223.

Two axioms of historical-critical methodology, though variously defined and implemented, nevertheless inform with some consistency historical-critical exegesis. I will limit this essay to those axioms: I will use George Brunk's "Journey to Emmaus: A Study in Critical Methodology"[1] as a point of reference to reflect critically upon the historical-critical method and to illustrate several of the axiological issues raised by this methodology. In addition to these formal and procedural limitations, I will further assume that historical-critical methodology is not simply a neutral technique of biblical interpretation, but that it is itself historically conditioned and carries with it certain philosophical and theological axioms, which may be, and in fact are, variously assessed as appropriate or apostate.

Historical-critical exegesis arose and gathered momentum in the seventeenth century as European Christendom's synthesis of Scripture, world view, and faith (dogmatically defined) was challenged by the scientific and philosophical reflections of the Enlightenment.[2] Doubtless the confessional and political conflicts of the preceding two centuries also riddled the credibility of Christendom's claim to an authoritative synthesis and nourished the scientific and philosophical reflection which gave birth to modern skepticism. If this is indeed the case, then ecclesiastical events as well as scientific and philosophical developments should receive some of the credit and/or blame for the birth and growth of historical-critical interpretation.

This assumption that historical-critical exegesis carries with it certain philosophical and theological axioms which are neither purely neutral nor strictly technical derives not only from a "guilt-(or praise-) by-association" reading of history, but appears to be a relatively widespread consensus among scholars otherwise divided in confessional loyalties as well as in their assessment of the method.[3] Others who by implication may regard historical-critical inquiry as relatively neutral, would nevertheless set certain limits to the method (e.g. George Brunk's summary) or argue that it need not be associated with skeptical presuppositions.[4] This, however, amounts to saying that it should be linked to certain presuppositions rather than defending its axiological neutrality.

Evaluation of "criticism"

Two years before the close of the nineteenth century, Ernst Troeltsch articulated the foundational concepts of historical-critical interpretation in his essay "On Historical and Dogmatic Method in Theology."[5] According to Krentz, Troeltsch's statement still "haunts" theology. Krentz's ghostly imagery may be neither historically nor theologically appropriate. Nevertheless, the rigor with which Troeltsch challenged German Protestant theologians of his day to choose between the "historical" and the "dogmatic" methods in theology provides a significant point of reference and continues to shape the debate about assumptions of historical-critical interpretation by both its critics and its apologists (Maier, Harvey, *et al.*). And the "foundational concepts" of historical-critical interpretation as listed by Troeltsch, namely *criticism*, *analogy*, and *correlation*, also continue to inform the discussion on presuppositions—even though they may be variously defined and/or supplemented. In the following remarks, both these concepts and the polemically formulated alternatives between historical and dogmatic method will be taken into account.

According to Troeltsch, criticism as a foundational concept of historical-critical methodology conditions our whole attitude toward historical traditions. Rather than simply questioning particular facts and details of the past, it signifies a comprehensive stance toward all historical traditions, namely that the continuity and relevance of the traditions for the present depends upon critical and discriminating judgment. In contrast to the dogmatic method which ostensibly does not depend upon historical continuity and/or contingency, a critical stance can lead only to judgments of probability rather than statements of certainty. Such judgments of probability, moreover, also establish higher and lower levels of probability by weighing the evidence and assessing it by the norms of critical reason. Contemporary critical reason rather than traditional authority becomes the arbiter of historical knowledge.

Troeltsch's observation that "criticism" implies judgments of probability rather than certainty seems to be confirmed by Brunk's description of the historical-critical method. Note, for example, the following statements of probability, as well as the different degrees of probability which these statements designate:

- "External evidence...is decidedly stronger for 60 stadia" (206).
- "If this reconstruction is true...we could conclude that the Emmaus appearance began as a legitimation formula...." (209).
- "Luke seems to depict an ideal 'day' of salvation history...." (210).
- "It is also widely accepted that the place name, the indication of distance...can only be explained by the rootage of the basic Emmaus event in historical memory" (211).
- "A definite feature of this form...is the recognition motif.... In all probability it was the center of the account at all levels of the tradition. If any feature of the account is traceable to a historical bedrock, it is the appearance experience of Emmaus when Jesus is recognized as present with Cleopas and his companion...." (215).

Brunk's description of the historical-critical method as used in the interpretation of the Emmaus story apparently confirms Troeltsch's observation that criticism issues in judgments of probability—even at those points where "historical bedrock" may be uncovered. Moreover these judgments of probability are themselves diverse: they may derive simply from weighing several textual readings against each other; they may reach tentative conclusions about the origin of the story based upon what seems to be the central intention; they may attempt to demonstrate the historical credibility of the events reported in the narrative. In any case, criticism as a stance cannot and does not intend to claim the kind of certainty presupposed by the traditional dogmatic method of theology.

In common parlance, the notion of criticism therefore often carries pejorative connotations: to criticize means to pass judgment on, to condemn, to catalogue errors. When associated with biblical interpretation, such criticism ostensibly presupposes a skeptical attitude toward the biblical documents, toward their dependability, historical accuracy, veracity, and authority. Etymologically, however, "to criticize" also signifies: "to sift out, to divide from, to distinguish that which is specific to." Whatever else does not correspond to the specific and distinguishing characteristics of a particular document or other object of investigation and evaluation, can presumably be "sifted out." That which is sifted out may be judged erroneous or simply as something which is not a distinguishing characteristic of whatever is being "criticized." In this sense criticism seeks to make discriminating judgments by following normative criteria. This aspect of criticism, however, also carries with it a negative component: whatever does not correspond with the normative principles of investigation and assessment may then be discounted as uncertain, not meaningful, or unreal. Whatever does correspond to the criteria of discerning judgment may be accepted.

Within the limits of this summary, it is not possible to examine and evaluate all the specific criteria which may have been used in Brunk's paper (or in historical-critical exegesis in general). Such criteria do need continual reassessment. Nevertheless, criticism as an epistemological stance, as a way of knowing and appropriating past traditions, may in several respects itself be problematical. As a formal epistemological concept, criticism is often a kind of empty sack which is filled with whatever seems reasonably evident and clear to the contemporary critic. But if this formal understanding of criticism (which derives from Cartesian methodical doubt and Kantian critical philosophy) becomes its own criterion, judgments of historical probability may often be more a reflection of contemporary assumptions about reason and reality than of the historical object of perception and study. The critical question of criticism as a method, therefore, has to do with its criteria and with the nature of probability expressed by critical judgment.

Particular judgments of probability may be an appropriate reflection of the object of investigation, namely the biblical narrative. Insofar as the biblical story refers to particular events and historical conditions, the probability of such critical judgments may well represent a more faithful interpretation of Scripture than the formulation of dogmatic statements which claim absolute certainty in the sense of exemption from the contingencies of time and space. If God has chosen to entrust divine revelation to the arbitrariness of historical events and existence and to particular people in particular times and places, such judgments of probability would not necessarily contradict the character of the biblical documents.

Some statements of probability may also simply reflect the degree to which an interpreter's questions and hypotheses do or do not correspond to the intention and the information of the text. In this case the factor of probability would in part be a commentary upon the interpreter's orientation and in part a recognition that the evidence available does not allow for a definite conclusion to the questions posed and the interpretive hypothesis being employed. It seems to me that Brunk's description largely demonstrates this orientation.

The notion of probability, however, may also reflect the introverted character of much, if not most, of modern criticism. According to Brunk's definition, the critical element "points to the function of the human mind, exercising intelligent judgments and discerning appreciation in the interrogation and evaluation of the sources" (204). This description apparently leaves open the question about the standard of intelligent judgment and discriminating appreciation. However, "criticism" as usually understood assumes that autonomous human reason functions as its own criterion for discriminating judgments.[6] In this case granting an event or a report a higher or lower level of historical probability means ascertaining the degree to which it corresponds to what may be considered self-evident and clear to the modern interpreter.

According to Collingwood, the critical historian, rather than relying on an authority other than himself, to whose statements his thought must conform…is his own authority and his thought [is] autonomous, self-authorizing, possessed of a criterion to which his so-called authorities must conform and by reference to which they are criticized.[7]

For Van Harvey this autonomy is not only a warning to be on guard against error, but "is grounded in the nature of historical knowledge itself."[8] Consequently the critical historian

> *confers* authority upon a witness. He reserves the right to judge who or what will be called an authority, and he makes this judgment only after he has subjected the so-called witness to a rigorous cross-examination…. If the historian permits his authorities to stand uncriticized, he abdicates his role as critical historian. He is no longer a seeker of knowledge but a

mediator of past belief; not a thinker but a transmitter of tradition .[9]

If criticism thus signifies an epistemological procedure for conferring authority upon the biblical witnesses, we may need to choose between being transmitters of that particular tradition and critical historians. I would suggest, however, that functioning as transmitters of the biblical tradition calls for greater rather than less critical awareness, because it means subjecting the autonomy of modern reason to criticism as well as developing an empathetic understanding of the meaning of the biblical documents in their historical setting. The alternative need not then be a flight into dogmatic timelessness, as Troeltsch defined the alternative to historical criticism. It would rather go in the direction of making explicit the standards of criticism, examining the degree to which they correspond to the reality of the historical objects (in this case, the biblical documents), and allowing them to be judged by their appropriateness to that historical reality, rather than by the self-confirmation of autonomous reason (however that may be defined). Otherwise the formal epistemological category of modern criticism tends to create not only an historical difference but also a spiritual distance between biblical revelation and contemporary understanding.

Evaluation of "analogy"

Troeltsch's second fundamental concept of the historical method is *analogy*. Whereas the axiom of criticism tends to remain a more formal concept, analogy provides the historian with more concrete material in the exercise of discriminating judgment. Troeltsch described the principle of analogy as follows:

> Analogy with what happens before our eyes and what is given within ourselves is the key to criticism. Illusions, displacements, myth formation, fraud, and party spirit, as we see them before our own eyes, are the means whereby we can recognize similar things in what the tradition hands down. Agreement with normal, ordinary, repeatedly attested modes of occurrence and conditions as we know them is the mark of probability for occurrences that the critic can either acknowledge really to have happened or leave to one side. The observation of analogies between past occurrences of the same

sort makes it possible to ascribe probability to them and to interpret the one that is unknown from what is known of the other.[10]

Troeltsch goes on to speak of the "omnipotence of analogy" which in turn presupposes a "fundamental similarity" although not an "identity" between all historical events .

Troeltech's understanding of analogy has not gone unchallenged.[11] Some would criticize the methodological doubt which Troeltsch's principle of analogy seems to imply; others would challenge the "tyrannical" omnipotence of analogy; still others would find the anthropocentric orientation problematic. Some would also focus on whether the category of uniqueness, rather than a common kernel of similarity, has been given adequate focus by Troeltsch's definition of analogy. Regardless of the challenges raised to Troeltsch's understanding, analogy remains an axiom of historical-critical interpretation. But rather than reporting on that debate in general, I would refer again to George Brunk's case study to examine one example of analogy as a means of historical interpretation. We may then return to the more systematic concerns with that example in mind.

Brunk employs the principle of analogy in several ways, particularly in the section on form criticism and tradition history (214ff). The first point of analogy has to do with literary forms. Based on the "recognition" motif of the Emmaus story, Brunk finds greater similarity between the Emmaus narrative and several Old Testament theophanies than between Luke 24 and hellenistic legends of a wandering deity.[12] This literary analogy thus serves as a basis for the judgment that the Emmaus story reflects an early Jewish Christian rather than a later hellenistic setting (or, for that matter, an apocalyptic milieu). The underlying issue thus has to do with the appropriate categories for understanding the Emmaus occurrence. Brunk finds these categories in what we may designate as the "biblical world" rather than in either the apocalyptic or hellenistic categories of perception and thought. An historically appropriate understanding of what happened would therefore depend upon our beginning with the analogy between the Old Testament theophanies and the New Testament christophanies.

The question of analogy arises not only with respect to the most appropriate categories of understanding, but also in relation to the objective referent of these categories. What kind of occurrence lies behind the Emmaus narrative? Can it be reconstructed by the tools of historical reason (in part or entirely), or does it lie completely outside the field of historical analogy? Brunk's response to this question is two-fold: based on the categories of understanding provided by the narrative

> the consequence of this situation is that the Emmaus event slips through the fingers of the historian *qua* historian but speaks to his understanding of the nature of resurrection faith. At the same time there is no reason to doubt the occurrence of an Emmaus appearance in *essentially* the manner described, but we cannot demonstrate what the actual event was.[13]

This conclusion derives however not only from an appreciation of the literary form, but also assumes the unique character of Jesus' resurrected existence, which on the one hand belongs to a new order of corporeal existence not determined by time and space,[14] and on the other hand breaks into the old order in a more than purely internal and subjective way.[15] Thus, the resurrection event has both a mysterious and an historical aspect.

The third major, albeit somewhat more implicit analogy, which Brunk's summary assumes is the continuity between the life of the church and the appearance of the resurrected Jesus to the early disciples. Although couched in terms of the reality and practices of the early church such as the interpretation of Scripture, community atmosphere, fellowship in breaking of the bread, the implication seems to include an analogy between the context in which faith in the resurrection of Jesus was acquired then and can arise now. Within the limits of his summary, Brunk at least assumes such an analogy between the situation of the church in Luke's time and the dynamic of the Emmaus event. Such an analogy would presumably also arise between the contemporary experience of the gathered Christian community and the disciples from Emmaus gathered in the presence of the resurrected Jesus.

These conclusions (or assumptions) differ markedly from an understanding of analogy which makes non-biblical categories of understanding primary, grants greater credibility to historical events similar in kind rather than to "unique" occurrences, and discounts the historical reality of what cannot be grasped by the contemporary community of critical historians. The concept of analogy is therefore one of the critical issues in historical method. For Troeltsch (as well as

Bultmann, et al.), the historical probability of an event depends upon its similarity with other events of the same kind. If one accepts this assumption, it follows that the historian as critical historian cannot confer historical reality upon an "event" for which there are no known analogies.

Without doubt, the comparison of the new and the unknown with the already known plays an important role in historical understanding as well as in human knowledge generally. If we have not the remotest experience of something, we cannot conceive what it is like. An historian quite properly interprets new data in the light of present understanding whereby "present understanding" includes much more than what has been mediated directly through empirical, first-hand experience. Thus, without analogy, it is impossible to understand the past. On the other hand, however, if the principle of analogy is employed with the rigor of Troeltsch (and his theological descendants), it seems impossible to do justice to the uniqueness of Christ as portrayed by the Bible. According to Van Harvey, "this dilemma" seems to inform much "discussion in contemporary Protestant theology over the nature of hermeneutics."[16]

Perhaps more directly than any other Protestant theologian, Wolfhart Pannenberg has addressed this apparent dilemma with respect to analogy. Pannenberg argues against the rigid and restrictive use of analogy by distinguishing between analogy as an instrument of historical research, on the one hand, and as the key to an anti-theistic world view or ontology, on the other hand. According to Pannenberg, Troeltsch's assumption that the principle of analogy requires a "fundamental homogeneity of all historical events"[17] raises the method of analogy to a criterion of ontological possibility. Pannenberg counters by maintaining that:

> The cognitive power of analogy depends upon the fact that it teaches us to see contents of the same *kind in nonhomogeneous things [das Gleichartige im Ungleichartigen]*. If the historian keeps his eye on the nonexchangeable individuality and contingency of an event, then he will see that he is dealing with nonhomogeneous things, which cannot be contained without remainder in any analogy. Provided that historical science is occupied above all with the particularity and uniqueness of phenomena, its interests must therefore be

focused more upon the ever peculiar, nonhomogeneous features, rather than the common ones first obtruded by analogies.... The cognitive power of analogy in historical study...is greater, the more sharply the limitation, of the analogy is recognized in each case.[18]

Pannenberg suggests that within Christian theology historical research should focus on the individual, the particular, and the contingent. Pannenberg goes on to say:

That a reported event bursts analogies with otherwise usual or repeatedly attested events is still no ground for disputing its facticity. It is another matter when positive analogies to forms of tradition (such as myths and even legends) relating to unreal objects, phenomena referring to states of consciousness (like visions) may be found in the historical sources. In such cases historical understanding guided by analogy can lead to a negative judgment about the reality of the occurrences reported in the tradition. Such a judgment will be rendered not because of the unusualness of something reported about, but rather because it exhibits a positive analogy to some form of consciousness which has no objective referent.[19]

Pannenberg thus apparently offers an understanding of analogy which reassuringly makes room for the "facticity" of the resurrection, even if it "bursts analogies" of otherwise usual and repeatedly attested events.[20] Rather than disallowing the historicity of Jesus' resurrection because it conforms to nothing within our present, critically informed beliefs of the world, Pannenberg's understanding of analogy would appear to reinstate the historical possibility (not necessarily however the probability) of the resurrection. If however historical research could demonstrate that the New Testament accounts of the resurrection correspond to forms of historical tradition which in turn relate to "unreal objects," a negative judgment on the resurrection would be forthcoming.[21]

I would suggest that Pannenberg's distinction between analogy as a help in understanding historical events and as ontological criterion of historical possibility can be taken as a corrective to the positivistic assumptions of Troeltsch. Furthermore, his contention that the unusualness of an occurrence may not be taken a priori as an argument against its reality is appropriate. Nevertheless, Pannenberg's understanding of analogy is embedded in a comprehensive view of "universal history" which may in turn evacuate the particular content of the resurrection reality. The biblical understanding of history and the uniqueness of particular biblical events hardly corresponds to a universal-historical frame of reference within which they receive their definitive significance.

> Characteristic for the biblical view of history is rather that very specific individual events arise as direction-giving points of reference for broad periods, and that from there material finds its place and historical questioning and thinking finds its response.[22]

This "perspectival" view may indeed correspond more adequately to the biblical witnesses than a developmental, existential, or universal-historical point of view. Moreover, Pannenberg continues to assume that the only reliable way to knowledge of the past is that of historical-critical research.[23]

This may amount to a mistake similar to what Pannenberg found in Troeltsch, namely that of translating one methodological tool which can be useful within certain limits into a criterion of historical reality. Brunk's description of the resurrection as both an eschatological and historical "event," as in part accessible to historical research, and in part eluding it, points in a direction which seems to me better corresponds to the biblical narrative. A view of the resurrection which relegates it to a solely eschatological reality (however defined) without objective referents in time and space cannot do justice to the witness of the early church. But a view of the resurrection which limits our knowledge of it to what is accessible by historical research (however defined) is hardly more adequate.

An acceptable understanding of "analogy" as an instrument of biblical interpretation, I suggest, needs to take the context of interpretation into account. As long as the concept of analogy remains primarily a formal epistemological notion, the content of what is historically "analogous" or "unique" will usually be defined in terms of a particular "world view." For Troeltsch and others, an understanding of the world as a continuum of cause-and-effect-relations ("correlation") provided the frame of reference for analogies which could be drawn between the present and the past. For Pannenberg, an understanding of the world as an open and future-directed totality of historical occurrences remains the point of reference for what may be considered historical analogies or within which unique events find their function. But if Brunk's interpretation of the resurrection is an example of a proper use of analogy, the normative point of reference will not be the totality of a particular "world" view, but the church as both an historical and a spiritual reality. We sometimes use the notion of the "hermeneutical community" to suggest that the locus of scriptural interpretation is most properly the church, or that all members of the church should participate in the interpretation of Scripture, rather than limiting this task to the specialists alone.

But the reality of the "hermeneutical community" goes beyond merely a functional dimension; it also includes an epistemological dimension and an historical/spiritual dimension. As such the church today as an historical reality and directed by the Holy Spirit becomes the place of analogy with the New Testament Church, rather than the contemporary world being seen as the place of analogy with the ancient world at the time of the New Testament. As Millard Lind puts it:

> ...by accepting the congregation as the context for the Bible's life situation, the process is quite a different one from that in which it is assumed that there is no twentieth-century life situation in which the Bible is truly at home. If the latter is true, the hermeneutical process is indeed questionable and largely meaningless. It is only within the life situation of the hermeneutical community that the fundamental analogies are experienced which make the Bible historically credible.[24]

This is not to suggest that the reality of Christian community and its perception of reality are at all points distinct from its historical environment. But it would suggest that the primary point of reference for analogies between present and past events is the "church" rather than the "world." At certain points those realities overlap, at others they are distinct. The sometimes similar, sometimes conflicting views of what may be "historically possible" therefore depend also upon the reality and perception of the community in question.

[1] Willard M. Swartley, ed., *Essays on Biblical Interpretation: Anabaptist-Mennonite Perspectives* (Institute of Mennonite Studies, 1984) 203.

[2] Klaus Scholder, *Ursprünge und Probleme der Bibelkritik im 17. Jahrhundeert* (Christian Kaiser Verlag, 1966) 9.

[3] See, e.g., Brevard Childs, *Biblical Theology in Crisis* (Westminster, 1970) 141; Van Austin Harvey, *The Historian and the Believer, The Morality of Historical Knowledge and Christian Belief* (Macmillan, 1966) 33ff.; Edgar Krentz, *The Historical-Critical Method* (Fortress, 1975) 55f.; Gerhard Maier, *The End of the Historical-Critical Method* (Concordia, 1977) 11; Wolfhart Pannenberg, *Basic Questions in Theology: Collected Essays, Vol. I* (Fortress Press, 1970) 40.

[4] See, e.g., George Eldon Ladd, *The New Testament and Criticism* (Eerdmans, 1967) 33.

[5] Ernst Troeltsch, "Historicshe und Dogmatische Methode in der Theologie," in *Gesammelte Schriften*, Vol. II (J.C.B. Mohr/Paul Siebeck, 1913) 729ff. (author's translation).

[6] Ferdinand Hahn, "Problems historischer Kritik," *ZNW* 63 (1972) 13.

[7] Harvey, 40.

[8] *Ibid.*, 41.

[9] *Ibid.*, 42.

[10] Troeltsch, 732.

[11] See for example, Colin Brown, "History and the Believer," in *History, Criticism and Faith,* edited by Colin Brown (Leicester, England: Inter-Varsity Press, 1976) 171ff.; Maier, 51; Pannenberg, 44ff.; Harvey, 40.

[12] George Brunk III, "The Concept of the Resurrection according to the Emmaus Account in Luke's Gospel" (Th.D. Diss., Union Theological Seminary in Virginia, 1975) 396ff.

[13] Cf. *ibid.*, 414f.

[14] Cf. *ibid.*, 384

[15] *Ibid.*, 387, 391, 409, *et. al.*

[16] Harvey, 32.

[17] Troeltsch, 732.

[18] Pannenberg, 46f.

[19] *Ibid.*, 48f.

[20] Cf. Brown, 172.

[21] Pannenberg, 48f.; cf. Ted Peters, "The Use of Analogy in Historical Method," *CBQ* (Oct 1973) 475-82.

[22] Hahn, 16.

[23] Pannenberg, 53.

[24] Millard Lind, "Reflections on Biblical Hermeneutics," in *Kingdom, Cross and Community*, ed. Richard Burkholder and Calvin Redekop, (Herald Press, 1976) 94 and 155 in this volume.

Chapter 18

Theology

Mennonite Encyclopedia V, Cornelius J. Dyck and Dennis Martin, eds. Herald Press, 1990) 881.

In classical Greek theology meant the knowledge of God or teaching about God and divine matters *(theo,* God; *logos,* word or study). The New Testament does not use the concept "theology." But the Bible knows and teaches about the one God who has created the world, called Israel and the church, and seeks to redeem humankind through Jesus Christ and the Holy Spirit. The Scriptures therefore contain theology understood as a distinctive knowledge and language about God, about God's speaking and acting in relation to humankind and the world, and about human responses to God's acting and speaking.

For definitional reasons, it is useful to distinguish theology from doctrine. Doctrines are teachings regarding Christian beliefs and practices which are considered normative for the Christian church, such as the doctrine of salvation through Jesus Christ, the Son of God. Judgments on which teachings should be normative for the Christian church, however, frequently differ among various groups and communities. Mennonites, for example, consider believers baptism and the rejection of violence as well as salvation through Jesus Christ normative doctrines. Such doctrines are normally correlated with theology, but are not identical with it. Theology usually seeks to interpret, justify, correct, and defend commonly held doctrines, their assumptions, and their potential implications. Theologies also frequently try to deal with everything which is desirable to teach as well as that which is essential. They may therefore range more widely and vary more greatly than would normally be the case for doctrines. For example, the doctrine of believers baptism may be interpreted and defended primarily in terms of the nature of the church or of the reality of faith or of following Jesus example. And it may be related to and explained in terms of a general theory of ordinances or symbols or sacraments.

Both theology and doctrine may be explicitly stated and formulated in spoken or written forms. Or they may be implicit and operative in worship, church, traditions and practices, patterns of personal and group piety, or standards of Christian conduct. Implicit and operative doctrines frequently, and perhaps even normally, become explicit and official through disagreements and disputes about what should be acknowledged as authoritative or normative. For example, controversy about the baptism of infants during the Protestant Reformation contributed to the development of explicit doctrines of believers baptism (by Anabaptists and Mennonites) and of infant baptism (by Lutherans and the Reformed) and their accompanying theologies. Or, controversy about the Incarnation contributed to the "heavenly flesh" doctrine, which was in turn later disputed and modified among the Dutch Mennonites.

In its explicit forms, theology can be understood as disciplined, discriminating, and comprehensive reflection on and articulation of normative Christian teachings and practices in a particular time and place. Christian theology arises and is carried out primarily within the community of faith in the attempt to articulate the presuppositions, content, and consequences of faith in Jesus Christ for the doctrine, practices, and spirituality of the Church and of individual believers.

In Western Christianity, theology as a discipline of study and teaching has frequently been further differentiated at least into systematic or dogmatic theology, apologetic or foundational theology, and practical theology. Systematic theology is primarily concerned with faithfulness to normative beliefs and practices. Apologetic theology seeks primarily to defend and explain Christian beliefs and practices in terms which can be intelligible to those who have not (yet) come to faith. Practical theology focuses on the application of normative beliefs and practices in the life of the Church and the believer.

In its concern for faithfulness, theology draws from specific sources and renders itself accountable to specific criteria. These usually include the Bible, learnings from tradition, contemporary experiences and insights of the faith community, and disciplined thought. Theologies differ considerably, depending on the relative weight granted to these sources and criteria.

Theologies also differ significantly in the degree to which they seek to be comprehensive (summarizing normative beliefs and practices as a whole) or occasional (focusing on specific issues). With the exception of the Dutch Mennonites in the nineteenth century and some contemporary North American Mennonites, most theological reflection and articulation among Mennonites has been occasional *rather than* comprehensive and has claimed to be rigorously biblical rather than also drawing significantly upon the resources of tradition, experience, and logic as appropriate.

Mennonites have frequently viewed "theology" with suspicion and distrust (*Mennonite Encyclopedia* IV:704). Their emphasis on the importance of discipleship and ethics most likely contributed significantly to Anabaptist and Mennonite suspicions of theology since the sixteenth century as they found it in the Roman Catholic tradition and the emerging Protestant groups. To some degree their distrust of theology was also conditioned by their experience of persecution and theological justification of persecution by both Protestants and Catholics. To a minor degree, their suspicions may have reflected an anti-intellectual stance. But in spite of these suspicions, one should not overlook the fact that early Anabaptist and Mennonite teachers were in conversation, through their writings and debate, with leading theological voices of their time.

The major reason for their suspicions of the dominant theologies was based on the ways they saw theological interpretation used to detract from the hard sayings of Scripture (for example, in relation to baptism or the rejection of violence), or to justify doctrines which appeared to make no demands (faith apart from discipleship), or to perpetuate a form of legalism by putting all doctrines on the same level. They also decried what seemed to be a lack of careful controls for interpreting the sense of Scriptures and the reservation of theology for the experts only. For them the true test of a theological statement was its compatibility with the life and doctrine of Jesus Christ and the apostles. The measure of true theological understanding depended not primarily upon the level of intellectual ability but upon the openness and abandonment to God's will as revealed in Jesus Christ and the teaching and example of the apostles. Throughout their subsequent history, Mennonites have frequently dogmatized this critique and expanded it into a general anti-theological stance rather than discriminating between good and bad theology.

Contemporary scholarship has characterized the theological orientation of sixteenth-century Anabaptism in several ways. These models represent attempts to understand sixteenth-century Anabaptist theology better and to articulate a distinctively Mennonite theological perspective in theology in the twnetieth century.

According to one view, Anabaptism represents a radicalized version of the Protestant Reformation. The Anabaptists pushed biblical authority to more consistent conclusions than did the Protestant reformers on matters such as baptism, nonresistance, and the authority of the congregation (rather than the civil authorities or the church hierarchy) to decide normative doctrine. H. S. Bender adopted a variation of this view and held that Anabaptist theology basically agrees with such major orthodox Christian doctrines as the Trinity, Christ, Scripture, justification by faith, and original sin. But it also constitutes a major theological type alongside Calvinist and Lutheran theologies with a distinctive focus in ecclesiology and discipleship.

Another variation of this view was proposed by Robert Friedmann. Anabaptists adopted an implicit and "existential theology" with a focus on the two kingdoms. This focus had implications for many traditional doctrines. Thus, the Anabaptists remained orthodox in their understandings of the Trinity and Christology, with the addition of seeing Christ not only as savior but also as the model for Christian life. But they differed radically from the Protestant orientation in their theological anthropology, soteriology, quiet eschatology, and ecclesiology.

A second view holds that the theological orientation of the earliest South German Anabaptism amounted to a radicalization of Catholic mysticism in a Reformation context. Werner Packull contends that the legacy of late medieval mysticism rather than the radicalization of the Reformation explains the early synergism and the later moralism of the Anabaptists, and their differences with Luther on anthropology, christology, and the outer Word. This orientation was modified in the Hutterites and the groups around Marpeck. According to Packull the Hutterites gave community priority over theology and remained theologically confused. Marpeck sought to clarify, purify, and systematize the theological convictions of the movement rather than choosing communitarian conformity or Swiss parochialism. He was thereby driven to accept a more or less Protestantized position on many theological issues, including the doctrines of justification and the Word of God. Blough has challenged this interpretation of Marpeck and argues that Marpeck was influenced by Luther in his anti-spiritualist emphasis on the humanity of Christ, but not in his understanding of justification.

A third interpretation of the Anabaptist theological orientation holds that it represents a position in its own right which is neither

Catholic nor Protestant, but combines some of the strengths of both. Walter Klaassen notes that the Anabaptists brought faith and works together. They incorporated the concerns of Catholic monastic movement while leaving aside its emphases on celibacy and restricted Christian vocation. They emphasized with the Protestants that the church rather than the hierarchy or the scholars alone interprets Scripture.

A fourth view has been proposed by Hans-Jürgen Goertz. He rejects the attempt to characterize the essence of Anabaptist theology in normative confessional terms and describes the various Anabaptists as "in, with, and under" the Reformation context. They represented a diversity of positions because they took up varying impulses in the context of the Reformation. The Anabaptist theological positions arose out of quite different attempts to implement the vision of an alternative Christianity. The concrete shape of this vision frequently was first developed in practice. Goertz further characterizes the life context of these Anabaptist movements as the milieu of anticlericalism in the Radical Reformation.

A variation on this view may be Durnbaugh's "believers church" thesis. Believers churches understand the Christian church to be a covenanted and disciplined community of those walking in the way of Jesus. Such groups, including Anabaptists and Mennonites, have articulated a variable set of common convictions on ecclesiology, eschatology, and following Jesus (discipleship) in somewhat adverse theological ways which are dependent to a significant degree on the particular context and the nature of the renewal they project.

Less scholarly attention has been devoted to theological developments among Mennonites since the sixteenth century. In contrast to the explicit elaboration of Protestant theology into comprehensive summaries of Orthodox beliefs, Mennonite theologies have traditionally been more implicit, operational, and occasional than explicit, formal, and systematic. With the exception of the Dutch Mennonites since the eighteenth century and North American Mennonites in the twentieth century, theological statements have frequently taken the form of confessional summaries, inspirational tracts, narrative accounts of history for internal use, or occasional essays rather than either extensive or comprehensive accounts of normative teaching.

The implicit theology of many North American Mennonites includes elements of traditional orthodoxy, pieces of Fundamentalist and Evangelical tenets, and selected practices of their sixteenth-century forebears. According to Kauffman's and Harder's survey *(Anabaptists Four Centuries Later* [1975]), American Mennonites scored higher in general orthodoxy (beliefs in the personal existence of God, the Incarnation, the divinity and humanity of Jesus Christ, two kingdoms, the return of Christ, life after death, heaven and hell) than the national average for Protestants and Roman Catholics. Mennonites have also frequently affirmed key Fundamentalist and Evangelical doctrines (biblical inerrancy, the Virgin Birth, a six-day creation, etc.). They also support their forebears' teachings on discipleship, suffering for the Gospel, baptism of believers, congregational discipline, rejection of the oath, practicing nonresistance, and separation from the world (nonconformity) to varying degrees.

The search for a theological perspective rooted in the renewal of the Anabaptist-Mennonite heritage among North American Mennonites in the twenieth century has thus been conditioned by a varied mix of doctrinal and ethical currents and undercurrents. The general lack of adherence to a specific doctrinal structure and the fragmentation of what seemed to be an implicit theological consensus has produced increasing theological diversity among Mennonites as well as proposals for Mennonites to formulate an explicit theology or at least a distinctive theological perspective.

One such proposal finds a common theological core in the Mennonite confessional tradition (Loewen). This proposal is based on the assumption that Mennonite confessional statements revolve around the three-fold axis of christology, the doctrine of the church (ecclesiology), and the doctrine of "last things" (eschatology), with Christ as the foundation for each. Accordingly christology and soteriology focus on redemption and regeneration; ecclesiology and mission emphasize the life of the church, its mission, and the life of discipleship; and eschatology centers on judgment and resurrection hope.

Other proposals emphasize distinctive perspectives in christology, ecclesiology, eschatology, and ethics. These perspectives would be informed by an understanding of Christian faith which includes following Christ in life, a concept of the church as a disciplined and missionary community of believers, the belief that the rule of God has already begun but is yet to be consummated, and the concern to incorporate normative Christian practices as well as beliefs into theological reflection and formulation. In spite of these proposals and the current discussions they represent, most contemporary Mennonite theological literature has remained occasional and thematic rather than systematic and comprehensive.

Nevertheless, at least three efforts to elaborate more comprehensive and systematic accounts of theology which are fundamentally informed by an Anabaptist perspective or take it into account are underway. C. Norman Kraus' Jesus *Christ Our Lord is* meant to be the introductory volume of a full systematic theology. Thomas N. Finger's *Christian Theology* draws on Anabaptist-Mennonite perspectives. The Baptist theologian James Wm. McClendon, Jr.'s volume on *Systematic Theology: Ethics* is to be followed by a volume on doctrine and one on apologetics.[1]

---

[1]Works cited or used in this article: Neal Blough, *Christologie Anabaptiste: Pilgram Marpeck et humanité du Christ* (Labor et Fides, 1984); Donald F. Durnbaugh, *The Believers Church: The History and Character of Radical Protestantism* (Macmillan, 1969; Herald Press, 1985); Thomas N. Finger, *Christian Theology, An Eschatological Approach,* 2 vols. (Thomas Nelson,1985; Herald Press, 1985, 1989); Robert Friedmann, *The Theology of Anabaptism* (Herald Press, 1973); Kauffman/Harder, *Anabaptists Four Centuries Later* (Herald Press, 1975) 101-17; Hans-Jürgen Goertz, *Die Täufer: Geschichte und Deutung* (C. H. Beck, 1980) 161ff.; Walter Klaassen, *Anabaptism: Neither Catholic nor Protestant* (Conrad Press, 1973); C. Norman Kraus, *Jesus Christ Our Lord: Christology from a Disciple's Perspective* (Herald Press, 1987); Howard John Loewen, *One Lord, One Church, One Hope, and One God: Mennonite Confessions of Faith, Text-Reader Series,* no. 2 (Institute of Mennonite Studies, 1985); James Wm. McClendon, *Systematic Theology,* vol. 1: *Ethics* (Abingdon, 1986) 17-46; *Mennonite-Brethren Profile, 1972-1982, in Direction,* vol. 14, no. 2 (Spring 1985); Werner O. Packull, *Mysticism and the Early South German-Austrian Anabaptist Movement, 1525-1531* (Herald Press, 1977); James Reimer, "The Nature and Possibility of a Mennonite Theology," *Conrad Grebel Review,* vol. 1, no. 1 (Winter 1983) 33-55; Willard M. Swartley, ed., *Explorations of Systematic Theology From Mennonite Perspectives, Occasional Papers,* no. 7 (IMS, 1984).

Chapter 19

Christology

Mennonite Encyclopedia V, Cornelius J. Dyck and Dennis Martin, eds. (Herald Press, 1990) 147.

The responses to Jesus' question "Who do you say that I am" have been decisive for Christian faith and witness ever since Peter's first answer that Jesus is the Messiah (Mt. 16:16 and parallels). In many additional ways and with a rich variety of images and concepts, the New Testament recounts, testifies, describes, and teaches who Jesus is, what he has done, and what he shall yet do.

Since New Testament times Christian churches have usually summarized this variety by speaking about both the divinity and the humanity of Jesus Christ (his person) and about what he has already done and will yet do for the salvation of human beings and the renewal of creation (his work). Christology addresses both major concerns. It thus seeks to articulate, in a disciplined way, a coherent and comprehensive account of the person and work of Jesus Christ for the church's life and witness, an account which is based on the Scriptures, learns from the church's teachings through the centuries, and meets the contemporary challenges to confessing him as Savior and Lord.

Because of its fundamental importance, Christology has been a focus of intense concern as well as controversy in church history. Especially from the seconnd through the seventh centuries, the churches hammered out basic formulations (dogmas) meant to establish guidelines for orthodox teaching and guard against heretical doctrines about the person of Jesus Christ. They sought to correct views which overemphasized his divinity at the expense of his humanity (sometimes called Docetism) or his humanity at the expense of his divinity (sometimes called adoptionism). Particularly the creeds of Nicaea (325) and Chalcedon (451) have been seen as foundational references for orthodox doctrine.

Throughout the centuries there has been less dogmatic unanimity about the work of Christ. Mainstream Western orthodox theology has generally adopted some form of the "satisfaction" view originally associated with Anselm of Canterbury (eleventh century). Other major views of the atonement have included the "moral influence" theory, originally elaborated by Peter Abelard (twelth century), and the classical or "victory over the powers" motif, most popular in western Christianity from the second through the seventh centuries, and revived more recently in revised forms.

Prior to the nineteenth century, Protestant theology generally adopted traditional Western Christian christological views. In addition, it placed great emphasis upon the Christian's appropriation of Christ's benefits through faith, rather than through a sacramental system (ordinances). And particularly in the Calvinist tradition, Protestant orthodoxy elaborated an understanding of Christ's world according to his threefold prophetic, priestly, and kingly "office."

Sixteenth-century Anabaptist and Mennonite Christologies were generally compatible with orthodox understandings in the sense that they affirmed both the divinity and humanity of Jesus Christ and salvation through his atoning death on the cross. However, they usually couched these affirmations in selected biblical categories and made little constructive use of the traditional dogmatic vocabulary. This preference for biblical terms has had both positive and problematic consequences for Mennonite theology and ethics since the sixteenth century.

On the positive side, this preference contributed to the Anabaptist and Mennonite teaching about Jesus as the model and example for believers. While affirming his divinity they also emphasized Jesus' humanity, teaching, and actions. While teaching his atoning work on the cross, they also emphasized Jesus' way of the cross as the model for Christian discipleship. These emphases had tended to recede into the shadows of orthodox Christology since the controversies of earlier centuries. To be sure, Protestants and Roman Catholics also found ways of considering Jesus Christ normative for Christian life. But these ways fit predominantly within the patterns of Constantinian Christendom. For the Anabaptists and Mennonites, following Jesus Christ and his teaching in life resulted in an alternative pattern of Christian and church life.

On the problematic side, this preference contributed to some deviations from traditional orthodoxy as well as from scriptural balance and most likely contradicted either one or both. These included the "heavenly flesh" teaching, adopted by Menno Simons and Dirk Philips largely from Melchior Hoffrnan's apocalypticism, and the Logos Christology represented especially by Hans Denck.

Menno and Dirk asserted that Jesus' humanity (flesh) was nourished in Mary, but that it originated in heaven and did not receive its substance from Mary. They based this position partly on John 6 and 1 Corinthians 15 and partly on the Aristotelian view that the mother's seed is entirely passive. By emphasizing that Jesus' humanity came down from heaven in the Incarnation as an entirely new creation they intended to support their distinctive views on salvation and the church. Through faith in the new Adam descended from heaven, human beings can be born anew and recreated to a new state of obedience. And this new creation manifests itself in the church without spot and wrinkle, the new community of those who are reborn and separated from the sinful world, having cast aside the weapons of violence and war.

The heavenly flesh doctrine became a major point of controversy between Mennonites and Protestants as well as between several Mennonite and Anabaptist groups in the sixteenth and into the early seventh centuries. Some maintained it until the middle of the eighteenth century. But it may have influenced some Mennonite concepts of church, salvation, and Christian ethics considerably longer, perhaps even until the present. The concept of the pure church, linked originally with the heavenly flesh Christology, has most likely contributed to both perfectionism and divisions among Anabaptists and Mennonites throughout their history.

In terms of traditional dogma, the celestial-flesh Christology emphasizes the divinity of Jesus Christ at the expense of his humanity. It has therefore been accused of being gnostic in the sense of assuming that matter and spirit are irreconcilable. It has also been considered docetic. Contemporary scholars differ in their assessments: the Melchiorite-Mennonite teaching is docetic (Klaassen in CRR 3), has docetic tendencies (Beachy), cannot be adequately described as docetic (Voolstra), or is not docetic (Keeney). Judgments differ along a similar scale on whether it is basically gnostic, has gnostic tendencies, or does not fall into gnosticism.

Denck's Christology has been markedly less influential. As are other areas of his thought, Denck's Christology is complex and difficult to categorize. Nonetheless, it had a mystical and universalizing tendency. It focused on the incarnate Word more than on the incarnate Christ. The eternal or inner Word suffered not only in the incarnate Lamb Jesus Christ, but had also suffered before and suffers since in the elect. Similarly, the eternal Logos which was victorious in Jesus Christ, has been victorious in the elect from the beginning and shall be so until the end.

This Logos Christology provides the basis for the theology of the divine in every human. Although the humanity as well as the divinity of Jesus is important for Denck, the two natures seem to remain somewhat separated from each other. The historical Jesus or the outer Word is important primarily as the teacher and example, namely, as the witness to the inner Word, which provides the means of deification for the disciple. Denck emphasized the unity of Christ's will with God's will, and the freedom of the will to be one with God. Some of his followers found his synthesis difficult to maintain and seriously questioned orthodox Christological and trinitarian doctrines.

Another Anabaptist theologian and church leader during the sixteenth century was Pilgram Marpeck. His influence at the time may have almost equaled that of Menno Simons. Although he shared an interest in relating Christology to the concepts of salvation and the church, he rejected the heavenly flesh Christology and articulated a distinctive view of Christ's humanity and its relation to his divinity.

Marpeck developed his views on the humanity of Christ partly as correctives to Lutheran and spiritualist (Schwenckfeld) Christologies. At the heart of Marpeck's thought is his view of the unity between the divine and the human natures in Jesus Christ. The essence (*wesen*) of reality is the unity between its inner and the outer dimensions. In Jesus Christ, the human (outer) serves the divine (inner). Simultaneously, the human (outer) also makes the divine (inner) visible and corresponds to it. In parallel fashion, the church as the visible and nonglorified body of Christ is enabled and called to correspond to the glorified and reigning Christ, who is the head of the body. Marpeck also extended this structure of thought to Christian discipleship, the sacraments, Christian liberty, and anthropology.

Contemporary scholars have devoted little attention to christological developments among Mennonites from the seventh through the eighteenth centuries. During that time, Mennonite confessions of faith generally perpetuated nondogmatic views of Christ's person and work, which they nevertheless gradually adapted to traditional orthodox and Protestant concepts. This tendency is most pronounced in the major twnetieth-century North American Mennonite confessions from the early 1920s through the mid-1970s. These confessions have also been influenced by Fundamentalist and conservative reactions to modernism, reactions that emphasized Christ's divinity and sacrificial atonement and tended toward doceticism. Simultaneously, Mennonites have continued to preach and teach that Jesus Christ exemplifies how Christians are called to live. This has both tempered the Fundamentalist and traditional orthodox influences and opened Mennonites to modern christological views which begin with the historical Jesus, emphasize his humanity and ethical significance, and frequently have adoptionist tendencies.

A representative voice for the conservative view tempered with a nondogmatic biblicism and Jesus as the example for Christian discipleship is J. C. Wenger. He generally adopts traditional orthodox and Protestant views on Jesus Christ's humanity and divinity and his threefold office as the framework for interpreting New Testament Christology. Wenger summarizes several biblical concepts for the atonement rather than attempting to develop a comprehensive synthesis. He also accepts several affirmations of conservative Christologies, including the preexistence, the virgin birth, the sacrificial death, and the bodily return of Jesus Christ. Wenger assumes the bodily resurrection without mentioning it in his account of Christology. His concept of discipleship appears not to imply any basic modifications of traditional christological assumptions, but belongs to an understanding of Christian life and holy living. This includes an emphasis on nonresistance and nonconformity.

The most influential book related to Christology by a twentieth-century Mennonite theologian to date is likely John Howard Yoder's *The Politics of Jesus*, which has been translated into several languages since the mid-1970s. In contrast to Wenger, it adopts current emphases on Jesus' humanity and his ethical significance. Yoder first put forth its major thesis in the context of conversations between the historic peace churches and mainstream Protestants in the late 1950s (Puidoux Conferences). It seeks to correct traditional theological ways of avoiding the pacifist content of Scriptures and rejects modern systematic divisions between the Jesus of faith and the real Jesus.

For Yoder, Jesus' life, his calling of an alternative community, teaching, and crucifixion reveal and incarnate a qualitatively new possibility of human, social, and political relations. Jesus' life, calling of alternative community, teaching, and crucifixion therefore remain normative for Christian social ethics. Although Yoder does not attempt to construct a comprehensive Christology, he claims to take Chalcedon's affirmation of Jesus' humanity more seriously than mainstream theologies which circumvent biblical pacifism and the way of the cross. In other writings, Yoder emphasizes Jesus' Lordship and affirms that the ordinariness of Jesus' humanness and crucifixion, as well as his resurrection, demonstrates the general application of Jesus' work of reconciliation. Simultaneously he criticizes theological and ethical approaches which limit the distinctiveness of Jesus, discipleship, and the church entirely to modern historicist and moral categories.

More than any other Mennonite author, Gordon Kaufman has attempted to reformulate theology from an historicist perspective. Rather than beginning with a conservative framework for Mennonite concerns like Wenger or with the christological foundations for Christian pacifism in a biblical realist and Barthian vein like Yoder, Kaufman comes to Christology from modernist systematic and epistemological considerations and grounds Christology in an understanding of the humanness of Jesus compatible with critical New Testament scholarship and contemporary historicism (the view that all of reality is essentially historical rather than based on supernatural, transcendent reality).

Kaufman therefore fundamentally reformulates most christological concepts. Instead of focusing upon the person of Christ as the unity of divine and human natures, he speaks about Jesus as the Servant, the Word, and the Son understood in historical-personal terms. Instead of adopting any traditional view of the atonement, he interprets the Christ-event as having established a community of authentic love and thus inaugurating a historical process which is transforming human existence into God's kingdom. Instead of the resurrection referring to an experienced event, it is a theological interpretation of Christ's appearances and means that God is Lord of history regardless of what human beings may do. Instead of the virgin birth being a touchstone for the doctrine of the incarnation, it represents a crude attempt to express the belief that Jesus is God's Son.

The most recent christological proposals from Mennonite theologians are being made by John Driver, Thomas Finger, and C. Norman Kraus. Finger reconstructs theology by adopting an eschatological orientation for the entire range of doctrine. Within this perspective, he understands Christ as the fulfillment of the promise of God's righteousness. He then develops a Christology around the life, death, and resurrection of Jesus Christ, rather than with traditional dogmatic categories.

Driver has focused on the work of Christ. His radical evangelical approach to the doctrine of atonement has arisen in the context of cross-cultural mission (in Spain and Latin America) seeking to disengage itself from the Constantinian assumptions of traditional theories and to do justice to the multiple biblical images of the atonement. Driver discovers even more biblical concepts for the atonement than Wenger and suggests that they reflect the contexts in which the early church carried out the missionary mandate of its Lord. Rather than reducing the multiple biblical images to one system, Driver recommends using them to enrich the understanding of the entire work of Christ. This pluralism of motifs also means that the saving work of Christ includes his ministry, his resurrection, and the actualizing power of the Spirit, as well as his death.

Kraus may be the first North American Mennonite theologian who attempts to construct, as an alternative to conservative as well as liberal Protestant approaches, a comprehensive Christology from a modern reinterpretation of Anabaptism. Like Driver, Kraus' approach has also been influenced by cross-cultural mission (in Japan). He contends that Christology in a historical and social-psychological mode best reflects the biblical and Anabaptist understandings of Jesus Christ and fits a missionary theology.

Kraus replaces the traditional metaphysical concepts of person and work of Jesus Christ with the identity and mission of Jesus, the Messiah. The identity of Jesus is described in terms of the man Jesus, the Son of the Father and the Self-Disclosure of God. Kraus's account of Jesus' mission focuses on how Jesus as Lord overcomes sin with love by having taken the way of the cross, on salvation as the renewal of the image of God and on the appropriation of salvation through Jesus' identification with us and our solidarity with him. In contrast to Western theological emphases on salvation from guilt, Kraus argues that reconciliation to God through the cross of Christ deals with shame as well as with guilt.

Driver and Kraus thus contribute crosscultural mission concerns to current christological discussions. In addition to such attempts to address Christology from a missionary stance, contemporary Mennonite teaching, preaching, and piety reflect both diverse motifs and some common interests. The diversity ranges from classical orthodox views filtered through pietist and evangelical lenses to modern images seen in historical and social perspectives. The common interests focus on discipleship and the community which confesses Jesus as the Christ.

Some sixteenth-century Anabaptists couched these common interests in terms vulnerable to Docetism. Some contemporary Mennonites express them in categories vulnerable to adoptionism. Christology therefore remains at the center of both doctrinal and ethical, as well as soteriological and ecclesiological discussion and debate, both among Mennonites and between Mennonite and other Christians.[1]

---

[1]Works used or cited in this article: Alvin J. Beachy, *The Concept of Grace in the Radical Reformation* (B. de Graaf, 1977) 79-86, 178; Neal Blough, *Christologie Anabaptiste: Pilgram Marpeck et l'humanité du Christ* (Labor et Fides, 1984); cf. *Mennonite Quarterly Review*, vol. 61 (1987) 203-12; Mitchell Brown, "Jesus: Messiah, Not God," *Conrad Grebel Review, 5* (1987) 233-52, with responses *CGR 6* (1988) 65-71; John Driver, *Understanding the Atonement for the Mission of the Church* (Herald Press, 1986); Thomas N. Finger, *Christian Theology: An Eschatological Approach* (Thomas Nelson Sons, 1985; Herald Press, 1985); idem, "The Way to Nicea: Some Reflections from a Mennonite Perspective," *Journal of Ecumenical Studies,* vol. 24 (1987) 212-31; cf. *CGR* 3 (1985) 231-49: Edmund G. Kaufman, *Basic Chistian Convictions* (Bethel College, 1972) 125-63; Gordon D. Kaufman, *Systematic Theology: A Historicist Perspective* (Scribner's, 1978); William E. Keeney, *The Development of Dutch Anabaptist Thought and Practice from 1539-1564* (B. de Graaf, 1968) 89-113, 191-221; idem, "The Incarnation: A Central Theological Concept," in *A Legacy of Faith,* ed. C. J. Dyck (Faith and Life Press, 1962) 55-68; Walter Klaassen, *Anabaptism in Outline: Selected Primary Sources, Classics of the Radical Reformation,* vol. 3 (Herald Press, 1981) 23-40; C. Norman Kraus, *Jesus Christ Our Lord: Christology from a Disciple's Perspective* (Scottdale, 1987); John H. Leith, editor, *Creeds of the Churches: A Reader in Christian Doctrine from the Bible to the Present* (John Knox Press, 1977), with confessional and creedal statements, including New Testament, Protestant and Roman Catholic, Anabaptist and Mennonite; Howard John Loewen, *One Lord, One Church, One Hope, and One God: Mennonite Confessions of Faith, Text-Reader Series,* no. 2 (Institute of Mennonite Studies, 1985); J. S. Oosterbaan, "Een doperse christologie," *Nederlands theologish Tijdschrift, vol. 35* (1981) 32-47; Sjouke Voolstra, *Het Woord Is Vlees Geworden: De Mechioritisch-Menninste Incarnatieleer* (Uitgeversmaatschappij J. H. Kok, 1982); cf. idem, "The Word has Become Flesh, the Melchiorite-Mennonite Teaching on the Incarnation," *MQR,* vol. 57 (1983) 156-60; J. Denny Weaver, "A Believers' Church Christology," *MQR* 57 (April 1983) 112-31; idem, "The Work of Christ: On the Difficulty of Identifying an Anabaptist Perspective," *MQR* 59 (1985) 107-29; John C. Wenger, *Introduction to Theology* (Herald Press, 1954) 62-70, 193-211, 334-59; John Howard Yoder, *The Politics of Jesus* (Eerdmans, 1972); idem, "But We Do See Jesus: The

Particularity of Incarnation and the Universality of Truth," in *The Priestly Kingdom* (University of Notre Dame Press, 1984) 46-62.

Marlin E. Miller

Born on November 29, 1938, Marlin had a childhood dream of being a missionary. When he came to Associated Mennonite Biblical Seminary as a guest lecturer in 1974, he expected to return to mission work in France, but stayed for 20 years. "A missionary on extended leave" is what Marlin called himself.

Marlin's dream to be a missionary was nurtured first in the Lower Deer Creek Mennonite Church near Kalona, Iowa, and then later at College Mennonite Church, Goshen, Ind., where his family moved. After graduating from Goshen College and studying at Goshen Biblical Seminary one year, he and Ruthann, his wife, moved to Europe where he continued studies and began fulfilling his dream.

He studied at the University of Basel (Switzerland) and was awarded the Dr. Theol. degree in 1968 from the University of Heidelberg (Germany), graduating summa cum laude. He then served with Mennonite Board of Missions in Paris, France, from 1968 to 1974. In this assignment he worked with international students in Paris, many of whom were from Africa and became the target of racism and chauvinism. He was ordained in 1971 by the Chatenay-Malabry Mennonite congregation near Paris as a pastor in a team ministry.

From 1974-75, Marlin taught at AMBS and in 1975 he became president of Goshen Biblical Seminary. In 1990 he also became president of Mennonite Biblical Seminary; thus he was the first person to serve as president of both institutions that make up AMBS. Marlin died unexpectedly on November 3, 1994.

Marlin left a rich legacy at AMBS. In just the last few years of his work there, AMBS introduced a new curriculum for the Master of Divinity degree which included renewed emphasis on pastoral ministry, preaching, pastoral care and spirituality; developed two new degree programs in Christian spirituality and Christian education; launched the Partners for Ministry comprehensive campaign; and legally joined GBS and MBS as one seminary.

Marlin's gifts extended far beyond AMBS. He served as co-chair of the committee shaping "Confession of Faith in a Mennonite Perspective" which was adopted by the Mennonite Church and General Conference Mennonite Church in July 1995. He served on several committees and projects of Mennonite Central Committee and wrote extensively for church publications. A book he co-edited with Barbara Nelson Gingerich, *The Church's Peace Witness*, was published by Eerdmans shortly after his death.

Marlin married Ruthann Gardner on June 12, 1960. Their children are Rachel Miller Jacobs, Lynelle Clark, and Eric Miller Sommers. The family included seven grandchildren at the time of Marlin's death.